Praise for
It's Ok Not to Share

"Bold. Unconventional. And downright useful! Through science, stories, and her Renegade Rules, Shumaker beautifully shows us why letting kids be kids may be the single most important thing we can do as parents."
—Anthony T. DeBenedet, M.D., coauthor of *The Art of Roughhousing: Good Old-Fashioned Horseplay and Why Every Kid Needs It*

"From 'Bombs, Guns, and Bad Guys Allowed' to '"I Hate You!" Is Nothing Personal,' the table of contents alone is music to my ears. Heather Shumaker is a healthy mom I can relate to—and I'll bet you will, too, when you hear out her logic."
—Paula Spencer, author of *Momfidence*

"These Renegade Rules will resonate with what you know to be true, speak to what you want most for your children, and teach you how to achieve it. Don't let this one slip off your reading list."
—Becky A. Bailey, Ph.D., author of *Conscious Discipline* and *Easy to Love, Difficult to Discipline*

"This beautifully written book celebrates young boys and all active preschoolers. It acts as a guide through the high emotions and roughhousing energy of the preschool years, and provides immediate, sanity-saving answers to tough parenting questions. I highly recommend it."
—Michael Gurian, author of *The Wonder of Boys* and *The Good Son*

"*It's OK Not to Share* is a refreshing change from the usual admonitions to parents to over-control their children. Instead, Shumaker's Renegade Rules are based on what children really need: room for play, freedom to express their emotions, choices during free play time, and understanding of what makes them tick. The results may not always be quiet or elegant, but it is what children need to thrive—and your life won't be dull!"
—Lawrence J. Cohen, Ph.D., author of *Playful Parenting*, coauthor of *The Art of Roughhousing*

"Shumaker's book is a must-read for parents and teachers. Finally, [here is] an author who recognizes the development of young children and which practices are needed. Heather gives permission to play and shows us how to develop spaces and curricula that support this endeavor. These Renegade Rules are a *must* for adults to follow. Some of my favorites are: '"I Hate You!" Is Nothing Personal,' 'Let Her Hog the Toy All Day,' and my favorite, 'Only Punch Friends.' If you are planning on having children, currently have children, or work with children, this is a book you will want with you all the time."
—Daniel J. Hodgins, author of *Boys: Changing the Classroom, Not the Child*

It's OK **Not** to Share

It's OK **Not** to Share

And Other Renegade Rules
for Raising Competent
and Compassionate Kids

◻ Heather Shumaker ◻

JEREMY P. TARCHER / PENGUIN   *a member of Penguin Group (USA) Inc.   New York*

JEREMY P. TARCHER/PENGUIN
Published by the Penguin Group
Penguin Group (USA) Inc., 375 Hudson Street, New York, New York
10014, USA • Penguin Group (Canada), 90 Eglinton Avenue East, Suite 700,
Toronto, Ontario M4P 2Y3, Canada (a division of Pearson Penguin Canada Inc.) •
Penguin Books Ltd, 80 Strand, London WC2R 0RL, England • Penguin Ireland,
25 St Stephen's Green, Dublin 2, Ireland (a division of Penguin Books Ltd) • Penguin
Group (Australia), 250 Camberwell Road, Camberwell, Victoria 3124, Australia (a division
of Pearson Australia Group Pty Ltd) • Penguin Books India Pvt Ltd, 11 Community Centre,
Panchsheel Park, New Delhi–110 017, India • Penguin Group (NZ), 67 Apollo Drive,
Rosedale, North Shore 0632, New Zealand (a division of Pearson New Zealand
Ltd) • Penguin Books (South Africa) (Pty) Ltd, 24 Sturdee Avenue,
Rosebank, Johannesburg 2196, South Africa

Penguin Books Ltd, Registered Offices: 80 Strand, London WC2R 0RL, England

Most Tarcher/Penguin books are available at special quantity discounts for bulk purchase
for sales promotions, premiums, fund-raising, and educational needs. Special books
or book excerpts also can be created to fit specific needs. For details, write Penguin
Group (USA) Inc. Special Markets, 375 Hudson Street, New York, NY 10014.

Library of Congress Cataloging-in-Publication Data

Shumaker, Heather.
It's ok not to share : and other renegade rules for raising competent and compassionate kids /
Heather Shumaker.
p.   cm.
ISBN 978-1-58542-936-3
1. Child rearing.   2. Sharing in children.   3. Child development.   I. Title
HQ769.S54533   2012   2012015523
649'.1—dc23

Printed in the United States of America
5   7   9   10   8   6   4

BOOK DESIGN BY NICOLE LAROCHE

ILLUSTRATIONS BY JOY KOLITSKY

While the author has made every effort to provide accurate telephone numbers, Internet
addresses, and other contact information at the time of publication, neither the publisher
nor the author assumes any responsibility for errors, or for changes that occur after
publication. Further, the publisher does not have any control over and does not
assume any responsibility for author or third-party websites or their content.

To my mother, of course

And to Rick,

who always believed

Author's Note

I am grateful to the many families and teachers who shared their stories to bring these ideas to life. While the age and sex of children depicted in the book have not been altered, names and some details have been changed to protect family privacy.

Contents

Section IV: Running Room: Kids, Power and Action

Section V: Creativity, Persistence and Empty Praise

Section VI: Bad Words, Polite Words and Lies

Section VII: Sensitive Subjects

Section VIII: Renegade Rules in the Real World

It's OK
Not to
Share

Introduction

The Renegade Rules inside this book are not entirely mine. The seeds for these ideas come from the accumulated wisdom of a tiny progressive preschool tucked near the banks of the Olentangy River in Columbus, Ohio.

In this forgotten spot, children can box and wrestle. They can paint their arms blue or climb a tree. No one has to sit still. Children don't have to share their toys. But because of these renegade ways, the School for Young Children (SYC) has produced confident, compassionate children for forty years, children who are masters in mediation and creative problem-solving.

I know all about it. I went to preschool there as a child. My mother is a teacher at SYC and has taught there for nearly four decades. Today I'm raising my own children following its philosophy.

This book came about because I realized how rare the SYC ideas are. The very title of this book—*It's OK Not to Share*—goes against some of our most deeply held notions about what's right and wrong when it comes to raising kids.

How renegade are these ideas?

- Rather than force a child to share a toy, the Renegade approach promotes generosity by letting a child keep a toy to herself all day long—relinquishing it to another child only when she's good and ready.

- When a child accidentally hurts someone, the Renegade approach encourages compassion by *not* saying "Sorry."
- Instead of teaching the ABCs to children when they're sitting down calmly and quietly, the Renegade approach suggests grabbing a pen and offering an impromptu literacy lesson when children are hollering and screaming.
- And instead of breaking up a fight when two children start wrestling, the Renegade approach suggests providing a wrestling mat and even giving kids boxing gloves.

These upside-down rules actually come with sensible reasons, all based in child development. The ideas really aren't that radical—they're just different.

When I first told Jan Waters the title of this book, she objected. Jan's taught at the school as long as my mother and served as director for seventeen years. "But the ideas aren't renegade!" she said. "They're not renegade or rebellious at all." "Well, they are unconventional," I said. "You'll have to admit that." Jan was undeterred. "They're Good Old Solid Child Development Principles That Work," she said. "Make *that* the title of the book."

There are other parenting books that give worthy advice on child nutrition, potty training and the like. This book is intentionally selective. The Renegade Rules don't focus on topics where we agree; they highlight where we differ: early academics, conflict, hitting and kicking, "No Girls" signs, social rejection and exclusion. This book sings the glories of rough-and-tumble play, and doesn't shy away from incredibly touchy topics like lying, swearing, weapon play, gender-bender play (think boys in dresses), sex education and death.

It all started in 1969, the year I was born, so you can see I had nothing to do with it. In 1969, the school's founders, Lee Row and Janet Stocker, set about to create a new type of preschool—one based not on rules, but on a set of Children's Rights. These rights included the Right to Uninterrupted Play, the Right to Choose Playmates, the Right Not to Share and the Right to Feel Safe. Over the years, of course, a few rules did evolve (for example: "Wear underwear" and "Clean up your lunch spot"). However, one main rule still guides every behavior: *It's OK if it's not hurting people or property.*

The School for Young Children itself draws on wisdom from early-childhood pioneers, most deeply from the work of author and child psychologist Haim Ginott and Ohio preschool teacher Mary Nicholaysen. Other important influences underlying the philosophy include Dorothy Briggs, Rudolf Dreikurs, Selma Fraiberg, Eda LeShan, Vivian Paley and Fred Rogers of *Mister Rogers' Neighborhood.* The philosophy has been enriched over the years through friends and educators like Bev Bos and Hedda Sharapan, plus advancing neuroscience knowledge on the importance of play and emotions.

People ask me: Does this progressive school have a name for its philosophy? Not yet. For now it's one of a kind, but I propose calling it a "playschool" philosophy. The ideas are play-based and embedded in a deep trust of the child.

When my first child grew old enough for preschool, I looked around seeking something similar to SYC. I live four hundred miles from Columbus, so my alma mater wasn't an option. But the more I looked, the more dismayed I grew. In program after program, little children sat still most of the day. There was scant time for spontaneous play. Adults structured kids' play and solved their problems for them. Everywhere I looked, the focus was on reading, writing and counting, when all the children wanted to do was jump, run, giggle and play.

During my search for a play-based preschool, I returned to Columbus and revisited SYC. It shocked me. I'd forgotten how bold it was, how fully it embraced childhood. Each day was filled with risk taking and creativity. Rough-and-tumble play, compassion and courage. As I watched, I saw three- and four-year-olds display advanced social skills and complex mediation abilities. I marveled. Then I resolved to share it.

The truth is, we don't all have a school like SYC in our neighborhoods. But the ideas can travel. I meet parents every week at the park or school yard who are yearning for something different. Some are exasperated by their kids; others are dismayed by school demands and social expectations. We all want our children to grow up to be whole human beings. We're all trying to raise caring, competent and compassionate young people. And we need to pool our wisdom.

This book shares SYC's secrets so you can replicate them at home. It's intended for you, the parent, teacher, grandparent or other caregiver, of children ages two to six. Here you'll find practical tips to cope with everything from a foot-stamping four-year-old who yells, "I hate you, Dad!" to a sword-swinging young superhero, to a child who announces, "Katie can't play with us." Along with sanity-saving advice, you'll find ideas to equip your kids with essential life skills.

The time for this book is now. Violence and bullying are in the news. No matter where you live or what preschools are locally available, like me, you want to raise children who can cope. Children who are both strong and compassionate. Children who can stand up against injustice and resolve conflicts peacefully.

This is the essence of *It's OK Not to Share*. Speaking up, setting limits and expressing feelings in appropriate ways. After all, this is what living together with other humans is all about. The Renegade Rules are not about greed and rudeness. On the contrary. A three-year-old can stand up for his rights and set an appropriate limit on another child when she takes his toy. The Renegade Rules do flip some popular views upside down, but they are really all about extending dignity and compassion in our parenting.

These Renegade Rules are also an antidote to the crushing pace of childhood. Play and recess are threatened across the country. Four-year-olds are expected to read. You'll rediscover why playtime gives children vital life skills—whether it's facing rejection, disagreeing with friends, coping with strong feelings or controlling impulses. Kids can best learn these skills as they always have—through play.

This book of Renegade Rules shares what works. The ideas have been time-tested through generations of families and represent the accumulated wisdom of seventy-five early-childhood educators over the course of forty years. Like me, you may have forgotten just what old-fashioned play looks like. How bold it is. How full of risks, emotions and power. But for the sake of our kids we can't forget. Kids need play desperately to develop social and emotional skills. Here's what it looks like. Here's how to get started.

This book contains twenty-nine Renegade Rules, but it can really be summed up with one, which I call the Renegade Golden Rule: It's OK If It's Not Hurting People or Property. When you're caught up in the whirlwind of parenting young children, refer back to this idea whenever you're in doubt. I have a three-year-old and a six-year-old at home, so I know firsthand time is short and precious for parents. To help you retrieve ideas easily, this book is laid out as a set of easy-to-remember Rules and Reasons, along with exact words you can pull out when you need them.

You may not agree with every "Rule" in these pages. Some of these ideas take getting used to. Some Rules may not be meaningful to you now, but deserve a second look as your child grows or as another child with a different personality comes along. One thing I've learned about parenting is that there are a variety of family cultures. We must respect one another's varying styles and values. At the same time, I know mothers and fathers have a lot to share and learn from one another. When you read this book, you can know that I'm sharing not only my experience, but forty years of collective wisdom and experience from a team of talented early-childhood professionals.

As you start to "Renegade" parent, take heart that you're not alone. Four thousand families before you have adopted this parenting style and sent their kids to SYC. "A special thanks for helping me deal with my child's immense love of guns and bombs," one mother wrote. "As a complete and utter pacifist, this has been a challenge for me." Or from another parent: "Thank you for touching Jack's soul, his sense of self, his emotions—ah, his anger—he knows this one well. I am grateful when he says, 'I'm so angry I feel like hitting and punching you!' and he doesn't. What a feat for a four-year-old!" "My love affair with SYC started like my arranged marriage," wrote another mother. "The more I saw of it, the more I liked it." Or simply: "You saved me from going off the deep end with Sophie."

At times I feel sheepish writing a book about parenting. My children often perplex me. Many days I'm not a model parent, but even then, my storehouse of knowledge from my mother and SYC gives me a tremendous advantage. Where would I be without it? Whenever I'm befuddled by my children's behavior and don't know what to do, I call my private hotline, my mother. We all need a hotline. So here's a hotline for you—a book of Renegade Rules. May it give you new ways of seeing your child, fresh ideas for parenting and practical tools for raising a competent, compassionate kid.

Section I

Reviving
Free Play

*Never let formal education get in the way of
your learning.*

—Mark Twain

Don't Steal Play

There's a sign on the wall at my childhood preschool quoting J. C. Pearce, author of *Magical Child*. "Every stage of development is complete in itself," he writes. "The three-year-old is not an incomplete five-year-old. The child is not an incomplete adult. Never are we simply on our way!"

This book of Renegade Rules is all about meeting your child where she is today. Not the first-grader she will become, but about your child's immediate social and emotional needs. How she thinks, solves problems and lives with her active body. When we meet our children's needs—where they are and who they are today—we're giving them what they truly need for the future.

If you're like me, however, "today" can somehow get mixed up with "tomorrow." It often comes when we try too hard to do what's best for our kids. We buy them flash cards when they prefer mud puddles. We enroll kids in peewee soccer when they're better suited to a ball in the backyard. Together with preschool teachers and policy makers, we often coax our kids to count, read, write, get the right answer and sit still.

What's most precious in these early years (ages two to six) is play. Free, unstructured, child-directed playtime. It's an old-fashioned idea with modern neuroscience backing it up. Kids need oodles of playtime. Efforts to "enrich" or replace play with academic lessons are missing the extraordinary value of early childhood. In fact, rushing academic skills often backfires.

Renegade Reason
Playtime is precious. Play builds brain pathways for thinking, creativity, flexibility, empathy and many other lifelong skills.

Today families are caught in a paradox. We're parenting during a time when scientists increasingly tell us free play is vital to the health of our kids, yet schools and policies are pushing us in the opposite direction—in an agitated rush toward early academics. The gap between what we *know* about young children and what we *do* with young children is widening each year.

We're also parenting in an age of acceleration. Not long ago—just two years in some cases—kindergarten was a half-day filled with play. Today, partly because of global competitiveness and educational policies like No Child Left Behind, the first-grade curriculum has crept into early childhood. Kindergarten is stretching to last all day. With the exception of a few child-based programs, this is happening across the country. To prepare for the rigors of kindergarten, three- and four-year-olds are increasingly drilled in early reading and math.

This is called "getting ready for kindergarten." It could also be called "stealing play."

Too often we think about preparing our kids for school in the same way we think about preparing ourselves for a job. Careful study, good work habits—in fact, years of diligent preparation. We need to take off our adult lenses. A child's "preparation" for school success looks nothing like ours. A child's preparation for life and school comes through boisterous play, spontaneous play, running and roughhousing, playing house and playing pirates. Yelling, screaming and crying are part of it. So is first friend-making (and rejection). Taking risks—creative risks, physical risks and social risks. Dressing up and storytelling. Trying out crazy (and messy!) art. Encountering conflict. Sorting it out. Young kids already have a full agenda: play.

Times have changed. But children haven't. Young kids are on the same evolutionary path they've always been on. It's our expectations that are off. We're trying to make children ready for the next stage of life before natural development allows them to be ready. It's like expecting ten-year-olds to drive a car safely, or expecting a four-month-old to walk.

"'Getting ready for kindergarten?'" said my mentor Jan Waters, long-time teacher at the School for Young Children in Columbus, Ohio. "Why ask kids to do that? That's not what young kids need. There's no 'getting' ready. Kids are ready for so much right now. They're ready for the present, not the future. Should we teach *you* to get ready for old age in your thirties? No. You're not there yet. We need to meet kids where they are now."

 Take Off Your Adult Lenses

Don't rush kids into academic learning before ages six or seven. It's a waste of their precious time. Child development moves at the pace of evolution. Accept its natural pace; don't try to accelerate it. Playing ball, blocks and dress-up is exactly what your child needs to do, learning in her own time, at her own rate. Young kids need ample time to explore and play—their brains and emotional health depend on it.

An understanding father once said, "You can't make corn grow by pulling on it." The same is true for children. We can push a three-year-old to study numbers or a four-year-old to study letters, but we shouldn't. Not unless she's ready—in her own good time.

Renegade Blessings

When we allow kids to play and grow at their own pace, they gain a multitude of blessings. Kids learn life lessons and think to themselves:

I'm OK just as I am.

My parents support and understand me.

I can try new things when I'm ready.

Books are full of fascinating stories. I love it when someone reads to me.

I can pursue what interests me most. I love to learn!

Life is marvelous.

Why It Works

Children's development can be quite uneven, especially in the early years. Some kids concentrate on physical tasks first; others are joyous early readers at age three. Some need to yell and jump endlessly. Others need to observe from a safe place. The whole child needs to be nourished and all aspects—emotional, social, physical and cognitive—given a chance to develop at the child's unique pace.

Brain researchers today are reinforcing the tremendous value of children's play. They're discovering children are designed to play. Play helps kids develop social skills, memory, emotional awareness, creative problem-solving, flexibility and impulse control. It helps them understand the world and their place in it.

The American Academy of Pediatrics and many doctors, psychologists and neuroscientists endorse free play as the best way to nurture young children. A CNN.com headline reads, "Want to Get Your Kids into College? Let Them Play." NPR reports, "Old-Fashioned Play Builds Serious Skills."

Psychiatrists, psychologists and other researchers are all finding that young children need free play desperately—and don't develop properly without it. But parents aren't buying it.

This is what I heard in the park the other day: "I worry about him. I don't see many worksheets coming home in his preschool backpack. What if he doesn't make the grade in kindergarten?" This mother voices a concern that so many of us carry. *He can't even write his name yet. Shouldn't I be working on his writing skills? . . . I'm worried about Ashley. She still gets mixed up counting to ten.*

Will our kids be left behind? What about preparing them for the global modern world? We can all relax. In many other countries (including much of Europe, with high literacy rates and first-world economies) children are playing. Formal reading instruction doesn't start in countries like Sweden, Finland and Poland until age seven. Why seven? Seven has historically been called the "Age of Reason." In every country in the world, children's brains undergo a remarkable shift at this age. Child psychiatrists Theodore Shapiro and Richard Perry called it the "age of seven, plus or minus one." Many cultural rites of passage recognize seven-year-olds' new abilities, whether it's the start of school in Finland or first communion in the Catholic faith. It's the time when young brains are naturally ready for formal school and a new level of thinking.

When I was six, I remember only looking at pictures in books. I couldn't read and didn't want to. Words were a bother to me. By the time I was seven, I read *Charlotte's Web* on my own and loved it. A child who's truly ready for academics can soak up these lessons quickly. There's hope. There's time.

But there's not enough time to play. A four-year-old will be a four-year-old only once. Concentrate on meeting his present needs. Don't foist future academics on him. If he's allowed to truly play now—spontaneous play with room for running, leaping, ka-powing, crying, dancing, painting, spilling and creative problem-solving—then he will be ready for academics later. When children gain social and emotional skills and confidence in the preschool years, academic learning naturally follows.

Stolen Time: Early Academics Hurt

"My son fidgets when he watches flash cards on TV with our learning-to-read video. He's three," one mother told me. "It's a battle every day. He's supposed to sit and give full attention to the screen."

Flash cards, testing and forced early academics for kids under age seven steal time away from play. We can make children memorize numbers and letters and study the calendar. If we're persistent, most four-year-olds can be trained to recognize letters well enough to read simple words. But at what cost? Early academics steal playtime, which is when nearly all of a child's emotional, social, physical and cognitive learning takes place. The child's brain is being asked to do something it doesn't need to do right now. As child psychologist David Elkind reminds us, "Miseducation teaches the wrong things at the wrong time." Social skills suffer. Joy suffers. Even future academic success can suffer. When a five-year-old drags home from school and yells, "Homework! I hate homework!" it's a painful state of affairs. A child like this learns: *I hate school. Learning is no fun.*

> Free play is freely chosen. It's child initiated and child directed.

Long-term psychology studies by Dr. Rebecca Marcon suggest that early academics in preschool can actually *set kids back* during elementary school. She found that kids who attended play-based preschools had better grades and better behavior once they reached elementary school. What's more, they were more creative and enthusiastic about learning than kids who started formal academics early. By the time they reached sixth grade, she was still seeing a difference. And of all the kids in academic preschools, boys suffered the most. This type of long-term research is backed by other studies. Dr. Lawrence Schweinhart tracked preschool kids into their twenties and found more future emotional trouble for kids who faced early academics. Neuroscientist Adele Diamond found kids who played during preschool developed better academic thinking abilities.

The loss of play literally hurts. Research from Yale University discovered kids were expelled from preschool more when they lacked the chance for dramatic play. Dr. Stuart Brown, who runs the National Institute for Play, says studies with animals show that play-deprived rats can't find mates or get on socially with other rats.

Every hour a child spends drilling academics, looking at flash cards or other "we'll make you smarter" stuff is lost time. And potentially damaging. Young kids become frustrated and stressed when they're required to sit still and handle academic tasks their brains aren't ready for. Too much stress can damage the prefrontal cortex, neuroscientists warn, an area critically important for memory and learning. Unless your child is reading joyfully on her own initiative or simply loves numbers, don't dwell on reading, writing or math yet. Young kids need to learn in the early years, but the way young brains learn is largely through free play.

Modern Kindergarten

The first kindergarten was set up by Friedrich Froebel in 1837. The word he coined, *Kindergarten*, means "children's garden" in German. It's no garden today. Froebel and early kindergarten pioneers banned letters and numbers from kindergarten. The Children's Garden was intended as a place for children to play in the "company of children under seven years old who do not learn to read, write and cipher."

"What do you remember about kindergarten?" I ask parents. "Oh," a father will say with a dreamy look in his eye, "we didn't do much. Just played mostly, sang some songs, had a snack, took a nap."

Kindergarten today is vastly different. Toys actually grow dusty. "We have blocks and a playhouse, but they don't get used much," a kindergarten teacher told me. "We don't have time for them." With so many structured lessons, including math, reading, social studies, science and more, free play is getting the squeeze. In many classrooms, kids take tests and have daily homework. It's common for five-year-olds to sit still for the majority of their seven-hour school day.

> *Play is the highest expression of human development in childhood, for it alone is the free expression of what is in a child's soul.*
>
> —Friedrich Froebel, father of kindergarten

Since many preschools today focus on academics, they ask kids to have social and emotional skills all figured out before they arrive. One school gave parents a handout called "Items Needed for Preschool." Along with a backpack and a jacket labeled with the child's name, it required all children to be able to get along socially with no bullying, hitting or pushing. This is absurd. Three- and four-year-olds shouldn't be expected to have mastered these skills already. This is the work of the preschool years.

Free Play Is a Child's Right

When Lee Row and Janet Stocker, the founders of my childhood preschool, set out to create the School for Young Children, they didn't start with a list of rules. They started by brainstorming a list of Children's Rights.

First and foremost was the Right to Uninterrupted Play. "Kids are learning so many things," Janet told me. "To interrupt, it's like someone interrupting you when you're deep in thought. We ought to respect kids' time and need for play." This Right to Uninterrupted Play informs many Renegade Rules, including choosing playmates and choosing not to share a toy.

A half-day preschool program is not the same as family life at home. Daily life does include interruptions, whether it's eating lunch or taking a nap. I've translated Janet and Lee's original list of rights to create Children's Renegade Rights for home life.

Children's Renegade Rights

A child has:

A right to unstructured free play.

A right to choose her own playmates.

A right to use props and choose his own play themes.

A right to uninterrupted play during playtime.

A right to feel safe.

A right not to have objects taken from her (forced sharing).

A right to move and use his body vigorously.

A right to be outside.

A right to experience and express the full range of her emotions.

A right to ask questions and know things.

A right to stand up for his own rights by setting limits on others' behavior.

A right to be listened to, to be respected, and to have her rights consistently supported by adults.

A right to grow at his own unique pace, following the natural course of child development.

Of course, rights and limits go hand in hand. One person's rights can't trample another person's. See Rule 2: It's OK If It's Not Hurting People or Property for tips on setting appropriate limits.

Reviving Free Play

Free play has many faces. It could be a child whacking two sticks together. It could be tree climbing, painting, making silly faces, digging in the sandbox or saying "Let's pretend." Whatever it is, the action is spontaneous, child initiated and child directed. The child follows her own ideas or the ideas of another playmate. When focused on play of their own interest, children are working at their optimum level of learning.

Free play evolves and flows; it does not conform to structure. Sure, she may enjoy more structured games from time to time, like board games or sports, but these should not take up much of a young child's time. She has other, better things to do.

Kids don't need much for free play, but they do need a few basics.

Free-Play Essentials

1. **Time for Play**

   Time is essential. Kids need plentiful unstructured time to play (in blocks of at least an hour). This means a child's early years should be free from formal academics, and his early days should have hours of unscheduled time.

2. **Space for Play**

   Kids need places to be where it's OK to touch, explore and get messy. Where can she be boisterous? Where can she discover the natural world? Your home does not have to be large, but you need to offer spaces (inside and out) where your child's play is welcome.

3. **Support for Play**

   Support comes in many forms. Resist encroachments on playtime. Rethink space. Dress your child in playclothes (clothes good for active movement and mess). Let your child be in the company of other children.

Free play demands large blocks of time of one to two hours or more. This allows kids to really engage in play. Dr. James Christie and Dr. Francis Wardle show that shorter play periods (less than thirty minutes) reduce the complexity and maturity of children's play. Kids will abandon sophisticated play to fit shorter time periods, but when they do that, free play loses many of its benefits. At my childhood preschool, teachers live by the mantra that kids need at least forty-five minutes to really get into good play with other children. Once deep play has started, of course, it needs time beyond that forty-five minutes to expand and play itself out.

False Free Play

Even preschools that purport to believe in free play actually give it little respect. Take a look at the daily schedules. If you see "free choice" time wedged in between multiple structured activities, group time and academic drilling, you'll know it's not truly the focus. Visit the classroom. Often "free play" is merely downtime while the teacher sets up the next structured activity.

I once watched a preschool teacher during "free choice" time. Instead of letting children freely play and explore, she directed the play by assigning them roles. "This is a restaurant," she told the five-year-olds. "You take the orders, Nicky. You can bring the food, Brenna. Who's going to cook?" Better to provide a play kitchen and let the children decide how to play with it themselves.

Playing *with* a child is fine. Contributing ideas is fine, too; that's part of play. But when you play with a young child, keep it child centered. Don't dominate. Make sure it's give-and-take.

Try This—Add to Your Toolbox

Sometimes as adults we fear free play. What are we going to do with the kids for all those hours? We rush to fill blank time with errands, TV and structured activities. Children's play engages their brains, but it can be tedious to adults. I've felt that panic myself, especially when the kids were very young and afternoons stretched so long.

Take heart. This is what your child was meant to do. As your family gets used to free play, it won't involve you so much. You can be nearby while your child plays on her own and with other kids—freeing you to do what you were meant to do.

Welcoming Free Play

1. **Make literacy joyful**

   Young kids don't need to study the alphabet. They need to fall in love with songs and stories. Sing songs, read nursery rhymes and do finger plays and chants. Read to your child over and over again. Write down kids' exact words to express their ideas and feelings (see Rule 7: Take Dictation from Your Tot), and use writing in their play. Let kids fall in love with storytelling and the power of words now—reading will follow later.

2. **Go outside**

   The world of free play opens up outside. Go to the park, walk in the woods or in the neighborhood. Play with balls. Seek out places with sand and water.

3. **Choose open-ended toys**

   The cardboard box is in the National Toy Hall of Fame (based in Rochester, New York). So are sticks and blankets. Give your child access to open-ended toys that promote imaginative play. Good ones: bells, flashlights, funny hats, old keys, buckets or baskets, blocks, dress-up clothes, blankets, clay or play-dough, ordinary dolls or stuffed animals (branded characters limit play possibilities). Don't forget sand, water, stones, puddles and the cardboard box.

4. **Offer space**

   Kids need room to play. Give children space to spread out with their "play du jour." Make room by rotating out extra toys and removing furniture. Find a spot inside, if you can, where rough, boisterous play is welcome. Look for places where you can say yes rather than no.

5. **Cut structured activities**

Does your daughter enjoy soccer at age four? She'll enjoy it more when she's nine. Kick the ball instead at the park or back-yard. Involve other kids. Make up your own games and laugh. For kids six and under, if you have two or more scheduled activities for your child a week, cut the number in half.

6. **Look for a play-based preschool**

This is harder to find than it used to be. If your child is already in preschool, go in and observe. Look for schools with at least three-quarters of the time devoted to free play and play-time in at least one- to two-hour blocks. Watch and see how much free play time kids actually get, both inside and outside, and how open-ended the play is. Change schools if need be.

7. **Slow down**

Young kids move at their own pace. Unpack your days. Parenting takes time.

WORDS TO TRY
Time to go outside!
What do you need for your boat (house, fort, game)?
Let's read a story together.

WORDS TO AVOID
What's this number?
This is the letter B. Can you say "B"?
Have you done your homework?

OUT AND ABOUT

"Oh, we can't do Thursday. That's Jason's swimming lesson, and after that he has violin." Kids are so scheduled it can be hard to set up a playdate. Seek out unscheduled families. You might find them at the park or library.

It's also hard not to compare your kids' activities with those of other kids. *Maybe Lucy is ready for violin lessons, too?* Even if you believe that your time picking dandelions with your child is valid, it can seem as if your family is being left behind. Stay grounded. When fellow parents ask "Are you doing music lessons with Lucy?" answer politely and proudly, "Right now we're mostly at home playing."

Rule 2

It's OK If It's Not Hurting People or Property

Free play is unstructured playtime, but that doesn't mean there aren't rules and limits. For example, three-year-old Samantha loved to pretend she was a dog. She asked her parents to put her supper in a bowl and feed her under the table. Next she demanded to eat "dog food" while sitting on top of the table itself. So night after night, that's how the family ate—two parents in chairs, and one creative three-year-old in command on top of the table.

Free play involves limits—both from adults and from other kids.

Renegade Reason
Free play is not a free-for-all. Set limits.

Samantha has a right to unstructured play, and a right to choose her own play theme (pretending she's a dog). However, her parents have the right to set limits on time and place. Not at the table. Not during mealtimes. Playtime comes after supper.

When it comes to play, parents have two main jobs: (1) to limit inappropriate behavior, and (2) to consistently support their children's rights. This means that when Jamie jumps up and down on the new sofa, he needs to be stopped. But Jamie also has a right to move and use his body vigorously. The play can go on, it just needs to be moved to a better location. Likewise, when Paige shoves her sister, she needs to be stopped. But Paige also has a right to play alone if she wishes, without her little sister. She has the right to choose her own playmates.

Children have rights, and adults do, too. Among others, parents have the right to personal sanity and the right to live in a home environment they like. Limits are the way people live together and get their needs met.

Renegade Blessings

Knowing what to limit and what to allow is the key to free play and successful family life. With the right limits, your child will learn:

> *Almost all my ideas for play are fine.*
> *Some things—like hurting people or destroying things—are just not acceptable.*
> *I'm not in charge; my parents are.*
> *Some places are for rough play, and other places aren't.*
> *I'm not the only one with rights.*
> *My parents will keep me safe.*

Setting Limits on Play

"I never tell children to stop running because they'll get hurt," says Jan Waters of the School for Young Children. "Running is normal. Kids are in motion. And, if they do get hurt, they'll learn it better."

What's appropriate play? What are appropriate limits? As parents, we sometimes hover and distrust our kids' play. Just look at the rules we make, like "no running" or "no sticks." We anticipate potential problems with safety, mess and hurt feelings. Although we may have enjoyed the same games as kids, as adults we're worried about things getting out of control.

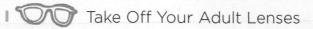

Take Off Your Adult Lenses

Children's play ideas are usually fine. Don't automatically ban the play your child wants to do. Change the timing or location. Set limits on his actions. Limits help everyone feel safe and comfortable and teach kids what's appropriate. Today limits are getting confused. We have both a quest for control and a desire for our children to like us. The result? We often overlimit play and underlimit other behavior. It's time to shift the balance. Loosen up in the world of play, but don't forget to set limits when they're needed.

Instead of stopping kids' play *in case* they get hurt, limit particular aspects of play. Sometimes that's the timing. Or the location. Sometimes it's how to use an item. For example, when kids run with scissors, we don't stop them from ever using scissors. We teach them to walk when carrying scissors; we teach them how to hold the scissors right. If running on cement floors is too dangerous, try skipping instead. That's what they do at Public School 3 in New York City's West Village. If you visit, you'll see kids skipping vigorously in the corridors. When it comes to outdoor play, limit the actual problem (throwing stones near people), not the play altogether (throwing stones in the lake).

Two-year-old Tyler liked to play with sticks. At the park he waved them around, accidentally hitting other kids. You could say, "Drop the sticks!" or you could redirect Tyler's play and teach him what's appropriate. "If you want to play with sticks, you have to do it away from other people. Move over here." That's a limit, not a ban.

Play also needs limits when it makes someone else feel unsafe. Cameron, age three, growled at Logan, another three-year-old boy. He said he was a tiger and tigers have to growl. Logan looked scared. Is this play OK? The tiger play was fine, but Logan didn't like being growled at and he has a right to feel safe. A good limit for Cameron would be: "You can growl, but not at Logan. He doesn't like it." Logan can even set this limit himself (see Rule 3: Kids Need Conflict).

When you set a limit, make sure kids stop. Be prepared to move them or physically restrain them. No need to get upset, just ask the child, "Can you stop or do I need to help you?" Then follow up.

Why It Works: The Renegade Golden Rule

Visitors sometimes stop by my childhood preschool. On a typical day, they'll see kids painting trees blue, kids racing tricycles wildly and kids wading in muddy water. Some kids are using real hammers. Others are coloring their arms green or running with toy swords.

Sometimes people ask if there are any rules at all at my childhood preschool.

There is one rule: It's OK if it's not hurting people or property. This is the Renegade Golden Rule, and it can guide play in almost any situation. How do you know if your child's play is OK or if it's out of line? Ask yourself: Is this play hurting people or property? The answer lets you know when to set limits.

Here are some examples. Chloe, age two, drips paint onto the dining room floor. It makes a neat-looking splot. Fascinated, she drops some more. Or maybe your niece and nephew come over and get into a wrestling match in the living room. The noise is deafening, and they're right near the fishbowl.

Try to find a way to say yes to play. Paint splatting itself may be fine. It makes interesting patterns, and young kids should experiment with art materials. Still, Chloe's play needs a limit. Make sure the paint's washable; put down a drop cloth or move the game outside. "If you want to drip paint, you can do it here. Otherwise, the paint stays in the tray." The same goes for wrestling. Wrestling next to the fish tank is out of line, and so is the noise. It's hurting others (tell them, "It's too loud for my ears") and could easily damage the aquarium. If the kids want to wrestle, make sure they know the living room's not the place. Send the wrestling match outside or to the basement.

When applying the Renegade Golden Rule, think of "hurting people or property" in the broadest terms. Hurting people includes feelings. It also includes the child herself (it's not OK for a child to harm herself intentionally). "People" can include living things (plants and animals should not be hurt). And when it comes to property, this means a wide variety of objects, including a picture a child drew, not just official "property," like a house or car.

The Renegade Golden Rule applies to most behavior in daily life, not only play. For example, your two-year-old is hopping mad and hits you. Not OK. People are not for hitting. This behavior violates the Renegade Golden Rule. As Becky Bailey writes, "All limits are based on safety. Any behavior that falls outside the boundary of that safety requires limit setting." Bailey, author of *Conscious Discipline* and other resources on limit setting, says limits keep young children safe from their own impulses.

Play can get wild—and that's OK—as long as it doesn't violate the Renegade Golden Rule.

Setting Limits Without Shame

It's all too easy to shame kids when we correct behavior and set limits. Haim Ginott was a strong proponent of setting limits on children without attacking their character or personality. He believed in the importance of saving face and advocated for a culture of dignity and respect when speaking with children. To do that, it helps to depersonalize discipline. Make it clear that it's the behavior that's bad, not the child herself. For example, say "I see toys and books on the floor" rather than "You're so lazy and you never listen! How many times do I have to tell you to clean up your room!"

> *Focus on what you don't like about the behavior, not the child.*

Ginott said kids accept limits better when the rebuke is not personal, but rather informational. Explain an object's true function, by saying things such as "The chair is for sitting, not standing" or "The blocks are for playing, not throwing."

When Benjamin, age three, throws sand at Lydia, his play has crossed the line. Sand in the eyes can really hurt. Lydia, also three, can set a limit and say "Stop!" (see Rule 3: Kids Need Conflict). If Benjamin won't or can't listen to the limit, you will have to do more. Place limit after limit on behavior like Benjamin's until the behavior is appropriate again. Here's how it unfolds:

1. Reinforce the limit.

   "Lydia said 'Stop.' You need to listen to Lydia and stop."

2. Describe and restrain behavior.

   "You're not stopping. I need to hold your hands until you can stop."

3. Ask for action.

   "Show me you're ready. When you tell me you can stop, I'll let go."

4. Follow through.

   "I can see it's too hard for you to stop throwing sand right now. I'm going to move you away from the sandbox. You'll have to play inside until you can tell me you'll stop throwing sand."

It becomes easier to set limits without shame when you realize what young kids can and can't do, according to their natural brain development. For instance, your daughter isn't being "bad" when she grabs the cookie package off the grocery shelf after you just told her not to; she really wants those cookies and doesn't have full impulse control yet.

Adele Faber and Elaine Mazlish, parent-child communication experts, talk a lot about the importance of setting limits in a respectful manner. They advise letting kids experience the consequences, not punishing. Instead of berating a child for breaking a limit ("Melanie! Didn't I just tell you not to do that? You're a bad girl. You never listen. Now get back here"), just enforce the limit. When a kid breaks a limit, you can give a shame-free warning first: "Oh, darn! Did you forget the rule? Remember, no crashing bikes." If the behavior continues, apply the next limit again, without shame. For example: "The rule is no crashing bikes into the house. You need to play with something else now. You can try again after supper." The consequence itself is enough.

Parents' Rights and Appropriate Power

On nights when my parents went out when I was little, my brother and I liked to play Doggie, Doggie with the babysitter. It involved a lot of barking and crawling around on hands and knees. Before my mother left, I remember her reminding the teenage babysitters that they had rights, too. "Remember, you don't have to play that game if you don't want to," she would tell them.

Adults have rights, too. Samantha's parents didn't like eating dinner with a "dog" on the table, but they didn't know how to stop it. Their three-year-old seemed to be in charge. Samantha was so verbal and insistent. They were nervous about curtailing her desires and wanted her to like them.

As parents, you are the child's primary teachers of what's appropriate and acceptable in our culture. You have the right to set limits on your child.

Young kids often demand power. Three-year-olds yell orders. Five-year-olds defy us. But believe it or not, kids don't always want what they ask for. When children this young get too much inappropriate power, they often feel insecure and uncertain. Setting limits is essential in play and daily life. Kids won't stop loving you. When you enforce limits, you send a clear message: Parents are in charge and will keep everyone safe.

"It can be very frightening for a child not to have limits," said Fred Rogers, beloved host of the children's TV program *Mister Rogers' Neighborhood*. "Not only can the world outside be frightening, but the world inside, the world of feelings, can also be scary when you're not sure you can manage those feelings by yourself."

Finding the right balance of power isn't easy. To get comfortable setting appropriate limits for free play, parents have to get used to the right balance of power and setting reasonable limits throughout the day.

Sometimes we ask our kids when we need to be telling them. Decide which questions are OK for your child to answer and which questions are not. For example, your son can easily answer a question like "Do you want the green shirt or the red one?" You don't care which shirt he wears; you just want him to get dressed. Don't ask your child a question when no is not an acceptable answer. Kids will often say no! Then you are left with two unpleasant options: either bowing to the dictates of your child or ignoring her completely and doing the opposite. For instance, here's a mother asking her two-year-old's opinion when she should be making the decision herself:

"Can Sarah use our wagon?" the mother asks.

"No!"

"Well, you're not using it. Sarah, it's OK for you to play with the wagon."

Involve kids in decision making, but choose your questions wisely.

Try This—Add to Your Toolbox

Limits for Free Play

Play sometimes needs different limits than we initially think. Pause and consider what the problem is before setting a limit on your child.

Setting Limits on Play

1. **Find a way to say yes to play**

   Maybe the play is OK, but not the how, where or when. Limit something specific. Try to offer an alternative when you set a limit. "Blocks are not for throwing. Do you want to throw? Here are some beanbags."

2. **Don't assume safety problems**

   Let kids take some tumbles in their play. Reserve "Stop!" for true safety problems (busy streets, the edge of a fast river) or hidden dangers (a dead branch when your child is climbing a tree; black ice on the driveway).

3. **Apply the Renegade Golden Rule**

   Examine the play. Is it actually hurting anything or anybody? The play theme might not be to your taste, but that's not a reason to ban it.

4. **Help kids listen to limits set by other kids**

   Limits can come from anyone, and peer limits are vitally important. Chances are, if kids are setting a limit, their rights are being infringed. Someone's not feeling safe or listened to.

5. **Set limit after limit**

   Kids can't always stop on their own. Acknowledge, "It's too hard for you to stop right now." Then help a child follow the limit, physically moving or restraining her body, if necessary. You may have to set additional limits: "You'll have to play next to me until you tell me you can stop."

Limits for Daily Life

The other day I was at the grocery store with my three-year-old. When he was younger, Zach always rode in the cart, but now he likes to walk.

That's fine, but I need to get the shopping done and make sure he doesn't knock all the crackers off the shelf. So we set some limits.

"You can ride or walk. If you walk, you need to hold on to the cart," I told him.

"I will!" Zach said.

Some days Zach can handle the freedom of walking next to me and other days he can't. Three-year-olds don't have strong impulse control. Often the temptation to touch things or run away is simply too great.

"I see you're not holding on to the cart. You're showing me you want to ride."

Then despite Zach's squawks, I slipped him back into the grocery cart seat.

"You're mad," I said to him. "You want to keep walking, but when you walk, you have to hold on to the cart. Next time we can try again."

The grocery cart incident doesn't merit yelling. Yelling usually happens when our patience reserves are depleted and we can't think of any other options. Use a firm and powerful voice for daily limit setting, but save your loud voice and high energy for serious events—when your toddler might tip a pot of boiling water or your preschooler runs into the street.

Learning how to set effective limits is central to parenting—in the preschool years and in the years to come. Here are a few ideas:

Setting Limits in Daily Life

1. Set expectations ahead of time

Let your child know what behavior you expect before you arrive. For example: "When we go to the library, we talk quietly and walk like little mice." Or "When we go into this store, there will be lots of things on the shelves. They're not for touching. Hands stay in your pockets."

2. Set the right expectations

This might require learning something more about child development. Should your four-year-old be getting dressed on his own? Can your three-year-old clean up her room? We often set expectations too high or too low for our kids. Learn more about what's age-appropriate.

3. Don't yell. Get fierce on purpose

Kids don't like being yelled at. They'll tune it out, and you'll get a headache. Match your energy level to the severity of the situation. Don't cry wolf with your kids by yelling routinely. Be fierce only when it matters (a child hits another child or runs into the street).

4. Don't ask the child, if you don't want no for an answer

Strike the right balance of power. It's fine to ask your child's opinion, but reserve decisions you care about for yourself.

5. Say what you mean

"I meant what I said and I said what I meant," chants Dr. Seuss's Horton the Elephant. Unfortunately, that's harder as parents. We tend to blurt out threats ("If you don't stop that, we're leaving this instant. I mean it!"). Then we backpedal. Try to avoid saying "I mean it." You should always mean what you say. To get the right words out, take a breath, buy time. Talk less, and when you do talk . . . mean it. Saying what you mean also involves following through.

WORDS TO TRY
Redirecting play
This is not a good place. Where could we do that?
This is not the right room for wrestling.
If you want to play with sticks, you need to move away from other people.
Blocks are not for throwing. We can get beanbags to throw.

Setting limits on behavior
I can't let you do that.
Can you stop, or do I need to help you?
I see it's too hard for you to control your body right now. I'm going to help you.
I will hold your hands until you can stop.
You're not listening to Brian's words. Until you can stop, you'll have to play in a different room.
I'm sorry that makes you mad. You can try again later.
I know you don't like it, but I'm here to keep you safe.
Show me you're ready. When you tell me you can stop, you can come back.

WORDS TO AVOID
No running!
Put that stick down!
No, you can't do that, and don't ask me again.
Because I said so.

OUT AND ABOUT
What to do when you allow your child to climb trees at the park or bang sticks on the ground, and other parents forbid it? One

tip that can help is to set limits for your child in a firm voice. This lets everyone know (your child and any onlookers) what's OK for your family and what's not. Other parents may not agree with your philosophy, but they will get the message that you are in charge of your kid and aware of what's going on. If no other child but yours is allowed to pick up a stick in the park, then move off to the side. There your child can bang her stick in peace, and it won't be such a temptation to the other children.

In public settings like the grocery store, it can be intimidating to stay firm about the limits you set. You may have to let the groceries melt. Or deny your child the chance to come with you next time. Think deeply before you set a limit. Then be sure to enforce it.

Rule 3 | Kids Need Conflict

My son Myles came home from preschool with a "Living in Peace" handout. It had a face he was supposed to color and lyrics to the tune of "Row, Row, Row Your Boat": "Let's all live in peace, let's play harmony . . ."

"Don't teach children about peace by singing about it," Jan Waters told me emphatically when I first started writing this book. Jan teaches at the School for Young Children. "That's just something cute that adults like. Children will sing it if they like the tune. But that's not *really* teaching peace. Children learn by having problems."

Developing conflict-resolution skills is perhaps the main job of early childhood. In these years, your child can gain practice encountering other people, having conflicts and learning how to work through problems in a way that doesn't hurt anyone.

Renegade Reason

Mediation takes practice. Kids gain vital social skills when they encounter—and learn to unravel—conflict.

Resolving problems is a social skill—an enormously important skill. Without it, nations head to war and families plunge into turmoil. UN diplomats are trained mediators. If given the chance, your child can become a skilled mediator, too.

As with any skill, kids need the chance to practice. Again and again, kids need to "bump into" other children during their play and experience conflict. *He has that toy—I want it! She took my spot. I was sitting there!* Each of these minor clashes is a tremendous opportunity to develop peace skills. With a little guidance, your child can assert her rights, stand up for others and gain the complex social skills of a mediator.

Children as young as two can learn conflict-mediation skills. Young kids can stand up for their rights, confront the other person directly and communicate their feelings—the first steps in resolving a problem. Older kids, ages four to six, can become true diplomats: sometimes mediating problems independently, coming up with a mutual solution and putting it into action.

Kids at my childhood preschool have been successfully mediating conflicts for forty years. The steps are simple, and resolving conflict may be the most important lesson you ever give your child. Because this Renegade Rule is so important, this is the longest chapter in the book. Conflict-resolution skills are fundamental to everything in our world. Whether it's a small issue, like who gets the bunny bowl, or a larger issue, like which nation controls oil reserves, conflict is always part of our lives.

Renegade Blessings

By experiencing conflict, your child can learn lifelong skills, including positive assertiveness, independence and mediation skills for managing future conflicts:

I can stand up for myself and stop things I don't like.

I know how to set limits on other kids.

When I have a problem with another person, I speak up and tell him or her directly and clearly what I don't like.

I have to listen to what other people say to me, and stop when they set limits.

Sometimes what I was worried about at first wasn't even the problem.

Our ideas might not be the same, but together we can work something out.

I don't always need an adult's help. I can solve many of my own problems.

Peace and Conflict

Conflict is part of everyday human life, yet we tend to wish it away. We don't teach kids how to deal with conflict, because we're scared of it. We just don't like it. Many of us avoid conflict and confrontation at all costs.

As parents we good-naturedly focus on peace for our children. We tell kids to "be kind" and "be nice to your sister." But "peace" doesn't last if it sidesteps conflict. Unresolved issues will pop up again.

Peace isn't found in a peace sign, song or slogan. Achieving peace takes work. The work of conflict mediation.

> *Peace isn't the absence of conflict. Peace is the respectful resolution of conflict.*

The minister at my church once asked us to write for five minutes starting with the phrase "Conflict is . . ." "Conflict is good," I wrote. "It gives us the chance to encounter new ideas and grow and change together." Mine was the only answer that addressed the positive side of conflict.

Conflict does not have to be violent. I like to think of conflict as two different ideas bumping up against each other. When ideas bump, there's potential for aggression and hurt feelings, but also the chance for growth, collaboration and creativity.

Of course, no one wants to dwell on that when the kids are squabbling over who gets the blue cup and why did Nora get to sit next to the window *again*?

That's the job of conflict mediation.

Why It Works

Developmentally, it can take years for children to understand what causes a conflict. Psychologist Kevin O'Connor says this sequence skill develops around age eleven. Most preschool-age children don't realize a problem has begun until they personally feel pain. Explaining what happened and offering basic information ("Your arm hit his body") helps children understand how their actions impact others.

Psychologist and educator Becky Bailey says conflict helps kids develop social understanding and empathy. Children's egocentric worldviews expand when they interact with other children. When conflict arises, children encounter a perspective different from their own.

Many early-childhood experts stress the importance of involving children in problem-solving their own conflicts. Let your child know it's her problem, not the adult's, and she needs to talk to the other child directly. You can be there for moral support. Child communication experts Adele Faber and Elaine Mazlish show how this empowers children and often results in the most satisfying and original solutions.

Take Off Your Adult Lenses

Talk of peace isn't meaningful to young kids. Neither is "being nice." Kids need chances to navigate conflict firsthand and learn what's appropriate. What do I do when conflict comes up? What do I say? How do I set a limit on another's behavior? Once kids know these answers they can mediate their own conflicts in most amazing ways.

My kids made a blanket fort the other day. All was fine until Zach, the younger one, threw a heavy plastic toy, which landed on his brother's head. Myles, age six, yowled and left the fort in protest. Zach, age three, cried, too—he'd lost his playmate. "What can you do to help Myles feel safe?" I asked Zach. As I watched, both kids came up with creative solutions I never would have thought of. Zach said, "Myles, I will only throw soft things. Then it's OK, right?" Myles said, "Will you show it to me before you drop it? Then I can say yes or no." Zach agreed and showed him a blue blanket. "This is great!" said Myles. They were back playing together, and Myles felt safe and in control.

Bullying

As a boy, President Obama was taunted about his big ears and funny name. He's no exception. Each year thirteen million U.S. kids are affected by bullying. That's one-third of the kids in school, or more if you also count the bullies.

Anti-bullying programs are on the rise, but most skirt the real issue of conflict. At my son's preschool, the kids stapled together little books called "Hands Are for Helping." At church, the three- to five-year-old group colored in leaflets that said "No Bullying Zone!" Neither of these activities helps kids prevent bullying. Effective anti-bullying programs give kids tools to respond to conflict. What to say. What to do. How to assert themselves and stop behavior they don't like. How to step in and stand up for others. And practice doing it.

Practice is absolutely essential. When we whisk kids away from conflict, we don't give them a chance to practice. Think about teaching a child to count. If she says, "One, two, three, four, six, ten," we don't punish her or give her fewer chances to practice. Instead, we encourage her and give her more opportunities to practice the skill. Conflict-mediation skills should be thought of in the same light. If a child has trouble coping with conflict, by all means don't limit her exposure to it. Encourage her, show her what to do, and support her so she will eventually be successful.

Free Play Brings Conflict Opportunity

Conflict is an opportunity to embrace in the early years—and luckily there is no shortage of it when kids play. Unstructured play is the absolute best way for kids to learn peace skills, because spontaneous free play provides countless chances to encounter problems. Free play lets children interact with one another and confront conflict firsthand.

I know many parents who send their children to preschool precisely to gain experience with other children. That's a terrific reason. But today's preschools rarely make room for free play and conflict. Too many classrooms focus on "peace" and order rather than letting the children interact and risk a conflict.

A classroom with too much structure is a terrible place to learn about peace. Why? Because it's a land of missed opportunities. Adults rush in to

Children learn about peace by having problems.

solve problems or squash conflict. When children learn to rely on rules and adults, they miss the chance to develop direct social skills with peers.

Here's an example of a teacher suppressing conflict: Three children are playing at the water table. Two more children arrive and want to play. "All right, boys," says the teacher. "Three more minutes. Then your time's done." After three minutes have gone by, she announces, "OK, time's up. Move on to something else." The new kids don smocks and the original three walk away.

This could be considered a success. New kids got a turn, and nobody screamed. But a few screams could have been helpful. The teacher in this case avoided conflict by deciding on a solution before the children even noticed there was a problem. Why was three children the limit? In a free play scenario, five, six or ten children could crowd the same water table. If the lack of space bothered the children, that would become a prime opportunity to bring in conflict mediation. *What's going on here? I see a lot of kids in one spot. Do you have enough room? What could you do?* View conflict as an opportunity. Don't rescue children (or blame or lecture). Give them tools and guidance.

Mediating conflicts with kids doesn't have to be hard. Of course, some conflicts do get sticky, but most mediations look something like this:

> *Daniel and Jason, both age four, are playing in a kiddie pool. Jason splashes water roughly.*
>
> DAN: Don't!
>
> *Jason keeps splashing.*
>
> DAN: Don't!
>
> ADULT: I heard you say "Don't." What don't you want him to do?
>
> DAN *(whispering to adult)*: Don't splash water on me.
>
> ADULT: Tell him.
>
> DAN *(to Jason)*: Don't splash water on me!
>
> *Jason stops splashing.*

Of course, we don't always have time or inclination to guide kids through every conflict. But the more we do, the better they will get. Cries for *"Mom!"* diminish. Practicing peace skills makes kids more independent.

Lacking Skills

Kids who don't have conflict-mediation skills are glaringly obvious. They expect adults to solve their problems, and they run for help whenever they encounter conflict. Here's what happened at the Gilbert home.

When the neighbor kids came over to play, they would shout, "Mrs. Gilbert, Kevin won't let me play with his truck!" or "Mrs. Gilbert, Adrienne isn't letting me be the princess!" She turned to them and said, "Well, *tell* him! Tell her!" The neighbor kids had no idea they could solve problems themselves. Moms and dads don't have to be dragged into kids' conflicts. It unfairly makes parents judge and jury. It wastes adult time. Most important of all, it deprives children of learning fundamental social skills.

Of course, young children need lots of guidance before they can handle peer conflicts independently. But even kids as young as two can start to learn. The joy of conflict mediation is that it builds patterns kids will adopt and follow on their

> Stating your feelings and wishes clearly is the first step in solving problems with another person.

own, without an adult around. Why? Because it works. Kids engaged in solving their own problems will expect to take an active role in working out problems they encounter throughout life.

Practice, Practice, Practice

Resolving conflict requires complex social skills. Kids aren't born with social skills; they need practice. That means plenty of time for spontaneous, unstructured human interaction. Play gives the best practice. Free play gives kids countless opportunities to "bump into" other kids and experience conflict. The more your child practices—when to speak up, what words to say, how to find the courage to assert herself—the more naturally she will be able to navigate the complex web of social relationships.

Try This—Add to Your Toolbox

Here you'll find specific tools to learn about conflict mediation for kids. The first part outlines ten steps for successful mediation, plus a step-by-step summary guide. The second part highlights strategies to use, including modifying mediation techniques for younger kids, ages two to three, and what to do when you witness a conflict but didn't see how it started.

Part 1: Ten Steps for Mediating Conflict with Kids

1. Help Kids Stop

First, help kids to stop behavior they don't like. Rather than rushing to rescue your child, ask questions and state what you see. This helps kids develop social awareness and learn to read body language.

Point out what you observe: "I see you putting your hands up. Do you want him to throw balls at you?" "I hear Sarah screaming and saying 'Stop!'" Or "I heard you say 'Don't.' What don't you like?"

Question behavior: "Did you like it when she did that?" "Did you want him to splash you?" "Did you like it when he knocked over your blocks?" Or "Did you want to be pushed?"

Go ahead and ask these questions. There may not be a conflict after all (*I like to be pushed—we're playing bulldozer*), but raising the question lets kids know they have a right to set limits and stop a situation they don't like. "Did you like what she did? No? Well, tell her!" This lets children know they have options.

2. Bring Kids Together

Some kids run from conflict. Others run for adult help. Bring the kids together. Kids need physical proximity to work out their problems. Walk the child back to the situation. You might put an arm on her shoulder for comfort. Touching reassures each child in a conflict, and helps them both realize you care about them. It's especially helpful to put your arm around the waiting child while you listen to the other. This simple action reassures the child. *My story won't be ignored. I'll get my turn to talk, too.*

3. Identify Feelings

Empathy is absolutely key. Kids will come together and talk to each other if they think you really understand their feelings. Voice feelings on both sides right away: "I bet you felt angry when he took your shovel. And John, you looked scared when he yelled at you. Is that how you felt?" Let kids know that you understand: "Sometimes I get angry when someone takes my things, too. And I don't like to be yelled at. Loud voices can be scary." Each child in a conflict needs to believe that you will truly support him. Otherwise, children may clam up and not be able to participate in the problem-solving. Build their trust through empathy.

4. Tell the Right Person—Direct Confrontation

"I'm telling! Mom, Danny pushed me! Mom!"

The problem with "telling" is that the child usually tells the wrong person. Mom can help, but the person who really needs to listen is the other child involved in the conflict.

Instead of running for Mommy, Daddy or teacher, kids can learn to deal directly with the child who caused the problem. The act of telling changes to "Tell him what you didn't like" instead of "I'm telling!" When a child runs up to you saying, "Danny pushed me," respond with, "You need to talk to Danny." Then go help her do exactly that.

It's important to feed the child the exact words she can say herself. "Tell him: 'I don't like it when you hit me.'" Older or more experienced conflict solvers may only need to be reminded, "Tell him."

Kids younger than six generally need you to be there. Guide them. Help them speak directly to the other child. If it's two kids on the playground and they don't know each other, introduce them. For example, Noah runs for help and points at another kid.

NOAH: He's bumping me!
ADULT: Sounds as if you didn't like that. You need to tell him.
Adult walks him over to Taylor.
ADULT: This is Noah. He's worried about something. Can you tell him what you're worried about?
NOAH: Don't bump me.
ADULT: He doesn't want you to bump him. Can you tell him you won't do that?
TAYLOR: OK.

5. Listen to Peers

Some kids don't listen when another child sets a limit. Listening can be a radical concept. Kids aren't used to listening to other kids. Usually adults set rules and kids conveniently overlook what other kids say. With peer-conflict mediation, children's words are taken seriously. The adult's job is to guide the talk and help kids listen to each other directly. Be there to back up your young mediator. Repeat your child's words to validate them. Speak loudly if your child whispers.

6. Define the Problem

Two- and three-year-olds may especially need your help to frame the problem. For example, young kids might only shout out, "No! No! No!"

This was the case for Gabe, who had built an elaborate road system for his cars and didn't want Scarlett to touch anything. "No! No! No! Go away!" he yelled. Help a child like Gabe define the problem. You might say, "Are you worried about your cars? You don't want Scarlett to touch your cars? Tell her: 'Don't touch my cars!' Help kids learn how to be specific when they set a limit.

7. Reinforce

The child's job is to speak up and express her wishes and feelings. Your job is to guide and reinforce her words. You can help teach listening skills by echoing and intervening when necessary.

Being an echo is a great teaching tool. In some cases, the adult is truly an echo—repeating the child's words loudly enough so both kids can hear. If a child murmurs a quiet answer, repeat it boldly: "She said: 'Don't touch me!' You may need to serve as spokesperson and talk for both kids: "I heard Jamie say . . ." "Rachel says she doesn't like sand in her face." If you model how it works, kids will catch on. Rephrase words so the message is always coming from the child.

Echoing isn't always enough; sometimes you have to intervene. Sometimes kids won't stop (or can't stop themselves). Other times kids don't understand. Let your child know you can always be called upon to help sort things out.

After church one sunny morning, the kids were playing on the swings outside. Six-year-old Emerson began throwing wood chips at my son, Myles, also six. Myles giggled at first. Then he yelled, "Stop! Stop throwing wood chips at me!" Emerson still thought it was a game and kept pelting him. Myles began to cry.

"Do you want some help?" I asked. "You clearly said what you didn't want, and he's not stopping." Myles said yes, and I turned to Emerson.

"Emerson, I heard Myles say, 'Stop throwing wood chips.' You need to listen to Myles. Stop when someone says 'Stop!'"

Instead of insisting on rules, this method focuses on listening. Listen to the limits another child sets. Adult intervention reinforces the child's words—even if you have to physically stop a child.

8. Problem Solve

Once both kids are clear about what the problem is and how they feel, it's time to problem solve. Ask them, "What could you do to solve this problem?" Offer ideas or information if they get stuck. "I know sometimes kids make a waiting list. Do you want to try it?"

9. Get a Commitment

Don't skip this step. Ask for a simple verbal commitment. For example: "Jimmy said, 'Stop throwing sand at me!' Are you going to stop?" A child who says yes or nods her head is more likely to honor her commitment to Jimmy than a child who doesn't answer (or one who says no!). You can also use a written contract to make a commitment. Consider the conflict still open unless you get a positive answer.

See more about verbal agreements, written contracts and kids who refuse to comply in "Strategies for Conflict Mediation" (page 50).

10. Put a Solution into Action

Kids are more likely to abide by their own agreements. So go ahead and try it, even if their solution is a bit off-the-wall. Tell the kids, "Let's try your idea and see if it works." If it doesn't, you can always problem solve again. "Hmm . . . that didn't work too well. Now let's try a new idea. How about . . . ?"

Ten Steps for Conflict Mediation with Kids

1. **Help kids stop**

   Point out what you observe. Interpret words and body language. ("I see you putting your hands up. Do you want him to throw balls at you?") Ask questions. ("Did you like it when he took your ball?")

2. **Bring kids together**

   Kids need to be close enough to see and hear each other. Bring back a child who runs away. ("You need to listen to Danny.") Get down at kid level. Touch, listen and look in their eyes. Support both kids.

3. **Identify feelings**

   Empathize. Show you understand each child's feelings. ("You feel mad he broke your castle.") Suggest feelings. ("Are you feeling mad that he took your toy?") Be matter-of-fact. ("You didn't like that. You wish you could have this toy.")

4. **Tell the right person—direct confrontation**

   Help kids face each other and speak directly to the other child. ("Tell her"/"Tell him.") Give children exact words. ("Tell her: 'I don't like it when you hit me!'") Stay with them as they talk.

5. **Listen to peers**

   Put the children in charge. Make sure each child knows he has to listen to the other child. Guide and support kids in this process.

6. **Define the problem**

   Help kids be specific about limits. ("I hear you saying 'stop!' What do you want Alexander to stop doing?") State what the child doesn't like. Restate it in the child's own words. ("Benny says he didn't like it when you pushed him.")

7. **Reinforce**

Echo what the kids say. Echoing reinforces the message and makes it louder. Intervene, if necessary, to help a child stop or listen.

8. **Problem solve**

Ask: What could you do to solve this problem? Offer information. ("I know playing in the water you might get wet.") Offer ideas. ("I know sometimes kids make a waiting list. Do you want to try it?")

Help kids define limits and set them on other kids. ("Jessica says you can play with the train if you don't crash the track.")

9. **Get a commitment**

Ask kids for a verbal agreement. ("Are you going to stop?") Or sign a written contract.

10. **Put a solution into action**

Try the children's solution first. Problem solve again and try a new idea if it doesn't work.

Part 2: Strategies for Conflict Mediation

Written Contracts

One way for kids to set peer limits is through a dictated letter. Here four-year-old Liam clearly states what he doesn't like and makes some promises of his own, so the letter becomes a safety contract.

> *Dear Max,*
> *Don't call me mean or don't call me stupid.*
> *Don't say I'll kill you.*
> *I won't push you or hurt you.*
>
> > *Liam*

Even if Max and Liam can't read and don't become friends, a letter like this carries authority, sets clear behavior limits and gives each boy a sense of safety.

Verbal Limits

Verbal limits work, too. To make a limit effective, make sure the child agrees to it before you consider the conflict resolved. A simple nod will do. Jessica, age three, was playing with trains. Brian came by because he liked trains, too, and crashed the track. With adult help, Jessica set limits on Brian and told him clearly what he needed to do if he wanted to play trains with her: "You can play with the train if you don't crash the track." "OK," agreed Brian.

Agreements like this take listening. Each child has a chance to say how she is feeling and what she doesn't want the other child to do. For some kids, listening to another child is a radical concept.

The key to these social contracts is putting the child in charge. It's one three-year-old who sets a limit on another three-year-old. It's Max and Liam who have an agreement. Kids who learn how to set limits on peers won't be easily bamboozled out of their rights when an adult isn't around.

> *Put the child in charge. Help kids listen to one another and set limits on peers.*

Conflict Mediation with Young Kids (Ages Two to Three)

Body language works great for the youngest children. Start with a strong stance. Coach kids by saying, "Put out your hand like this. Use a loud voice. Say 'Stop!'"

Speak and echo for kids who don't or won't talk. Make sure the dialogue is coming from the child. (For example: "Rachel says, 'Don't take my blocks!'") Young kids will catch on quickly and mimic you. Don't be afraid to empower young kids. The earlier they start, the more conflict mediation becomes second nature. You are teaching skills for a lifetime.

When Kids Refuse

Kids don't always do what we want them to, even in conflict mediation. Sometimes a child refuses to participate or won't agree to stop the problem behavior, even after it's been talked about. Make a good attempt to involve both kids. After that, you might have to continue one-on-one with a reluctant child.

You know you have more work to do if you ask "Are you going to stop throwing sand?" and the answer is "No!" or silence. Stick with the situation. First reinforce: "You have to stop when Jimmy says 'Stop.'" Next, take action: "I have to move you away. I see it's too hard for you to stop right now."

Sometimes moving away is all that's needed. Other times a child needs more time with you. Focus back on feelings: "You look angry." Something inside her is still upset and needs more time and patience. At this point in the conflict, your role changes to helping that one child express more feelings (draw an angry picture, run fast; see Rules 5 to 7 in the Wild Emotions section for ideas). Take care of these feelings first and problem solve when she's good and ready.

When You Didn't See What Happened

You walk into the room and see two children screaming over a toy. Who had it first? What would be fair? What really happened?

We anguish over these situations because we want to be fair judges. But peer mediation helps us avoid the judge role. Didn't see the conflict start? State what you do see: "Looks like you both want this toy," or "Wow, you look mad!"

You don't have to be an eyewitness to unravel a problem. Sometimes it's even easier if you aren't; it forces you to help the kids work it out. Relax and use basic conflict-mediation steps. Make statements. Ask questions. Don't worry about what you don't know; stick to what you do know. State the obvious and focus on emotions to help kids untangle the situation.

> *Two kids are screaming and tugging at the same toy in the sandbox. An adult appears.*
> ADULT: What's happening? You look upset. You both want this shovel. (*State what you see.*)
> GAVIN: I had it first!
> RAJ: I was playing with it! It's mine!
> ADULT: You sound mad. You both think you had it first. (*Stick to what you know.*) You both wish you could play with it right now.

Remember, even if you witness a conflict start, you don't always know what kids are thinking. It's no different here. Ask and involve the children in the solution. Piece the story together and reflect back the kids' answers: "Sounds as if you were digging and then went to the bathroom." Or "The problem is that Gavin wanted to dig, so he took your shovel." Or "You need to dig a big hole, and Gavin is worried your digging will mess up his road. What can we do?" Reflecting back shows you're listening and helps move the conflict to a solution.

You're not a detective. You don't ever need to know exactly what happened. All you need to do is identify feelings and help the children listen to each other and make a plan.

Keep Things Neutral

Conflicts can happen even when one child is unaware there's a problem. Assume neutrality when you help kids discover the problem. Even if one kid is "at fault," helping him save face can make him more willing to cooperate in a solution.

Will and AJ are shoving and pushing each other.
ADULT: What's happening?
AJ: He hurt my hand!
ADULT: Did you know the way you moved hurt his hand?
(*Offering neutral information*)
WILL: No.
ADULT: AJ, you can tell him, "Be careful of my body!"

Parents: Work hard to stay neutral. Don't pounce on your own kid, or automatically support the youngest sibling. You do your best parenting work when you don't take sides, even emotionally. Many of us have a tendency to come down harder on older kids (younger siblings are experts at exploiting this one!) or to unfairly pick on our own child. It's easy to do. We feel embarrassed. We take our child's behavior personally and feel judged by other adults. Remember, all children have feelings, and it takes two to tango.

WORDS TO TRY
Help kids stop the behavior
Stop! What's happening?
Did you like it when she did that?
Do you want Bobby to push you? Tell him to stop.
Put your hand out like this. Use a big voice. Say "Stop!"

Bring kids together; tell the right person
You need to talk to Danny, not me.
I'm not sure Rachel knows that. Let's tell her.
Tell her in a big voice. Tell her loudly so she can hear.
Tell him what you don't like.
Rachel has something she wants to tell you.

Dan, come back. You need to listen to Rachel.

Can you say it, or do you want me to help?

I'll hold the ball while we work this out.

Define the problem; identify feelings

I heard you say "Stop." What do you want him to stop?

I heard you say "Don't." What don't you like?

You don't like that. It makes you mad. You wish you could have the train now.

Peer listening and reinforcement

I heard Sam say, "Stop throwing wood chips." You need to listen to Sam.

When someone says "Stop," you have to stop.

He's not listening. Say, "I need help!" You can always ask an adult for help.

Jessica, Rachel does not like pushing. She says no pushing on her body.

Get a commitment

OK, that's your rule. If you want to play with the trucks, you have to follow Sarah's rule.

Can you do that? Are you going to stop?

He said "Stop," and I see it's too hard for you to stop. I have to move you away.

When you didn't see what happened

I hear two kids yelling. What happened?

Looks like you both want this toy.

You sound mad. You both think you had it first.

You both wish you could play with it right now.

WORDS TO AVOID

All right, you two. Break it up.

I don't care who started it. You're both in trouble.

He's younger; give him the ball.

If you can't play nicely with it, I'll take it away.

I don't want to hear it.

OUT AND ABOUT

By teaching your child how to face conflict and speak up directly, you may encounter culture clash. Children are often eager to share their feelings and help solve a conflict. Adults you meet might be uncomfortable. You can't change that. Try explaining your goals: "We're working on problem-solving with Teresa. Do you mind if we let the kids try to work out the problem they had in the sandbox?"

Be prepared for a variety of reactions if you take this technique out in public. One morning at a toddler gym time, another boy pushed my son and tried to take his bike, then ran away when I came up. Myles was three at the time. "Did you like it when that boy pushed you?" I asked. "No!" said Myles. He looked mad and also a little scared. "Let's go tell him how you feel," I said. "You can tell him not to push you again." We found the boy standing by his mother's leg. After saying hello, I let Myles do the talking. "Myles has something to tell your son," I said. Myles told the boy he didn't like being pushed. The mother stood in shocked silence. Then she grabbed her child by the arm and pulled him away. "We know when we're not wanted," she said. "We don't need to take this. Come on, let's get out of here."

Other times, it works like a charm, even with kids who are completely new to the idea. At the playground one afternoon, a girl complained to Karen about her son. "You should stop him," she said. "He's got a big stick on the climber." "Sounds as if you think that's a bad idea," said Karen. "Let's go tell him." Together they walked over, and Karen opened the mediation: "There's something worrying Layla and she wants to tell you about it." Layla spoke up and Karen's son listened, both kids gaining good practice in conflict mediation.

Section II

Wild Emotions

The best way out is always through.

—Robert Frost

Rule 4 · All Feelings Are OK. All Behavior Isn't

Benjamin, age four, was furious at his mother. He didn't want to be at preschool. When he first arrived, Benjamin swung his lunch box hard and hit his mom. His mother looked embarrassed but didn't stop him. Instead, his teacher jumped up.

"Hey!" she said, raising her voice to match his energy level. "People are not for hurting. You can be mad, but you can't hit people. And that includes your mother."

Renegade Reason

Mad, sad and scared feelings are OK. Show kids what is appropriate and what's not when those feelings arise.

Parents often say, "I just want my child to be happy." True happiness is not about being happy all the time, but about having the skills to cope with the full range of human emotion. You can teach this skill.

I remember sitting cross-legged on the rug at preschool, singing, "If You're Happy and You Know It, Clap Your Hands." My four-year-old feet shook the floor as we sang the next verse: "If you're mad and you know it, stomp your feet!"

If you don't know the lyrics, here's a popular version:

If you're happy and you know it, clap your hands (repeat).
If you're happy and you know it, then your face will surely show it.
If you're happy and you know it, clap your hands.

This children's classic has the potential to teach valuable lessons on life emotions. But beware—the lyrics change depending on who's singing it. In my childhood preschool, we all wailed loudly for the sad verse ("If you're sad and you know it, you can cry") and added verses for all sorts of emotions (scared, excited, lonely). Many modern versions keep repeating "happy-happy-happy" on each verse, as if the goal is to keep the whole world smiling.

The truth is, we're not happy all the time. As parents, we know firsthand that young children are not happy all the time, either. They explode with joy one moment and implode with rage, frustration or fear the next.

Kids' feelings are so powerful, it's easy to get shaken by their intensity. So we say things to push those ugly, unwanted emotions back in the box. We tell kids, "That's nothing to cry about. Be a big boy." Or we say, "That's not nice. You shouldn't feel that way." Part of parenting is learning to accept uncomfortable feelings—especially if they're directed at you.

Angry kids, weepy kids, clingy kids, whiny kids. We need to accept the feelings behind it all, but we don't need to put up with antisocial or irritating behavior. Even happy kids sometimes need limits on their behavior.

Renegade Blessings

Accepting your child's feelings and teaching emotional skills are gifts that will last your child's whole life.

I don't have to hide my feelings.

I don't have to be happy all the time. My family will still love me.

It's OK to feel all sorts of ways.

Feelings come and go.

People listen to me. My feelings and ideas are important.

I know how to express my feelings without hurting anybody or anything.

Why It Works

"Fish swim, birds fly and people feel," said Haim Ginott. A child psychologist, Ginott wrote the best-selling classic *Between Parent and Child*, which has guided generations of parents in accepting children's feelings, especially hard-to-take negative feelings. "If a child is to grow up honest," wrote Ginott, "he must not be encouraged to lie about his feelings, be they positive, negative, or ambivalent."

When it comes to young children, feelings are their world. A block-throwing, screaming two-year-old is feeling mad, but probably also scared, out of control and misunderstood. He's engulfed in volcanic rage and doesn't know how to cope. That's our job. As parents and caregivers, we need to teach him appropriate coping skills. Gradually, during the preschool years, children learn to handle powerful emotions by simply identifying, accepting and directing emotional expression.

Emotions and actions tangle together, but don't forget to handle them differently. As Ginott explained it, most discipline problems are made up of feelings and acts. Handle each part separately. Feelings have to be identified and expressed. Acts may have to be limited and redirected. The adult's job is to help children find an appropriate way to express

Take Off Your Adult Lenses

Children's emotions can make us feel out of control. Focus on what you can control: kids' actions. Stop whatever behavior is inappropriate, but allow kids to own and experience their feelings. Acknowledging a feeling, like anger or sadness, won't make it worse. And unwanted feelings won't go away through wishing; we can no more make a child feel a certain way than we can make him sleep.

these inner feelings. The block-throwing two-year-old needs to be stopped from throwing blocks, but he still needs to express his feelings.

No one likes being scared. Or unhappy. Or lonely, embarrassed, angry or overwhelmed. But one of the surest ways to get rid of these feelings is to express them.

We often try to deny or downplay our own negative feelings and those of our children. "Aw, that didn't hurt. There's nothing to cry about!" or "Don't talk to me like that," or "You don't really feel that way." Sometimes we just want to make every bad feeling go away and instantly make everything better. Or we cut off a child's feelings because they are painful to us. Psychologists like Dorothy Briggs and Selma Fraiberg said these methods hurt. Briggs and Fraiberg steadfastly supported a child's Right to Feel.

If we teach children to show only happy feelings, we deny part of their humanity—and set the stage for trouble. Repressed feelings don't go away; they go underground. These suppressed feelings can create roadblocks to learning in school and disrupt social relationships throughout life.

Psychiatrist Stanley Greenspan calls emotions the "architect of the mind." His research shows how vital emotions are to a child's developing brain. As children experience feelings, they are also building neural pathways that are needed for future academic learning.

Lay the groundwork for good emotional habits. Each feeling a young child experiences gives us an opportunity to teach him how to cope with the full range of life's emotions.

Emerging Emotional Intelligence

Young kids can be fireballs of emotion, but their ability to cope and understand human emotions is just beginning. A three-year-old may not know that the surge of rage or fear he feels will ever go away. It's helpful for both parents and kids to remember that feelings are always changing. Feelings are intense and real in the moment.

Kids are developing "emotional intelligence"—a term made popular by Daniel Goleman in his book *Emotional Intelligence: Why It Can Matter More Than IQ*. Young kids don't know if the emotion engulfing their body has a name or if other people ever feel this way. Often a child can't read emotions on others. *Oh—she's sad? I didn't know.* On top of that, kids don't understand what to *do* with these big feelings, and they can't control their bodies well. Preschoolers lack good impulse control. A child may strike out and be unable to stop hitting without adult help.

Aggression, Anger and Feelings in Disguise

Kids often lash out aggressively when they feel worried or scared. If a child feels anxious, he may hit, push or kick someone nearby. That's a common reaction. Instead of getting into a "who started it" cycle, try addressing a fear. Here's an example, in which two three-year-olds are fighting over a fire truck. Sam approaches Zeke, who had the fire truck first. Zeke screams and begins to push.

ADULT: Zeke, I hear you yelling. Are you worried he might take your truck? *(Find the fear.)*
Zeke nods.

ADULT: Sam, are you going to take Zeke's truck? *(Get information.)*
SAM: No.
ADULT: I heard Sam say he won't take your truck. *(Reinforce the message.)*

Practice looking beyond behavior to see your child's emotions. If it's hard to do at first, try watching kids at the playground who aren't your own. Sometimes it's easier to see in others. When you observe angry or aggressive behavior, stop and think whether it could be driven by fear, worry, embarrassment, frustration or another emotion in disguise. Ask questions to understand the underlying emotion. "Are you scared Sam will hurt you?" "Are you worried about something?" "Are you feeling disappointed because you wish _____ could be different?" "Is something scaring you?"

Try This—Add to Your Toolbox

Emotional learning is not a quick or easy lesson. Many adults never master it. But practice makes better. The more practice young children get, the better they will be able to express their emotions *and* control their behavior.

Name It

"You're feeling sad. You miss your mommy."
   "You are so mad! You really want to go outside now!"
   "Look, Joey's face looks scared. I don't think he likes your mask."
   The first step is to state the obvious. Name the emotion you see. When you name it, your child gains an awareness of her current emotion. *Oh, this is what being mad feels like.* Identifying a feeling also helps her realize

that other people feel it, too. Being mad, sad, glad or terrified is part of life.

Kids need names. Although they are learning language rapidly, it's hard for many kids to express themselves with words. When a powerful emotion floods their brains, children really struggle with their limited verbal skills. They need words to cope with these feelings. Kids age three and younger need basic names (mad, sad, happy). At about age four, children are ready to develop nuances in their emotional language and name feelings like jealousy, disappointment, frustration and so on.

However, resist the urge to label a child's feeling by saying "You're just tired." While this might be true, it dismisses the child's real feeling. We all have fewer coping skills when we're tired, but the inner feelings are still valid.

If a situation stumps you or you need to buy yourself more time, try asking the child a question about her feelings. "Are you feeling angry at Sydney? What did she do that made you mad?" Or simply: "How are you feeling right now?"

Limit Behavior

Kids can have their feelings, but at the same time they need clear limits on what's appropriate and what's not. Hitting your mother or little brother is out. So is smashing the kitchen lamp. Calling someone names that hurt their feelings is another type of harm. Is it hurting people or property? Step in and stop the inappropriate behavior.

Use Physical Outlets

It's hard for young kids to sit still at the best of times. When an intense emotion charges through a child's body, get ready for some *action*. Powerful body movements like running, ripping, kicking and pounding can give kids much-needed emotional release. Don't try to bottle this energy up. Channel it into safe outlets. You can redirect physical energy into plenty of appropriate alternatives. See Rule 5: Let Kids Hit and Kick.

Find Alternatives

My five-year-old once handed me a picture he'd drawn of poisoned olives. I loved it. It showed huge growth in his emotional coping skills. We were having tacos for supper—his favorite—and Myles was impatient and angry. A few minutes before, he had shrieked and stamped his foot because supper wasn't ready yet. Then, on his own initiative, he had disappeared into his room and become busy with his markers. When he handed me the picture, we both smiled. "I wasn't mad anymore after I drew it," he said.

Kids can write out, draw out, pound out and run out their feelings. The important thing is for the children to find a safe way to express the emotions inside. If you give kids concrete options to try, you may be surprised when they automatically turn to these tools without any prompting from you.

The Renegade Rules in this section, Wild Emotions, offer appropriate emotional alternatives. See particularly Rule 5: Let Kids Hit and Kick and Rule 7: Take Dictation from Your Tot.

Depending on your child's temperament, a quick affirmation of feelings may do. Five-year-old Stella, for example, would spiral into deep funks whenever her mother attempted to help her express her upset feelings. Some kids will wallow. It's OK to help your child move on—just make sure you acknowledge and accept the feeling first.

Steps to Emotional Competence

1. Recognize and label

Help children identify their feelings. "You're mad." Help children read facial expressions and other emotional cues. "Look at Joey's face. He looks scared."

State an observation. "You pushed over the chair and you're stomping your feet. You look angry!" Ask a question. "Are you scared Sam will hurt you or take your trucks?"

2. Accept and value

Accept your child's feeling. Make room for all emotions—including negative ones. It's OK not to be happy all the time. Give kids time to be sad when they are sad, mad when they are mad. All people have this feeling sometimes, even grown-ups.

Powerful feelings come and go. Feelings can change quickly.

3. Express feelings appropriately

Feelings often need to be expressed before they go away. It's OK to have a strong feeling, but set limits on behavior (for example, hitting). Find appropriate outlets: "You can't kick Nate, but you can kick this box."

Tailor it to the child; try new things.

WORDS TO TRY

Acknowledging and accepting feelings

You're really mad at me.

You want more cookies and I said no. That makes you mad!

You are so mad you want to kick.

Your face looks sad. You miss your mommy. I feel sad when I miss someone, too.

It's OK. You can cry when you feel sad.

Wow! You are so frustrated with that puzzle.

That's the way you're feeling *right now*. I know feelings can change.

Limiting behavior

You can be mad at me, but I can't let you hit me.

You can be mad, but you can't hit Mason.

People are not for hurting.

I can't let you run out the front door even if you miss your mommy.

You can be frustrated, but it's not OK to kick the game. You might break it.

It's OK to feel _____, but I can't let you _____.

Feelings in disguise

Is something scaring you?

Are you worried about Anthony?

Were you worried he was going to take your toy?

Were you worried he was going to hurt you?

WORDS TO AVOID

You're OK—that didn't hurt.

Don't cry.

Big boys/big girls don't cry.

You don't really feel that way.

I know you don't mean it.

Come on, smile.

OUT AND ABOUT

When one of my children is crying, strangers often like to step in and try to cheer him up. "Crying never helps anything," they'll say, or "It can't be that bad. Big boys like you don't cry. Where's a smile?"

Not everyone you run into will be comfortable with "ugly" emotions. As long as your child hears from you that her emotion is valid, don't worry about the commentators. People mean well and are trying to help. Sometimes the distraction of a new face does help your child calm herself. If your child's noises or actions are bothering others, leave the area. Find a place where your child can finish getting her feelings out.

It also helps to make a calm announcement when a new person arrives on the scene, say, your spouse or a babysitter. "Joey is really feeling sad right now. He misses his grandma. I told him even big people feel sad like that sometimes." This creates a safe, welcoming atmosphere for the feeling.

Let Kids Hit and Kick

Hitting, kicking and biting are unacceptable behaviors. Or are they? Hitting, kicking and biting *people* is not appropriate, but sometimes young kids need to smash, pound, kick, punch and scream their emotions out. The key is finding a safe outlet to do it.

Renegade Reason

For some kids, a burst of physical energy is the key to reaching calm. If an angry child needs to hit, let her hit a safe target.

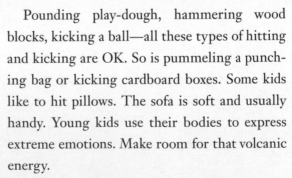

Pounding play-dough, hammering wood blocks, kicking a ball—all these types of hitting and kicking are OK. So is pummeling a punching bag or kicking cardboard boxes. Some kids like to hit pillows. The sofa is soft and usually handy. Young kids use their bodies to express extreme emotions. Make room for that volcanic energy.

Jack, age four, bit, spat, kicked and hit on a regular basis. His preschool teachers had their hands full helping him learn to control his anger. What worked best for Jack was to run around a fir tree in the school's courtyard. Jack ran circles around that tree, burning out the intensity of his feelings. When he was exhausted, he was also calm. Eventually, Jack learned to stop potential outbursts before they happened and would run around the tree all on his own.

A four-year-old like Jack has mastered a lifelong lesson. As he makes his way through adolescence and adulthood, he will know that he has to find alternative ways to express mad feelings.

Action and anger go together. When kids are in the throes of a burst of adrenaline, it's premature to try to calm them down. A child like Jack is too furious to think straight, let alone go through the complex cognitive steps required to sort out conflict. First, children have to cope with a surge of overwhelming energy. Move the child to a place where she can be loud and active, and give her options for releasing that physical power. Remember the Renegade Golden Rule: It's OK If It's Not Hurting People or Property.

Give your child a chance to use his body in a powerful way. Physical exertion and exhaustion help release emotional energy and allow many kids to reach a point of calm again. Once the burst of high energy is gone, children can begin to problem solve.

Renegade Blessings

These lessons are huge for any young child:

Hitting any person—including my mom or dad—is strictly off limits.

I can be mad, but I still can't hurt people.

I know ways to let off steam that don't hurt anybody or anything.

When I'm mad, I feel like hurting something, but there are better ways to solve problems.

> *My parents will still love me even if I get mad sometimes.*
> *My parents will keep me safe. I can trust them.*
> *Adults will help me when my feelings are too powerful for*
> *me to control.*

Why It Works

As a four-year-old, my son Myles went through an extremely angry phase. It lasted about three months. During this time, big and trivial events alike set him off, and instantly he'd lash out with arms, legs or teeth. My reflexes got quick. "I can't let you hit me," I'd say, grabbing his arm. "People are not for hitting. If you need to hit something, you can hit the sofa."

You may be thinking, *If I let him hit the sofa, won't he get more riled up? I don't want to make things worse, and I don't want to encourage violence.*

Think about it as letting off steam. Your child might need to pound at the sofa for a while, but with each punch he exhausts both his emotions and his body. Vigorous physical action is a perfect way for young kids to get rid of negative emotions, says psychologist Dorothy Briggs. Some psychologists who work with children use punching bags in their offices. As adults, we release stress and anger physically, too—we walk, go for a run or play a hard game of basketball. The tension leaves our bodies as we move.

> *Young kids express emotions with their bodies.*

Of course, adults often use words when we're angry. But young kids are still learning to use language. When anger engulfs children, they let fly with their fists and heels. Fred Rogers, of *Mister Rogers' Neighborhood*, said that's perfectly normal. As kids mature, they gain more impulse control (the ability to stop) and can express anger more creatively in a picture, story or conversation. But for now, children are their feelings. And their feelings are their bodies.

Take Off Your Adult Lenses

A child who is hitting is too furious to think straight. Stop the harm, but don't necessarily stop the action. The ultimate goal is conflict mediation, but she needs time to be ready. Take care of the burst of adrenaline first. If your child needs to hit, direct the hitting toward a pillow, sofa or other suitable target. This simple act of substitution reinforces the idea that people are not for hitting. After the first raw energy is released, then it's time to calm down and start talking.

Hitting, kicking and smashing things help release wild energy. Just pick the right targets. Even when children are mad, they need to learn early on what's off-limits and what's not.

Substitute Targets Are OK

Stopping a child from kicking or hitting altogether can backfire. The energy has nowhere to go. Dorothy Briggs says it's far preferable to hit a substitute object than to repress the urge to hit. In the world of the young child, bodies equal emotions.

Substitute targets work. Instead of banning the motion the child wants to do—head butt, kick, punch—the action is simply redirected. If a child is expressing himself by hitting, then follow his lead. Somewhere he has a great need to hit right now. This technique helps partly because the child feels valued and understood, even in the midst of all the mayhem. His "need to kick" is recognized. Instead of being thwarted, he is allowed to do what his body wants.

Redirecting Hitting and Kicking

1. Match the child's energy level to get her attention. Be loud, move fast.
2. Stop the inappropriate behavior. Hold the child's arm or leg.
3. Repeat simple sentences.

   "I can't let you hit me" (Mia, the cat, the lamp).

   "You can be mad, but you can't hit Mia."

   "People are not for hitting."
4. Offer an alternative. "If you need to hit, you can hit the sofa. The sofa can't get hurt."
5. When things are more calm, move on to listening and problem solving.

Psychologist Haim Ginott said substitute targets are the key to setting effective limits. Limits need two parts, he said: (1) what behavior is not acceptable, and (2) what substitute can be accepted. When we tell kids "Don't hit your brother," that's only half the information they need. Kids also need to understand what's a suitable substitute (a pillow). What's more, it's perfectly acceptable for an angry child to pretend that the pillow *is* her brother. Substituting the pillow for her brother reinforces the idea that real people are not for hurting.

Making room for hitting and kicking does not teach violence. The very act of substituting an object ("You can't hit the dog, but you can hit this pillow") reinforces the message that hurting living things is not acceptable.

> Action and anger go together. Don't rush to calm your angry child right away.

"But what about yoga?" I hear parents ask. "Deep breathing is very calming."

Yoga and other calming techniques can work with kids, but many parents and teachers make the mistake of trying to calm a child too soon. That stage comes later. Stay with the wild emotion first. Time and again, children whose need to hit or need to kick is accommodated soon calm down. The initial burst of adrenaline has dissipated. Now the child is ready to cry, talk, do yoga breathing, or sit on your lap.

Temperaments do vary. Some children attack with words ("I hate you!") and others with their screams or fists. This chapter focuses on handling physical energy. See Rule 6, "I Hate You!" Is Nothing Personal, for more on verbal anger.

Moms and Dads Are Not for Hitting

Jason was in a grumpy mood. His mom tried to reason with him, but he wasn't listening. He was just plain old mad. As his mother kept talking, Jason started hitting. I watched the scene unfold nearby. I knew Jason and his family; our kids were in the same preschool class, and I felt comfortable stepping in. When Jason hit his mom, she looked embarrassed but took no action to stop him.

"Hey, Jason!" I said, moving into his personal space and using a strong voice. "Your mom is not for hitting."

Surprised by the intervention, Jason stopped immediately.

"Thank you," his mom said to me. Then she paused a moment as if just thinking of it: "You're right, moms are not for hitting. That's true. Thank you."

As parents, we quickly stop a child from striking his younger sibling, but often neglect ourselves. The "no hurting" rule must include moms and dads. Our message to kids should be all inclusive: Do not hurt people, animals or property. Do not hurt people's bodies or feelings. The rule applies to all people—including the child herself and her parents.

Children feel terrible guilt when they strike a parent. They may not be able to stop themselves, but they want to be stopped. That's up to you. Take control. A child should never be allowed to hit a parent. Provide secure limits: I won't let you hurt me.

Don't Be Scared

A raging child may seem like a powerful beast. She may even scare you with her ferocity, but don't be fooled. Chances are, this child is feeling scared and out of control. As Dorothy Briggs reminds us, tantrums are nothing more than intense communication of the message "I've lost all control! I'm extremely frustrated!"

I distinctly remember what it feels like to be that raging child. As a girl, I threw first-class tantrums. The all-out screaming, yelling, body-flung-to-the-floor, knocking-into-kitchen-chairs kind. My tantrums weren't about trying to get something (a candy bar); they arose from being confused and overwhelmed. These tantrums carried on to an embarrassingly late age, so I vividly remember the feelings inside. The intensity of my own emotions engulfed me. When I was in the midst of a tantrum, the original trigger no longer mattered; I just wanted someone to step in and take control. To save me from myself.

Remember, you can offer safety and control. When dealing with out-of-control children who are hitting, kicking or in another emotional frenzy, remind yourself that kids crave limits. "I have always been amazed at the relief in a child's face when a parent says, "You simply cannot do this. I'm here to stop you,'" says T. Berry Brazelton, a pediatrician and well-known author on child development.

You may need to restrain some children so they can't hit you or somebody else. Use your strength to keep children from hurting themselves, objects and others. I've sat on my children and pinned their arms when they couldn't stop hitting—yes, even in public, even in the church hallway on a Sunday morning. Other times you might move your flailing child to a location where she can let out her energy for a while without hurting anything. When the child is calm, address her fears and other emotions.

Our job as parents is to reassure children. As Ginott said, the message children need from us is this: "You don't have to be afraid of your impulses. I won't let you go too far. It is safe."

Try This—Add to Your Toolbox

Make room for action. Give your child a chance to use his body in a powerful way. Physical exertion and exhaustion help release emotional energy and allow many kids to reach a point of calm again.

There are myriad safe ways to redirect your preschooler's aggressive feelings. They all release physical energy. Most of them make satisfying noises. These ideas work particularly well for active kids or less verbal kids who just need to let their feelings out. Once kids are physically exhausted, they may be able to talk and problem solve, or at least stop the original damaging behavior.

Make Room for Hitting and Kicking

Shredding newspaper (or other large paper) is a tried-and-true method for channeling anger. An adult holds out a big sheet of paper (you can also tape the paper across an open doorway) and invites the angry child to rip it with a karate chop. Destroying the newspaper gives the child a powerful outlet and produces a loud ripping sound that matches the child's energy level. Another great hitting action is pounding clay or play-dough.

If your child needs to throw things, help her make a target. Let her draw a picture of what she's mad at and then encourage her to throw beanbags at it. Reinforce with your words: "You're mad at Daddy. I can't let you hurt Daddy, but you can throw beanbags at this picture. That can't hurt him." Once I did this with Myles, and the target was a traditional bull's-eye set of circles with the words "pick up toys" in the middle. He was mad; he didn't want to pick up his toys. After he worked the feeling out, he was able to help clean up.

Consider a Pummeling Dummy

Classrooms at the School for Young Children have a "Dummy." This is a four-foot-long human-shaped rag doll whose job it is to get punched and pummeled. Dummy has a nondescript face and no clothes, just long limbs and a soft body and head. Dummy has helped countless generations of kids express their frustrations. "I can't let you hurt Mia," the teachers say firmly. "But you can hit Dummy. Dummy can't get hurt when you hit him."

Some adults shy away from the idea of an effigy as a substitute target. It still works, though, because it trains kids to redirect their impulses away from hitting real people and reinforces the message that they have to find an appropriate, inanimate object. If this method bothers you, stick with sofa hitting.

Active Ideas for Expressing Anger

Hit or kick something that can't get hurt

Karate kick a cardboard box

Punch a pillow

Shred newspaper (rip it or karate chop)

Hit the sofa

Hit a big stuffed animal or "Dummy" figure

Strike a punching bag

Throw mud at a tree

Throw beanbags at a target (which can be a picture of what the child is mad at)

Be loud and active

Go outside and yell

Go in the bathroom and yell

Run around a tree fifty times

Pound play-dough with fists or mallets

Hammer wood

Knock blocks down

Jump on Bubble Wrap

Do a Demo

If other kids are around, the sight and sound of an angry child ripping newspaper or karate chopping cardboard universally draws a crowd. This is a side benefit. When other children gather as spectators, they can share the lesson in anger management. "Danny is angry. I can't let him hurt a person, but he can chop this box." It's a perfect model for siblings, neighbors and classmates, since these kids are in a rational state of mind and can absorb the lesson in front of them: Anger is OK, but you need a safe outlet for it.

Follow Through

Releasing anger is only step one. Don't stop there. Remember, physical action can help relieve tension, but it doesn't address the underlying problem. Keep going—move on to problem-solving (see Rule 3: Kids Need Conflict).

WORDS TO TRY

You're mad.

You can be mad, but you can't hit Mia.

People (moms, brothers, animals, lamps) are not for hitting.

You can be mad, but I won't let you hurt me.

I will hold your hands until you stop.

I can't let you hit me, but you can hit the sofa (cardboard box, pillow, tree).

Get your mad feelings out: Hit the sofa hard. It can't get hurt.

WORDS TO AVOID

Just calm down!

You can't act like that.

No hitting!

We don't kick.

Nice girls don't hit.

OUT AND ABOUT

As with other Renegade techniques, it helps to be vocal as you parent in a public setting. Go ahead and say, "I can't let you hit the car, but if you need to hit, you can hit this tree." Not everyone will like it. Some will worry about violence in your child; some will worry about the tree. Given the loud and volatile nature of temper tantrums, hitting and kicking, you will probably move yourself and your child away from others as soon as possible.

"I Hate You!" Is Nothing Personal

Y ou're so mean! I wish you weren't my mommy. I hate you!"
Words like that are guaranteed to give you a jolt. You may slip into soul-searching shock and think, *How could you say such a thing? After all I've done for you. What happened to my sweet baby, and where did this monster come from? I love you. Why, I'm your mother—I gave birth to you!*

Take a deep breath and take it for what it is: an angry outburst from a small child who is trying to express herself. These moments pass. The intensity is real, but the meaning is rarely true. Feelings come and go.

Renegade Reason
Harsh words only mean that your child is temporarily upset. Focus on his feelings.

I remember screaming "I hate you!" to my mother when I was about five. The words scared me. I knew they were dangerous words, and deep inside me I knew they weren't true. I loved my mother with all the ferocity of my little heart. But I was in out-of-control dervish mode. All I knew was that I was mad and I grabbed the strongest words available. As soon as I'd spoken the words, I felt desolate and vulnerable—*would my mother stop loving me, too?* My heart froze until I heard my mother's reassuring voice:

"I know you're angry right now. I love you even when you're angry at me."
She didn't negate my words ("No, you don't! You don't feel that way!"). I
imagine that would only have riled me up more. Instead, she was a source
of strength when I needed her most.

Keep a calm head when your child is losing his. Don't bother giving
any deep meaning to the insults. He is lost in the intensity of his emotions. Remember, he needs your help right now; he's relying on you.

Renegade Blessings

Your child will carry these early lessons into her adult life:

I can cope with my strong feelings.
I have options. I know what works to help me feel better.
It helps to have someone listen.
My ideas are important. I can help solve my own problems.
*My parents understand me. Sometimes I say the wrong
    thing, but my family knows I still love them.*
*My parents are strong enough to lean on when the world
    seems too much.*

Why It Works

"We don't say 'hate' in this house."

Rules like that are unenforceable. You may wish you could ban words
like "I hate you," but you can't stop a child from speaking, especially
when he's riled up. Child psychologist Haim Ginott reminded us, "Strong
feelings do not vanish by being banished." When a listener simply accepts difficult feelings with sympathy, emotions lose their edge. On the
other hand, when kids get a charged reaction from adults, they may use

harsh words more often. Disregard the words your child shouts; go directly to the feeling underneath it.

Jennie, age six, experimented with shouting "I hate you!" at her parents when she got mad. She noticed a funny thing. Whenever she said those inflammatory words to her mom, her mother reacted in spectacular fashion. She took personal affront and tried to stop her daughter. "You can't say that. You don't mean that, Jennie. You can't act that way." When Jennie said the same words to her dad, her father replied in a calm voice, "I can tell you're angry, but those are strong words. You can hurt people by saying that." Jennie stopped saying "I hate you" to her father, but kept using it against her mother.

 Take Off Your Adult Lenses

Don't let harsh words devastate you. Remember, the speaker is a very young child who is focused on his own issues. Even if he's mad at *you*, it's nothing personal. In fact, it likely means that you're being a good parent and setting a necessary limit. Listen for the feelings underneath. Chances are, he's angry or sad and needs help expressing those emotions more appropriately.

Young kids need you to support them while they grapple with their feelings. Adele Faber and Elaine Mazlish, authors of *How to Talk So Kids Will Listen and Listen So Kids Will Talk*, say many techniques work to help kids express emotions, but most of all children need acknowledgment of their feelings, not criticism, denial or advice. Faber and Mazlish support physical action (pounding clay, punching pillows, striking a punching bag) and paper-and-pencil techniques like drawing. When kids share how they feel, they can let go of their emotion. If hearing "I hate you" upsets you, it's just fine to tell your child how it makes you feel. Faber and Mazlish say the important thing is to keep your cool and suggest saying something like "If you're angry about something, tell it to me in another way. Then maybe I can be helpful."

Remember, "I hate you" may seem like an insult, but it's really not at all personal. A young child is extremely egocentric; it's all about him.

Saving the Worst for Home

When I was five, I astonished my preschool teachers by throwing an all-out tantrum. "Oh," said my mother when she picked me up. "I think that means she's growing comfortable at school."

Young kids work hard emotionally when they're away from home. Many kids try to "hold it all in" and control their emotional reactions. But keeping emotions in check is hard work, especially for preschool-age kids. By the time they reach home, they've used up all their energy reserves. They're plumb exhausted. Four-year-old Jillian, for example, let it all loose at home, flailing and screaming whenever she lost a card game. At preschool, however, this would never happen. A child like Jillian is more likely to scream "I hate you!" at the ones she loves best. She's comfortable at home, and simply has no energy left to cope.

Try This—Add to Your Toolbox

I know firsthand a yowling child can be intimidating, but keep perspective. With the right tools, you can handle this situation with calm and confidence.

Some kids are screamers. Others kick and fight. Some children lash out verbally with "I hate you!" One child might withdraw into a quiet corner while another freezes with his body rigid. Equip your child with more effective tools than these. Whatever your child's style or temperament, there are tools to help him express his feelings, develop impulse control and practice problem-solving skills.

A combination of emotional tools works best. In the heat of the moment, give your child active ways to express her feelings. Reinforce ideas with books and puppets another day when your child is calm.

In the Heat of the Moment

Techniques that work best in the heat of the moment are often vigorous and physical (See Rule 5: Let Kids Hit and Kick). Remember not to hurry through the child's first urge for physical release. However, some children do better with quiet or solitary expression. Children may turn to calmer activities when their physical energy is spent.

Draw It Out

Some kids like to draw out their feelings. Give them paper and say, "Show me how mad you are. Show me on this paper!" You can also make a picture yourself. Help your child draw a picture of what she's mad at or who she misses. Put it on the wall. If it's an angry picture, tell her, "You can throw beanbags at it."

Write It Out

Grab some Magic Markers or crayons. Find some paper. Writing a letter that captures how your child currently feels can make all the difference in the world.

Don't be afraid to write the raw, stark feelings she is experiencing in the moment. For example: "Rebecca is so mad she wants to scream for a thousand million years and never stop screaming, not even to eat." If your daughter yells "I hate you, Mommy!" don't blink, just write it down.

It can help to restate it this way: "Rebecca is *so* mad, she is saying, 'I hate you, Mommy.'"

Remember, you're not making the sentence true by writing it down, you're helping her express her emotions and letting her know you hear her. No matter how ugly and unlovable she feels right now, someone cares enough to listen and stand by her. (See more in Rule 7: Take Dictation from Your Tot.)

Make Mad Faces

Tell your child to make mad faces in the mirror. Kids are fascinated by their faces, and mad faces often begin to look silly, which can relieve the tension. You can also do the "mad face" idea with windows. After losing a board game, my son Myles likes to go outside and run around the house five times. Each time he runs by the kitchen, he makes a mad face at the window. From inside, I make a mad face back. By the fourth or fifth lap, Myles usually dissolves in giggles. This method works because it's allowing the mad face, not smothering it. Myles starts to smile again because he is done with that emotion.

Count and Breathe

Numbers and patterns can be comforting. If your child can count, teach him to count to ten over and over when he's upset. Show him how to put a hand on his chest and take deep breaths. Yoga for kids can work. So can going outside. The change of scene refreshes kids, and nature can be especially calming.

Punch It Out

Don't forget the importance of vigorous action. Punching pillows, kicking cardboard boxes, throwing beanbags or hitting a tree with a stick are all effective and appropriate activities for kids in the heat of a strong emotion. See Rule 5: Let Kids Hit and Kick.

Ideas for Coping with Intense Emotions

In the Heat of the Moment
  Create space for physical action
  Pound something that can't get hurt
  Write a dictated letter together
  Draw a picture
  Make faces in a mirror or window
  Count or take deep breaths
  Go outside

When It's Calm
  Read books about feelings
  Use puppets to portray emotions
  Play stop-and-go impulse control games
  Talk over play-dough
  Ask your child for solutions
  Make a written agreement

When Things Are Calm

Repetition is critical for young kids. Although children feel emotions as genuinely as we do, they lack impulse control and have trouble remembering what to do with their emotions from one time to the next. Kids need repeated experience to develop coping skills.

Whether it's a game of Red Light, Green Light or a homemade puppet show, there's lots you can do to reinforce emotional learning in daily parenting. Pick a time when your child is calm and in a regular mood. It could be later that day or some time the same week after an emotional outburst.

Books and Songs

Your library has many excellent stories that can help young children learn about feelings. See the books recommended for kids and adults in the appendix. Reading about emotions helps kids recognize and accept their feelings, and lets them know their feelings are a normal part of being human. Depending on the book, your child might also get ideas about how to express anger and other emotions appropriately. Reading books together is a great way to talk about hard subjects.

You might try music, too. Many good children's songs can help kids accept difficult emotions, such as Barney's song "I Can See It on Your Face," *Free to Be You and Me*'s "It's All Right to Cry" or *Sesame Street*'s many songs about feelings including "Mad," "Sad" or "Everyone Makes Mistakes."

Puppets

You don't have to be a puppeteer for this one. Grab a stuffed animal or doll and give it a try. Your only audience is your child.

Puppets help children to see their emotions and behaviors clearly because kids view the emotion separately from themselves. There is no shame when three-year-old Tommy watches Brown Bear get angry and kick over the trash can—even if Tommy did the same thing himself the day before. When Brown Bear asks for help, Tommy will give him good ideas. *What else can I do?* the puppet wonders aloud. *I get so mad sometimes, I just want to kick something!* Reenact a scene from your child's day or focus on an emotion your child struggles with. Let the puppet do the work. It's magical to see how universally kids react to help a puppet friend in trouble. Once you get used to using puppets in your parenting, you'll find you pull out puppets to teach all sorts of valuable lessons— holding hands to cross the street, eating at Grandma's house, coping with a new baby.

Games

Games like Freeze Tag and Red Light, Green Light offer a fun way to practice impulse control. A major part of coping with strong emotions is gaining control over impulses, and you can strengthen this emerging skill. Stop-and-go games can strengthen the prefrontal cortex of the brain, which is important for impulse control. The more young children practice stopping their bodies and controlling their impulses, the better they get.

Try any stop-and-go game. Simon Says is a good one. Wild dancing to music is also great for this. Have your child freeze when you turn off the music or shout "Freeze!"

> *Stop-and-go games teach impulse control.*

Ask the Expert

My mother tried everything to stop my childhood tantrums. One day when I was calmly playing, she asked *me* what would help when I felt like that. I answered: "Hug me." She tried it next time and it worked.

Go ahead and ask your child for ideas that might help her. Just make sure to ask when your child is calm. Promise you'll listen; don't promise you'll use her suggestion (though you might be surprised how often her idea works). Try these steps: (1) "We have a problem"—for example: Getting dressed in the morning takes too much time and gets me mad. (2) "What can we do to fix this problem?" (3) "What's your idea? What else could we do? Here's my idea." You can even take this approach one step further and codify the plan in a contract. For instance: "Next time I get really mad and scream, Mommy will hug me." See more about writing agreements with kids in Rule 7: Take Dictation from Your Tot.

Play-Dough Talk

There are times when simply talking is easiest. When you are talking to young children about their behavior and emotions, it can help to give them something to do. Let kids mash play-dough while you discuss a touchy subject. Throw a ball back and forth as you talk about fear, jealousy or anger. This technique often works especially well with boys, who find it easier to express themselves when they move their bodies.

Get Creative

Active kids may respond well to the running and yelling techniques. Quieter kids may prefer to draw their feelings with crayons. Tailor it to the child. Emotional outlets are as different as kids.

Don't be afraid to try out new techniques. Your child is constantly changing, so what works one week may not work the next. Introduce new concepts and see what works for your family. Encourage a quiet child to express himself more vigorously. Help an active, volatile type to find an appropriate outlet before blowing up. Think up new ideas and ask your child to add her own. Some of the best ones come from kids themselves.

Model Feelings

There's lots you can do to model emotions in daily life. Go ahead and cry in front of your child. Tell him, "I'm sad. I'm crying because . . ." Practice looking beyond your child's behavior to view his underlying emotions. When he hits or pushes, for example, ask him, "Are you scared about something?"

Set Up a "Mad Corner"

Find a spot in the house where your child can go when she's mad. Stock it with beanbags, pillows, a punching bag, paper and crayons, a mirror for making faces, drums, play-dough for pounding, etc.

WORDS TO TRY

I know you're feeling that way right now.

Let's write that down. Rebecca is so mad, she is saying, "I hate you."

You are really mad at me right now.

Show me how mad you are. Show me on this paper.

When I feel like that, this is what helps me.

WORDS TO AVOID

Don't ever say that to me.

You don't mean that, honey. I know you love Mommy and Daddy.

You shouldn't feel that way.

We don't say "hate" in this house.

Bad girl! Bad boy!

OUT AND ABOUT

You can't control when your child is going to have an emotional outburst. You can control your reaction. The best way to prevent a showdown in public is to immediately acknowledge a child's feelings. It won't always work, but if your three-year-old yells, "I hate you!" when it's time to leave the park, acknowledge his feelings first, then enforce the limit. "You're really angry with me. You don't want to stop playing. But it's time to go home."

Take Dictation from Your Tot

My son Zach started crying in the car the other day. He suddenly missed his blankie, which was lying at home forgotten under the sofa. From the front seat, I tried to comfort him—"Zach's sad. . . . You miss your blankie. . . . You wish we had brought Blankie in the car"—but his wails continued. We parked, and I fished about for a piece of paper. "Let's write a note and tell Blankie how much you miss him," I said. Zach stopped crying. This is what Zach's note said:

> *Dear Blankie,*
> *I miss you. I love you.*
>
> > *Love, Zach*

Zach's tears dried up and he held the note tightly for the rest of ride.

Renegade Reason
Writing down your child's words makes feelings real and clear.
Kids feel respected and understood.

Whether your child is mad, sad or nervous, dictating a letter can greatly ease her anguish. Expressing the feeling is what's most important here—plus making it tangible. She can hold the letter, look at it and touch it. You might not be able to fix the situation, but don't underestimate the power of writing feelings down. It means someone has heard; someone understands.

Three-year-old Abigail was homesick at preschool. Her teacher asked her what to say, and she dictated a letter:

> *I miss my mom because I feel scary when I'm by myself.*
> *—Abigail*

Abigail put the letter in her cubby. After that, she was ready to move on to play.

Don't worry if your child can't read or even if she doesn't know the ABCs. I started writing letters with both my kids when they were two. They couldn't read, but they understood the power of the tool. If you have books and papers around the house, kids already understand that written words have meaning. Letter writing works for the preliterate child.

Writing feelings down is one more way to label an emotion. Writing makes a child feel valued and listened to, and often that's more important to her then getting her way.

Renegade Blessings

Letter writing builds a treasure trove of trust with your child. He can learn:

> *Grown-ups know how I feel.*
> *My feelings and thoughts are important.*
> *I won't get forgotten.*

> *Writing can express my deepest feelings. Written words have real meaning for me.*
> *Someday I want to learn to read and write. Writing is powerful.*

Why It Works

Letter writing with young children is a powerful tool for harnessing intense feelings. It's a tried-and-true method that captures their exact feelings and helps kids move on.

Why does writing work so well? Letters sum up and validate the emotional moment. The very act of dictation helps kids get out their mad-lonely-scared feelings. Letters also make feelings tangible; your child can touch and hold the paper, knowing his feelings are summed up right there.

Writing can express a child's innermost feelings. It works for the preliterate child.

Letter writing packs a powerful literacy lesson, too. Just think, your child's letter personally connects her to reading and writing and teaches her that *her written words have power*. Research by Dr. Stanley Greenspan shows how closely emotions are tied to learning. Emotions are critical to developing symbolic thought (letters, numbers and so on). Young kids need to make an emotional connection with events to remember and derive meaning. Greenspan says young brains use emotions to build symbolic thought processes. Drilling the ABCs is devoid of emotional meaning, whereas letter writing is just the opposite. What better foundation for kids to learn to read later on? They've learned that written words matter. This is what I call "meaningful literacy." Not only do words tell stories, but writing can express their innermost feelings. That's a powerful lesson.

┌───┐
│ 👓 Take Off Your Adult Lenses   │
├───┤
│ Why write with a child who can't read and who is wailing and beating │
│ her feet on the floor? It may seem counterintuitive, but give it a try. │
│ Kids understand the power of words and gain tremendous calm from │
│ writing dictated letters. In addition to emotional regulation, this │
│ technique offers a personal and deeply meaningful lesson in literacy. │
└───┘

When to Use a Letter

When our toddler is furious, everybody knows. My husband swears the neighbors three blocks away can hear. I knew we'd hear some squalls when it was time for Zach's bedtime one night. Zach, age two then, was intent on squashing green watercolor paint onto a soggy sheet of paper. No way did he want to stop. But bedtime is bedtime in our house, I'd already warned him, and Zach was past tired.

I told Zach painting was all done, it was time for pajamas. He yelled. I told him again and took the paint away. He dissolved into dervish mode. When I thought he could hear me, I spoke above the ongoing howls: "Boy, are you mad! Zach wants to paint. You like to paint! You don't want pajamas. You are mad at Mama." Next I carried him away from the table, saying, "You can be mad, but painting is all done. It's bedtime."

Remember what it's like to be a child. Not only are you mad, but typically you feel powerless and hopeless. Simply put: You don't trust the adult. How does a child really know if she will ever get to go back and do that fun thing again? That's why I like the Renegade method of writing a letter together.

Zach's letter that night said this: "Dear Mama, Zach wants to paint tomorrow." I signed his name. Then he signed the letter with his mark. The crying vanished. We read it over several times so he knew exactly what the words said. We talked about where to put it. He decided to stick it on his bedroom door, at knee level, where he would be sure to see it. He referred to our letter several times that evening, confident, cheerful. The next day he painted again.

Good Times to Write

When your child is mad.

When she has to wait.

When you need to postpone something he wants to do right now.

When she misses somebody—Mommy, teddy, Grandpa.

When he is hurt or scared.

When she wants to communicate an important thought to another child.

When you both need to remember something.

When you are problem-solving and making behavior action plans.

Kids of many ages and temperaments benefit from letter writing. Some letters are angry:

> *Dear School, I hate you! I don't want to be here! School is no fun. Nothing at this school is fun.—Leo*

> *Dear Mommy, I am really, really mad! I want to play outside right now! You won't let me. Love, Jake*

Or lonely:

> *I want to go home.—Caleb*

Mommy, I miss you.—Milo

I'm feeling sad. My mommy just leaves. I love my mommy. I love my mommy. My friends just came over at my birthday party.—Jesse

Letters can share difficult times:

Dear Mom, I fell down and hurt my elbow. It hurt a lot. I cried. Love, Batman

I had a bad day.—Hanna

Or make a plan after a conflict:

I will clean up the fort by 8:10 p.m.

Zach gets a Popsicle after his nap.

I'm worried about the boy grabbing the backhoe and the shovel. I want help if he grabs again.—Ian

Tomorrow Ben gets to play with his firefighters first thing.

All letters express emotion and validate a child's thoughts and feelings. A letter is a way of sharing.

Sign an Agreement

Jackson couldn't control himself. When he got mad, he hit other kids. His teachers at preschool couldn't trust him, so Jackson had to stay inside to play. He desperately wanted to rejoin the games outside, so he made a plan with his teacher. Together, they wrote it down with markers:

Jackson's plan so that he can play:
Tomorrow I'm not going to hit.
Make a sign: No hitting.
If I'm mad I'll move away.
If I hit I come inside.
I can do blocks or drawing in a safe place.
Call a teacher for help.

Within a week of this problem-solving, all of Jackson's hitting had stopped. He was invested in a plan that he helped create, and he had true incentive to make it work.

Make a contract with your child. If your child is preliterate, don't let that stop you. Write down behavior expectations together. Add pictures or symbols, if you like. For example, four-year-old Darby's plan said, "No Hitting, even when I'm mad. If I'm mad I will tell whoever it is if I like it or not. Say Stop. I will rip paper except Daddy's."

Read the contract aloud. Make sure your child knows what's on the paper. Sign your name to bind the agreement, then give her the pen and let her sign it by scribble or splotch. Don't worry what it looks like; tell her, "Now you write your name." Young kids see you writing all the time. Getting a chance to participate in an adult world is often exciting to young children, and they take their part seriously. Post the agreement where your child can see it best. Maybe that's on the wall next to her bed, on the refrigerator or by the back door.

Try This—Add to Your Toolbox

I admit it. At first it does feel mighty odd to reach for a pen and paper when your child is screaming mad or wailing with heartache. Taking dictation from a two-year-old is not second nature. But it works—with kids of many ages.

1. Grab a pen

If you and the child are both new to writing letters about feelings, some standard questions can help. Prompt her by saying, "Let's write that down! Let's write how you feel in a letter. What should we say? How about: 'Dear Mommy, Rebecca is mad. She didn't want to come inside. . . .' Once your child gets the idea, stop prompting. Write down whatever words she says.

For two-year-olds, you might start by drawing a picture as part of the letter. Say, "Here is your face crying. Here are the tears." This helps very young kids connect ideas with symbols on the page.

2. Put it in her words

Write down the child's words exactly. The grammar might be bad; there might be words like "poopyhead." The idea is to capture the child's thoughts and turn them into a written letter.

Don't be afraid of the power of his words. Writing words down will not make them come true. Hurtful feelings will change and go away. What *will* last is the all-important feeling that he has been listened to.

Sometimes a child is too upset to speak. In that case, write down what you *think* she's mad about. If you're wrong, your child will most likely correct you. That's huge progress—all of a sudden you are engaged in dialogue, sorting out the issues.

3. Read the words aloud

Repeat each sentence as you write. Read it out loud as you go, and read the whole letter aloud at the end. This helps your child know that the words she speaks are directly connected to the words on the paper. Children love repetition, and chances are she'll want you to read the letter through more than once. The experience of hearing her own words coming back to her—repeated just the way she said them—gives a child deep confidence in the process.

4. Ask for a signature

Most children are so curious about the letter-writing process by now that they have stopped crying. Involve your child further. Ask if she wants to write something. Give her the pen. Say, "Now you write your name. This is your letter." Don't worry what it looks like; the act is what's important. Your child understands she is helping to write the letter. Let her scribble all over it.

5. Set expectations

Before writing an I-miss-you letter, kids need to understand that the letter itself will not make their mother appear, but it will let their mom know how they are feeling. In the same vein, writing down a wish won't make it come true. Kids need to know that the letter isn't magic, but it can help them express their frustration or sorrow.

6. Address the right target

I feel a little funny when my children direct mad letters at me. Why all this anger pointed at me? I'm not doing anything wrong; I want to be liked. Keep those thoughts private in your head. You are not here to worry about yourself—you are here to help your child deal with his emotions. The right person to address a letter to is the one at the crux of the child's emotions. If she misses Nana, have her write to Nana. If she's mad at Daddy, address the letter directly to Daddy. If she's mad at you—write the letter to yourself.

7. Read and post the finished letter

When you're done, let the child choose where to put the letter. Some kids like to pin it on their door, post it on the fridge or other visible spot. Some kids enjoy putting it in a real or imaginary mailbox. Others simply don't care. When they are done, they are done. Wherever you put it, don't forget to read the letter aloud when it's finished.

8. **Receive letters calmly**

If you are on the receiving end, sad or angry letters can be a shock. It's hard to have all that anger directed at you. You may feel guilty about leaving your child, or wish you could've been there in her time of need. Try to react calmly. Remember, these letters from your child are snapshots in time. Just like a photo, they capture your child's feelings *at that moment*. Writing them down doesn't make angry feelings come true, and feeling sorrow is not bad. Sorrow shows deep love, and it's a natural part of being human. Take the letter as a piece of information, a part of your child's day she wanted to share with you. Read the letter and ask her if she wants to talk about it. Chances are, she has already moved on.

9. **Stay low-tech**

Yes, we live in an instant, digital age, but stick with old-fashioned paper, crayons and pencils when it comes to letter writing with children. Kids need something to see, hold and touch. Also, if you zap out a text message, suddenly the child expects an answer. You likely feel guilty: *Oh! My child is crying and missing me—I need to run to her!* Letter writing is not about instant rescue. It's about emotional expression. The letter can help your child accept sad parts of her life, express her sorrow and move on. Stay low-tech, rooted in the world of early childhood. Let the child touch, draw and cry on the paper letter, put her special letter to you in a "mailbox" and get on with her day.

10. **Follow through**

Some letters include a plan: "We will get the paints out again tomorrow." If you agree to something in a letter, stick to it. You might find it convenient to ignore a promise (Oh, that's right, I said he could paint again, but he's going to make a mess and . . .), but it's vital you follow through. If your child forgets, show him the note and remind him. Good follow-through builds trust between you and keeps future letters effective.

WORDS TO TRY

Let's write that down!

Let's write down how you feel in a letter.

You want your mom right now. Let's tell her how you feel.

Your letter won't bring your mom here, but it will let her know how you're feeling.

What should we say in your letter?

How about: "Dear Mom, Hanna is sad. She wants her teddy bear."

How about: "Dear Daddy, Caleb is mad. He's so mad he feels like kicking."

Here's a picture of your face crying.

WORDS TO AVOID

It'll be OK. Now, stop crying.

No tears today, even if you miss me.

Stop that this instant.

You don't feel that way.

OUT AND ABOUT

I can't count the number of times I've whisked out a pen and paper on the go. Pack a stash of writing materials. Letter writing is my number one favorite technique for staving off public meltdowns. Plus, it's a great way of sharing this Renegade writing idea with other parents.

Go Ahead: Let Him Hate the Baby!

Most of us expect some jealousy when a new sibling arrives, but still we insist on a basic level of love. "Deep down, you love your sister," we will say.

When we're cold, we make our kids put on sweaters. When we're hungry, we often assume that the whole family's hungry. It's no surprise we expect children to mirror our emotions, too.

Jeff, age two and a half, asked to hold his baby brother. The next minute he scowled and tried to throw his brother backward over the sofa. You may love the baby, but don't expect your older child to feel the same way. Right now your preschooler has his own set of volatile and equally valid emotions.

Renegade Reason

Jealous feelings need acceptance. Protect the baby from physical harm, but don't worry about the intensity of an older sibling's reaction.

Julius frequently attacked his baby sister. At age two, he was an active, energetic child who loved to romp outside. The new baby took his mom's time, and all the extra naps meant Julius was stuck inside more than usual. He punched Ella, knocked her over and attacked his mother, too.

Above all, protect the baby physically. Restrain your older child—pin his arms or sit on him if you have to. Let him know he can be as angry as he wants, but he still can't hurt someone. A high-energy kid like Julius needs to hear this message multiple times: "People are not for hurting. You can be mad, but I can't let you hurt the baby."

Renegade Blessings

When you accept your green-eyed monster, your child benefits in many ways. He or she learns:

My family still loves me.

My parents understand it's not easy to have a baby around the house.

If I don't like the baby, that's OK, but I still can't hurt her.

I can share my feelings, even ones that scare me.

It's safe to be honest in my family. I don't have to pretend false affection.

It's OK to change my mind. Feelings change sometimes.

Why It Works

If your three-year-old screams, "I hate babies! I wish Ella would go away and get blown up and go out with the trash!" chances are he's mad. Don't panic when you hear violent words. Your child is simply expressing a strong feeling. Maybe the baby knocked over his block tower for the umpteenth time. Maybe she drooled on his Legos or spit up on his shoe. Babies aren't always easy companions.

Accept your child's emotion. Let him know you understand how he's feeling. Help him rephrase and clarify the problem. For example: "You're feeling mad. You wish she'd go away. You're tired of Ella knocking your tower over." Empathy does wonders. Besides, you can probably agree with him: "It's not easy living with a baby in the house."

We all want siblings to get along, but we shouldn't try to whisk angry feelings away. It may be tempting to say, "Oh, you don't mean that. You don't really feel that way!" But the truth is, he does. He probably is wishing he could blow up the baby or cart her away in the trash. He's sending you a clear signal that he's frustrated and angry. Don't contradict him. His feelings are real, and most of all he wants sympathy and understanding.

Psychologist Dorothy Briggs says a child must "own" his feelings and that it's healthy to acknowledge feelings, no matter how bitter and ugly they may seem. "Understanding never makes feelings worse," Briggs reminds us. "It only gives them permission to be revealed."

Take Off Your Adult Lenses

It's especially hard to accept a child's negative feelings when they're directed at someone we love—another child in the family. Don't hurry love. Show *your* love for everyone in the family, but don't expect the big brother or sister to mirror your feelings. Your goal is to create a caring family environment. Remember, affection comes at different times for each family member.

Haim Ginott was another psychologist who didn't worry when children feel extreme anger toward their siblings. It's far better for a child to say, "I hate my brother!" than to pretend affection, he said. Many times kids are scared of these dark, intense feelings. They hide them, perhaps thinking, *If she knows how I really feel, my mother won't love me.* The authors of *Siblings Without Rivalry*, Adele Faber and Elaine Mazlish, base much of their understanding of children on Ginott's work. A caring sibling relationship, they say, allows for honest emotional expression.

Jealous kids are vulnerable. They need our support just as much as the baby does. The bottom line: You can be as angry as you want at your brother or sister, but you cannot hurt him or her.

Physical Attacks

Jealousy often shows up as aggression. Be fast and firm if your child tries to hurt her sibling. Just as with any hitting or kicking behavior, stop the action and make sure your child knows that people are not for hurting. You may have to set strong limits on your older child until you can trust her. For example, "I can't trust you to be in the living room with the baby. Until you tell me you won't touch her, you'll have to play in the kitchen instead." Establish zero tolerance for physical attacks.

Don't Force Love

"Nonsense! Of course, you love the baby!"

Brothers and sisters will discover affection in their own time. You can't force love, so don't demand it. Don't even expect it. Doing so can make your child feel inadequate and possibly afraid of losing your love. Make sure your older child knows that your love for him will never go away. You might say, "I love all the kids in this house. I love you even when you're mad. I love Ella even when she's a baby." There's no reason siblings should like each other or love each other. Most do, but let it evolve naturally.

Ongoing Jealousy

Four-year-old Molly loved her baby brother and thought he was cute. But when baby Adam started crawling, he annoyed her and disrupted her play. Sibling rivalry might be on your mind when you first bring the new baby home, but then you expect the kids to get used to each other. As the baby grows, watch for other significant flashpoints.

> ### Parent Tip: Common Times for Early Sibling Clashes
>
> Birth and Homecoming
> (attention on baby; parents short on sleep)
> Crawling: Age 6 to 10 Months
> (mobility means getting into big sibling's stuff)
> Talking: Age 2 Years
> (new competition in conversations)

Try This—Add to Your Toolbox

Your angry and jealous child needs limits, honesty and empathy. Accepting a new baby also gives kids an excellent foundation for coping with others throughout life. This is the first major lesson in tolerance: There will always be people I don't like or don't agree with. I still have to treat them with respect.

Offer Information

Kids live in the moment, so it's well nigh impossible for them to imagine a day when baby Ella won't knock over their play tower or stick marbles in her mouth. Having a baby sister or brother seems *endless*.

Reassure kids and remind them babyhood is not a permanent state. Say, "I know babies grow up," or "I know Ella won't always be a baby." Show kids pictures of when they were younger so they can see their own bodies change over time.

Kids also need to know their own feelings might change. "That's the way you're feeling *right now*. I know feelings change," or "I know kids sometimes change their minds." Sentences like these help kids realize they won't be trapped in this mad and jealous feeling forever. It also gives children a face-saving out to avoid embarrassment later when they do become buddies.

Create "Special Time"

When relationships in a family are going through stress, carving out Special Time helps tremendously. This means twenty to thirty minutes alone with one child, time when she is fully the center of your attention. Say, "I'm going to spend this Special Time with you, and we can do anything you want." Accept whatever activity she chooses. Put down your phone and gadgets. Find a time when other siblings don't need you. You might end up doing something together or simply watching your child play. Make Special Time regular, maybe not every day, but several times a week. Special Time can develop into a time of intimate sharing, a period you both will value even during times of low stress.

Special Time helps because the child knows her time is coming; she doesn't have to fight for attention. Your complete attention gives her confidence and security. Even if you are with your child all day, as a parent you are often distracted by your own agenda. Remember, you are an all-important person in her life.

Use New Methods for Older Kids

My older son, Myles, took an instant dislike to his baby brother. At the time, he was three. "I don't like Zach," he'd say. "I wish he'd never been born." We expected some sibling jealousy at first, but Myles's intense dislike carried on for two years. He would tell strangers, "I hate babies." He would glue Zach's Valentine hearts upside down. "They're upside down because I don't like him," he'd say.

As the baby grows up, alter your methods. Big siblings can belt out, "I hate the baby!" when the baby is just an infant, but by age one or two, children pick up on unkind words. Even if she can't talk, the little sibling can understand.

Keep accepting your older child's feelings. Make room for free expression, but limit how and when he can say it. You might say, "Hearing those words would make Ella feel sad. She can't talk yet, but she can understand. If you want to say those words, you need to go to your room to say them." Remember to accept the feeling: "It's OK to feel that way, but don't say that in front of Ella. She can hear you." Give your older kid a way to express himself nonverbally: "I can't let you say that in front of Ella, but you can draw how you're feeling."

Just as before, let your older child express his feelings, but protect the younger one from harm. And don't fret. Chances are, the older child won't even remember his strong feelings. Myles doesn't. Now he and his brother play together joyfully and hug each other on the street.

WORDS TO TRY

Accept and empathize

You're feeling mad. You wish she'd go away.

You're tired of Ella knocking over your tower.

I know you're mad at Ella, but I can't let you hurt her. People are not for hurting.

It's not easy having a baby in the house.

That's the way you're feeling right now. I know feelings change. I know babies grow up.

When you were a baby, you dumped food on the floor, too.

Growing siblings

Hearing those words would make Ella sad. She can't talk yet, but she can understand.

If you want to say those words, you need to go to your room to say them.

You can draw your feelings, or you can write them, but you can't say them in front of Ella.

WORDS TO AVOID

Of course you love your brother.

You don't really feel that way.

That's not nice. Don't let me hear you say that.

Why can't you be good like your sister?

Give your brother a kiss.

OUT AND ABOUT

When people ask, "And how do you like being a big brother?" and your child answers, "I hate babies," let him know that his feelings are welcome even in public. "James is getting used to having a baby in the house. It's not always easy." Friends and strangers may make a special effort to interact with your older child. Bless them if they do, but don't steer the conversation toward the baby. Remember to respect your older child's interests: "James wants to tell you about his Lego ship."

Sharing People and Toys

Friendship is born at that moment when one person says to another, "What? You too? I thought I was the only one."

—C. S. Lewis

It's OK Not to Share

Y ou're reading a magazine when suddenly someone takes it from you and starts reading the feature story. "I want it," he says. "You've had it a long time." Do you get mad?

As adults, we expect our friend to wait his turn before grabbing the magazine. We don't like to be interrupted. When we're done, we gladly hand it over. The same turn-taking concept should apply to young kids. A child's turn should be over when she is "all done."

Renegade Reason

"Sharing on demand" interrupts play, erodes parent-child trust and teaches false generosity. Take turns instead.

Here is one of my favorite scenes of childhood: watching a three-year-old rush up to another child and joyfully hand over a toy. Not just any toy. The same toy these two kids were competing over a few short minutes ago. The same toy this three-year-old had clutched to his chest and refused to be parted from. What's more, the toy is offered up without any parental prompting. Suddenly everyone is all smiles.

Fantasy? I see it happen all the time. By protecting your child's right to play with a toy until he is all done, by building trust together so your child knows he can count on you to protect his rights, and by coaching him to tell the other child when he's all done, you can witness this joyous scene of true generosity.

Almost any young child can do it. Why not yours?

Renegade Blessings

Simple turn-taking lessons teach your child positive lifelong skills:

> *Giving something away to someone else feels good.*
> *Rules for keeping a toy are fair. I can understand them.*
> *I have some rights. I can stand up for myself and adults*
>   *will support me.*
> *I can wait. I know my turn will come. I can control my impulses.*
> *I trust that someone will come get me when it's my turn.*
>   *They care about me.*
> *Adults believe what I'm doing is important. I'm important.*
> *I trust my parents.*

Why It Works

You can wish your two-year-old could share, but developmentally, she's not ready. Sharing comes in stages. Young kids can be trained to give up a toy on command to please an adult, but experts on children's moral development, like William Damon, say a notion of true, altruistic sharing doesn't begin until elementary-school age. Children younger than five share sometimes, most often to get something they want.

Teaching delayed-gratification skills, on the other hand, can do your child good. Impulse control (waiting for a toy and not grabbing) is a vital part of brain development and can be strengthened through practice. Impulse control is part of what's termed "executive function." Neuroscientist Adele Diamond's research examines executive function (impulse control, memory, adaptability, problem-solving, reasoning and other skills) in young children and shows how strong executive function can lead to later academic success.

Child development experts, such as Dorothy Briggs (author of *Your Child's Self-Esteem*), say young kids need to experience "owning" before they can share. Ownership is not legal ownership. It could mean owning a stick or a pinecone found at the park. Ownership to a child is control over an object. This means he's using it and he's the boss. He gets to hold it and decide who else can touch it. As early-childhood expert Eda LeShan writes, "Teaching young children to be generous starts with allowing them to be selfish."

> *Young children aren't ready to share. They are ready to take turns.*

Studies by child development experts such as Nancy Eisenberg and others show that adult insistence on sharing has little effect. What's more, true generosity is slower to develop in children who are forced to share on demand. Kids will often get sneaky, share only to please an

---

 ## Take Off Your Adult Lenses

Keeping a toy when another child wants it is not the mark of a selfish child, but simply a busy one. Protect your child's right to play and teach her to say, "I'm not done yet." Interrupting play—and instantly rewarding the other child—does not benefit either child. Waiting for a turn teaches great lessons in delayed gratification. Young children aren't ready to share; they are ready to take turns. Turn-taking empowers kids and helps teach courtesy, awareness and spontaneous generosity.

adult, and never share if an adult isn't watching. True generosity, however, can be habit-forming. The glow of generosity comes in part because the brain releases neurotransmitters, reinforcing the "reward circuitry" in kids' brains.

Cultural Ideas of "Nice"

We expect young children to share their toys. We expect them to be "nice." But typical adult views of sharing trample kids' right to play and teach them the wrong lessons.

Here's a typical example:

> *Max is playing with a truck. Hayden comes up and reaches for it. Both kids are three.*
> MAX: Hey! That's mine!
> HAYDEN: I need it!
> MAX: I had it first! I'm playing with it!
> HAYDEN: *(Crying)* He's not sharing.
> MAX'S MOM: Max, be nice. Remember, we have to share. Hayden hasn't played with it yet. If you can't share your toys, I'll have to put the truck away.
> *Hayden gets the truck. Max cries and sulks.*

The preschool years are summed up best by the image of two kids tussling over the same toy. "I had it!—I want it!—No, mine!" When that happens, we expect young kids to do what we should not do ourselves: passively give up and hand over the object to the aggressor.

What's more, we often pressure and scold our *own kid*, saying, "Be nice and share. Let Hayden play with it now." We are embarrassed when our child won't share. Our instinct is to give in instantly, *as soon as someone asks*.

It's easy to sacrifice our own kids in favor of others. We all want our kids to be liked. We try to teach them to be kind and generous people. Too often, however, forced sharing, or sharing on demand, backfires. Here's why.

A child like Max learns:

> People get what they want in life by grabbing.
> In social situations I can't count on my mother to protect me.
> My mother likes the other child better.
> My own play is unimportant.
> Sharing means giving up something I like.
> Sharing makes me feel bad and mad.
> I won't share unless I have to.

Sharing on demand hurts both kids. What did Hayden learn?
A child like Hayden learns:

> I get what I want in life by grabbing and whining.
> If I demand I shall receive.
> What I want right now is more important than anyone else's rights or feelings.
> Being loud, fast and persistent wears other people down.
> Adults will take my side if I use the word "sharing."
> I need adults to get what I want.

What should be more important here is protecting Max's right to un-interrupted play. Let Max keep the truck. He is busily engaged and his play is important. It doesn't matter if he has a long turn with a toy and Hayden is kept waiting. Delaying gratification teaches a far more valuable life lesson than giving in to demands. The key to taking turns is making it happen on the child's schedule. His turn is done when he is all done with the toy.

Sharing can be a confusing topic for adults because we mix up the right to property ("It's mine!") with the right to play (the child is busy).

This is especially strong since American culture gives so much weight to individual property and what "belongs" to whom. But turn-taking is not really about property at all. It's about learning social awareness and protecting precious playtime.

Consider this. What if someone says, "Hey! Can I use your car? Can I borrow your purse?" We want to trust somebody before lending them our car. Some items are very personal: a purse or wallet to an adult, a blankie or favorite toy to a child. Sharing is a social choice. For true generosity, sharing should be built on trust and infused with the warmth of giving.

> *Share food. Take turns with toys.*

As adults, we:

Don't share things with people we don't trust.
Don't share things that are personal or valuable.
Don't readily share things until we are finished using them.

And if we do, we don't feel good about it. We feel pressured and worried. If we give something up, we do it just to please. Yet we expect young children—who have fewer social skills than we do—to share on demand. "Sharing is a desired behavior in our society," says Jan Waters of the School for Young Children. "But it's fruitless to force it at the preschool level."

Being All Done

Being all done may take seconds or hours. The key is that the child herself decides. Her play is done when she decides she is done. Don't think about the clock. Young kids don't have a concept of time. Saying "Five more minutes, then the doll goes to Katie" is confusing to kids and puts unnecessary pressure on their play. When a child keeps a toy until she is truly finished, she willingly hands the toy over to the waiting child.

Of course, play needs to be interrupted many times a day for necessary events, such as meals and outings. There may be times when waiting for your child to be all done just isn't feasible (see ways to cope in Rule 10: Let Her Hog That Toy All Day!). This makes uninterrupted playtime even more vital. Not sure if a child's done yet? Ask him.

Here's what turn-taking looks like. This example shows an adult helping young kids learn the method.

> *Joey and Danny (both age three) want the same airplane. Joey had it first. Danny grabs the airplane.*
>
> JOEY: Hey!
>
> MOM: Danny, I see Joey has the airplane right now. He's using it. I can't let you take it from his hands. Can you give it back, or do I need to help you? *(Mother returns toy to Joey.)* Let's ask Joey if he's finished yet. Joey, are you finished with the airplane?
>
> JOEY: No.
>
> MOM: Will you let Danny know when you're all done?
>
> *Joey nods. Danny cries and grabs for the toy.*
>
> MOM: That makes you mad. You want it right now. It's so hard to wait.
>
> *Mom helps Danny move away and holds him.*

Sharing for adults is about trust, friendship and generosity. All these take time to nurture. Sharing for kids centers around possessing and controlling. A young child can learn lessons of trust and generosity best when she is allowed to hold on to an object until she is fully done using it.

Direct Communication Skills

Child-directed turn-taking packs some powerful life lessons. It forces kids to confront one another directly. Communicating differences with a peer is a huge social step for young kids, and truly, for a person of any age.

How many of us parents have the courage to speak up, confront someone directly and clearly communicate our needs? William Ury, coauthor of *Getting to Yes* and author of *The Power of a Positive No*, coaches adults to say no gracefully and set limits on others. Your preschooler can learn that. Setting healthy habits of positive assertiveness will be a life blessing.

This puts the kid who won't share in a different light: It's good and healthy when she protests when asked to give up a toy. It shows she's busily engaged and can't be bullied by another kid. Here's an example of a confident four-year-old who can stand up for herself and her right to play. The second four-year-old also shows emotional maturity when he doesn't get what he wants right away.

> *Four-year-old Tess is playing with a flashlight. Aiden grabs it from her.*
> TESS: Stop! Don't take my laser out of my hand!
> AIDEN: I want it!
> TESS: I'm not done yet.
> AIDEN: Oh, man! I need a laser, too! *(Hands it back.)*
> TESS: Well, you know, there's a list for it. I don't want you to steal it.
> AIDEN: *(Looks at the list and adds his name after Sarah's.)* I'm waiting for the list.
> *Five minutes later, Tess puts the flashlight down.*
> TESS: I'm all done!
> AIDEN: Who's next on the list? *(Hands the flashlight to Sarah.)*

A friend of mine couldn't believe this scenario happened. "It unfolded too easily," she protested. Tess and Aiden are real kids. Just four years old. They managed this conflict seamlessly because they had confidence and practice with a fair turn-taking system. Your family can adopt this system, too.

It's not hard to switch. A family in Massachusetts adopted Renegade turn-taking in just two days. "My two- and four-year-olds 'get' taking turns. I've bought in fully to letting kids take long turns," said their mother. "What a relief it is for me not to make any limit calls on timing or sharing resources anymore!"

Benefits of Renegade Sharing

Giving up something feels good, and true generosity develops with joy.

Play continues uninterrupted. Learning follows to its natural conclusion.

Fair and easy to understand.

Less stress on parents.

Kids get practice setting limits on other kids.

Kids gain enhanced awareness of others.

Great lessons in courtesy (telling someone when you're done).

Direct communication with peers.

Delayed gratification and impulse control.

Experience of ownership and power.

Concepts of sequence (your turn, then his turn, then my turn).

Practice handling tough emotions (it's hard to wait).

Independence—ability to deal with sharing situations without an adult.

No Time for All Done

There are times you need to end play before your child is all done. Acknowledge that reality, stop the play, and if possible, find a way to extend the turn later. See more about extending turns and coping with long turns in various settings in Rule 10: Let Her Hog That Toy All Day!

Try This—Add to Your Toolbox

Taking turns works. Young kids can do it and often master the idea quickly. "This morning I tried long turns," reported a mother from Wisconsin. "Cameron [age six] really likes it, and he did hand over the toy joyfully just like you said." Turn-taking is fair and lets kids be independent—making life less stressful for *you*. When a child hands a toy to the waiting child, she experiences the warm glow of true generosity. It's a good feeling, one she will want to repeat over and over in her life— whether a parent is watching or not.

Offer Information and Reassurance

Don't forget that young kids really don't know much. They are a bundle of emotions without experience, so offer basic information to reassure kids. A child who screams "Mine!" may be scared. Is that toy gone for good? Will the other child get to take it home with her? Reassure her by saying, "Brenna's playing with it now. She won't take it home. This bear lives at our house."

A hug offers comfort (and physical restraint). You might say, "I will hold you while you wait," and sympathize with the child's plight. It *is* hard for kids to wait. Sitting together can help a child endure the waiting period and know that someone understands. Help a child decide what to do while she waits, or offer an alternative favorite activity.

Write a Note

Writing makes a wish visible—and makes sure no one will forget. A note works well when only one child is waiting for a turn. For example, Sam wants the crane truck when Zeke is done. Ask the child what to say. For example, "Alexis really, really, really wants the lion puppet now." Help your child understand the solution: "Alexis can play with the lion puppet when Lucy is all done."

Make a Waiting List

Start a waiting list when more than one child wants a toy. Kids as young as two love waiting lists. It makes their need real. Spoken words like "You're next" may not have meaning for young kids. But take a bold, red marker and write their names. Suddenly their wish is real. They can see and touch the paper. They begin to understand sequence. "Let's look at the waiting list. I'll put your name on it. See, here's your name. You're next after Danny."

Waiting List for Swing
1. ~~Hayden~~
2. ~~Gloria~~
3. Danny
4. Jack
5. Nate

Give Kids Another Chance

Controlling the impulse to grab is hard work for young kids. Sometimes they will slip up. When they do, don't be angry or surprised ("You know better than to grab it!"). Just reinforce the limit and give them another chance. There's no need to punish kids in a time-out, though you might need to move a child away from the situation temporarily. Let the child know she can come back and try again just as soon as she's ready. "You can come back in the toy room when you tell me you won't grab the train again. Are you going to grab the train from Kelsey?" As soon as a child tells you she won't grab this time, give her a chance to practice.

Clarify Group Space and Private Space

Sharing is not just about objects. Sometimes taking turns is about space. Space might include furniture, the climber or the sandbox. Think about which spaces in your family belong to everybody, and which spaces can be private. For example, "The sofa belongs to everybody. If you don't want to sit next to Sophie, you need to move. Your bed is a special place you can have all to yourself." Outside, you may decide that everyone can use the sandbox, but the top of the climber can be "owned" by one child for a long turn. Be clear about what's private and what's shared space.

Take Turns with Group Items

Four-year-old Eli had a friend over. At first they shared a puzzle, but then Eli wanted to use it just for himself. His mother felt doubly upset—not only was Eli grabbing, he wasn't treating Hannah as a friend.

The "all done" rule still applies. When two kids are playing with something together, whether it's a puzzle, board game or play-dough, it's typical that one child will get done first. Since it was a joint game, both kids need to be done before either one takes it all. Eli's mother could say, "I see Hannah was playing with the puzzle, too. She's still playing with it. You can be done, but I can't let you take all the pieces from her."

Playdates are exciting but can be tough. A child may get worried when another child uses his toys, or simply so excited he can't control his body. Tuck extra-special toys away ahead of time. Conflicts are natural and kids still have lots to learn about friendship (See Rule 11: We're Not *All* Friends Here).

Accept "Overabundance"

Kids often want more than what we consider is enough. More sand. More dinosaurs.

Two-year-old Brandon found a box of necklaces and draped all eight over his body. Myles saw what fun Brandon was having and wanted a necklace. Here's what happened:

> BRANDON'S DAD: Give one to Myles. You need to share.
> *Brandon clutches his necklaces protectively.*
> BRANDON'S DAD: Come on, Brandon. You have a lot of them. Why don't you give one to Myles?

To the dad, eight necklaces were an overabundance. Why not give one to the other child? This idea seems perfectly reasonable to adults. But Brandon was only two and not ready to play collaboratively. To Brandon, eight necklaces were exactly what he needed; it was the right number because that's what he was playing with at that moment. Protecting Brandon's right to play meant letting him keep all the necklaces.

Distract and Supply Multiple Objects

Even two-year-olds can grasp the turn-taking system, but you may not have the energy to teach higher ideas about emotions and generosity every moment of the day. In a group setting (classroom, day care), it helps to have at least two copies of popular toys, especially for toddlers. If you're at the beach, bring more than one shovel. Distract and move on. There will be plenty of chances to practice.

Drawbacks of Sharing on Demand

Giving up something feels bad.

Meaningful play is interrupted because of another child's wish.

Rules for keeping a toy are arbitrary and confusing.

Sharing is just to please adults; it doesn't have intrinsic value.

True generosity may develop more slowly.

Children can't trust adults, especially in a social situation.

Sharing on demand involves parents' constant policing.

Children also learn these negative lessons:

Don't share if adults aren't looking.

Invoking "sharing" magically gets you what you want. ("You have to share! I'm telling! Mom! Jake's not sharing!")

Running to an adult and being helpless are good ways to solve your problems. ("He's had it a long time"—*sob*—"I never get to play with it.")

It's OK to give up and let people walk all over you.

WORDS TO TRY

Protecting play

I see Brenna has it. It looks as if she's still using it.

I see Carly has her hands on that toy. I won't let you take it out of her hands.

She can have a turn. When she's all done, you can have a turn.

You can play with it until you're all done.

Are you finished with your turn? She's not done yet.

Did you ask if she was done? You need to ask.

Do you want to play with him or keep playing by yourself?
Did you like it when he grabbed it? Tell him to stop!

Courtesy
Will you tell Jimmy when you're all done?
I'll let you know when he's all done. I'll come find you.
Sam, I see you're all done. Go find Jimmy. Remember, he's
    waiting.

Comforting the waiting child
Oh, it's so hard to wait!
You are so mad. You really want to play with that truck right now!
You wish he were all done.
I'll help you wait. I'll hold you.
Oh, darn it! You still wanted to play with those blocks, but you
    walked away. Now someone else is playing with them.
Let's start a waiting list. I'll put your name at the top.
Tell him you're tired of waiting.

WORDS TO AVOID
Be nice and share.
We share with our friends. Another friend wants it now.
You can both play with it together.
You've had it a long time. Let Gavin have it.
You don't need all those. Give one to Betsy.
Five more minutes, then it's his turn.
I'll set the timer.

OUT AND ABOUT
Allowing your child to take a long turn in a public setting can be
intimidating. Some parents get mad. Your job is not to please all

adults. Some will disapprove no matter what you do. What's most important is to stand by your child. Don't betray him.

Allowing your child to take a long turn in public is also a terrific teaching opportunity. The other day at open gym time, my son Zach refused to give up a doll another child wanted. I spoke aloud to reassure both kids. "Zach's not done yet. When he's done, would you like a turn? Zach, will you give this boy the doll when you're all done?"

The other mother said nothing, but pulled her child away. Zach played with the doll for ten minutes. Then, without prompting, he raced across the gym to find the other child, held out the doll in both arms and said joyfully, "Here you go! Here you go!"

The boy smiled and took the toy. And the mother? Her face registered shock. Pure, unadulterated astonishment. It's hard to believe the power of child-directed turn-taking until you see it in action.

Let Her Hog That Toy All Day!

When my son Myles was four, he learned how to pump a swing by himself. Delighted with his newfound skill, he would swing for hours a day. In fact, he swung so long his hands developed blisters before we realized, and we had to wrap his palms in gloves and bandages. Still, he would swing. Back and forth, back and forth. Up and down and up again.

Tom, age three, used to stand at the water table every day at preschool. All morning long. Week after week. "Why doesn't he try something else?" his mother would worry. Other children were painting, riding bikes, playing with play-dough and exploring ants outside. Tom kept playing with water.

As parents we often balk when kids crave "long turns." The repetition bores us. Our sense of fairness needles us into stopping their play (Janey's been waiting!). We worry there's something wrong with our child. How could so much of the same activity be normal? Yet young kids need repetition, safety and comfort. Long turns let kids fully explore an intense interest or feel safe in their comfort zone. Kids who enjoy the trust and safety of knowing they can have a long turn also relax and typically end their turns more quickly.

Renegade Reason

Long turns give kids time to fulfill their needs. Trust them.

If you stand up for your child's right to uninterrupted play (see Rule 1: Don't Steal Play, and Rule 9: It's OK Not to Share) and shift to child-directed turn-taking, be prepared for some *lonnng* turns. Long turns can take ten minutes or all morning. All day. During playtime let your child decide when her turn is truly done—even if it takes until bedtime. Chances are your child is fulfilling a need. Sticking with one object or activity is precisely what she needs to do right now. Respect long turns just as much as short ones.

Renegade Blessings

Trust yourself enough to trust your child when it comes to long turns in play. She'll learn:

I can do what I need to do.

My interests are valued.

I can feel safe in social situations.

I deeply trust the people around me.

My actions have an impact on other people (my friend is mad she's still waiting).

Practice and persistence are great ways to master a new skill.

Why It Works

Kids hog a toy (or a space) for a number of reasons. Young kids learn through repetition. They are following a deep need when they try things over and over. Kids who are highly sensory learners may benefit from a certain motion. Practicing a new skill is a common reason for long turns, and young kids are constantly learning new skills—whether it's pedaling a tricycle, bouncing a ball, singing a new song or stacking blocks.

Sometimes long turns indicate a child isn't feeling safe. A child may hog a ball because she doesn't trust other kids not to steal it. Hanging on to the ball for an extra-long time can give kids a sense of safety. Other kids have a need for control. A child who holds a toy tightly just so others can't play with it might announce, "I'm never going to be done!" The need for control is still a valid need, says Stephanie Rottmayer, director at the School for Young Children. This drive for control and power could be a signal that this child needs to experience more ways to feel powerful in his life. See Rule 16: Give Kids Power.

 Take Off Your Adult Lenses

Trust your child at play. Her reason for a long turn may not be obvious, but it fulfills an inner need. Long turns are a fundamental part of child-directed turn-taking. Protect a child's right to have a long turn even as you sympathize with a waiting child. Kids who feel safe often take shorter turns. When it's playtime, let kids decide when enough is enough.

When children's play is self-initiated, it usually fills a need. Sometimes the motion of a swing or rocking horse meets that need. Maybe being cuddled up in blankets meets the need. Or practicing something over and over and over. "Sensory learners may really enjoy a certain feeling," says Deb Baillieul, senior teacher at the School for Young Children. "A child who swings all morning has a need that's being met by that swing. Sometimes the motion just really feels good."

In other cases, a child may stick with one activity—say, the sandbox or swing—because it gives her a safe place to observe. According to sociologist Mildred Parten, who researched children's free play, one of the stages of play is "onlooker" play, which means a child observes play but doesn't actively join in. Children need time to feel safe before they interact with peers. A child may be overwhelmed and simply need a quiet place to observe the action before jumping in with greater social participation. See more about the stages of play in Rule 11: We're Not *All* Friends Here.

Kids who are forced to share on demand will typically hog the ball and take extra-long turns when first given the opportunity to keep an object as long as they like. This makes sense. They simply don't trust the system. At any moment, their precious ball or action figure may be taken away. They react by taking extremely long turns. They hog it with all their might.

Over time, these kids change. They relax. When children truly trust that you will consistently support their right to continue playing, and trust that they can keep something as long as they like, they usually stop hogging an object. They feel safe and don't need the object to prove it.

> ## Reasons for Long Turns
>
> Practicing a new skill
>
> Safety or ownership
>
> Intense interest
>
> Chance for control
>
> Fulfilling a need (such as feeling a swing's motion)
>
> Chance to observe as an onlooker
>
> Rarely having a chance to take a long turn

Coping with Long Turns

Long turns are especially hard for parents to accept when a child needs a long turn and another child is waiting. This gets back to our instincts to be nice and socially accommodating, but long turns are an integral part of children's right to play and child-directed turn-taking. Here's what typically happens when an adult decides how long is "enough."

Three-year-old Nathan is happily swinging. Jeff, age six, wants a turn.
JEFF: Can I have the swing?
GRANDMOTHER: Sure. He's been swinging a long time.
Nathan screams and hangs on to the swing. His grandmother pries him off.
GRANDMOTHER: You've got to learn to share!

This section deals with waiting for long turns at home, in a classroom or in a public area that's not overly crowded. Do you live in New York City? Chicago? If extra-long turns would not be tolerated (in a big-city playground, or a crowded science museum) read about options in "Out and About" (page 138).

Of course, long turns mean other children get tired of waiting. Protect each child's right to have a long turn, but go ahead and help waiting children express their frustration.

> LUCY: Zoe's still got the blue bike!
>
> MOM: Tell her you're tired of waiting! You can tell her you've been waiting all morning and it makes you mad.

Kids like Zoe will learn that their actions have impact on other people. Lucy gets mad when she has to wait a long time. Zoe might not give up the bike right away, but she has gained an awareness of others' feelings and has realized that her actions have consequences. To fully protect Zoe's right to a long turn, her mom might say (within earshot of both girls), "Zoe doesn't have to give it to you. She can have as long a turn as she wants. But you can tell her how you feel."

A simple way to help kids wait during a long turn is to remind them the rule applies to everyone. "When it's your turn, you can have a long turn. I won't let anyone take it out of your hands. You can play with it until you are all done. No one is going to take it away from you." This reassurance does wonders. Using a waiting list also reassures kids their turn will come (see Rule 9: It's OK Not to Share). Once a child experiences this system, it becomes easier for him to wait next time.

Once in a while there's a child who displays an extreme need for a long turn. A long turn that lasts for days instead of hours. If so, change the situation, not the child. For example, Mitchell, age three, needed to paint and hogged the easel day after day at his preschool. His need to paint was so great that his teacher set aside a special painting area just for Mitchell so other kids could paint, too. Brooks, a two-year-old with autism, intensely focused on one Clifford book. He always needed that book in his arms. The solution was to get a second copy of the book. Solve the space or physical problem, don't stop the child.

Try This—Add to Your Toolbox

How Long Is Long?

Depending on the child, long turns can go on for several days. If someone's waiting, set a reasonable rule in your house. For example: A long turn can last all day. The next day starts things fresh and the child who's waiting gets a turn.

No Time for Long Turns

Sometimes there's just no time for a long turn. Acknowledge that. Tell your kids, "We can't have long turns now. We have to go to Grandma's [or it's nap time, supper time . . .]." If you preserve their right to enjoy long turns during playtime, it's easier to stop when you have to. Remember, you're in charge of the family's daily rhythm, and even playtime must come to an end. Your child's still not done? Write a note: "Alexa gets to play with the chalk again *first thing* after we get back from Grandma's." Or: "Aiden isn't done with the circus train. He gets to play with it before breakfast tomorrow." Acknowledging that your child's not all done is sometimes all a child needs. Empathize with his feelings: "Oh, that's too bad! You're not done yet, and it's time to go home." Extend the long turn by letting the turn continue after your break. Make a sign or otherwise keep her playthings safe. Knowing she can return to her game later keeps the trust in turn-taking.

WORDS TO TRY
Protecting long turns
It's OK to have a long turn.

Yes, she's having a long turn. When it's your turn, you can have a long turn, too.

I see you are digging a long time today.

You're not done yet. Let's write a note and save it.

Danny is still playing with the shovel. He can play with it again after his nap.

Coping with long turns

It's hard to wait.

Yes, she's having a long turn. When it's your turn, you can have a long turn, too.

Go tell her you're tired of waiting!

Zoe doesn't have to give it to you. But you can tell her how you feel.

You don't have to give it to him. You can say yes or no.

I see Devon's face is mad. He's tired of waiting.

We can't take long turns now. We have to go in for supper.

Sharing public space

The climber is for everybody.

I see lots of kids waiting for a turn. When will you be done?

There are lots of other kids here. We need to take fast turns.

At home you can have a long turn. At the park it's different.

Your turn's done. If you want to do more, wait for another turn.

WORDS TO AVOID

You've had that long enough.

Michael wants a turn. You have to stop.

Five more minutes, then you're done.

Come on, try something else.

OUT AND ABOUT

Long turns get tricky in public places. Adeline, for instance, a long-turn-taking two-year-old, loved to sit on top of the playground slide. Lines of kids piled up behind. Her mother found a way to protect Adeline's need to be up high but still let the other children play. She helped Adeline scoot off to the side. Adeline would continue to sit up there for fifteen minutes while other kids slid down the slide.

See if you can accommodate others and meet your child's need for a long turn the way Adeline's mother did. Consider what the need might be. Does she need power? Being up high? Being alone? Climbing up something? Find an alternative way to meet the need. For example, "If you want to be up high, the climber is high. You can stay up on the climber for a long time, but the slide is for sliding."

How long you allow your child to play is a matter of personal preference. You may feel comfortable sticking to long turns no matter what. You may decide to set different rules at home versus the city playground. Most people balance the social need with the long-turn need. If there's only one bubble machine at the science museum, and hordes of kids want to use it, make sure your child is clear that the rules are different in this context. When headed to a crowded place like a museum or playground, set expectations early on (before you arrive) and give reminders. For example: "There are lots of kids at the children's museum. We have to take fast turns."

When situations come up, problem solve by making observations: "You want a long turn on the horse, but I see other kids waiting. There is only one horse." Or offer information: "The park is for everyone. It's different from home." Sometimes you may feel the best thing is to cut play short: "The playground is crowded today. If you want to play with that digger some more, you need to wait for a new turn." Then help your child get back in the lineup.

Rule 11

We're Not *All* Friends Here

My mother cringes every time she hears an adult talk about young kids as "friends." Why? "It's a lie," she says.

When children are gathered together in a group we suddenly call them "friends." Yet oftentimes young children in a group barely know one another. Even if they've played together before, young kids are egocentric and frequently wary of each other. A two-year-old may even view another child as an intruder into his territory. That's far from a friend.

Kids' social fears are real and demand our respect. The first step is to be honest about what a friend is and allow your child to make social choices. The second is to help kids gain friendship skills (called "getting into play") and the ability to set limits on peers.

Renegade Reason
Kids are not all friends. Accept social fears and favorites. Guide children toward better friendship skills.

The truth is, kids are not all friends. One child doesn't necessarily like another child. Even if they like each other, they might not want to play together. When we try to force friendships, we ask the impossible of small children in the social arena at a time when they possess few skills to cope.

Of course, kids are thrown together all the time. Parents get together and our kids rub shoulders with the other kids. Kids share space in a neighborhood, day-care program, preschool or family reunion. At these times, children may play together, play solo or play side by side. Whatever it is, don't assume kids are all friends just because they are all roughly the same age.

Respect your child's social choices. Kids might have to be in the same space together, but they don't have to play together. Better learning unfolds when you don't try to force friendship.

Renegade Blessings

Friendships are confusing enough without calling all children "friends." When you respect true friendships and help kids gain additional social skills, children blossom. Here's what your child can learn:

> *Friends are special people in my life.*
> *I know how to get into play. I can make new friends.*
> *Friends don't have to always agree. You can still be friends.*
> *Adults respect me and my play. I have some control.*

Why It Works

Jamie, just turned three, sits possessively in a little red car. Another child approaches and Jamie eyes him warily.

"Now, be nice. Another friend wants a turn," says his mother.

Jamie lunges forward in his car and crashes into the other boy's foot. "Jamie, be careful! You hurt your friend's toes."

When we call young children "friends," we confuse them and devalue friendship. A friend is not just anybody. A true friend is someone to be treasured—somebody who laughs with you, cares about you and simply enjoys your company. Storybooks for kids are full of examples of true

 Take Off Your Adult Lenses

Kids are not magically all friends just because they are all little. Young kids are just learning about friendship, and applying the term "friend" to every situation is confusing. Young kids will play with some kids and ignore others. That's OK. As an adult, you don't like everyone you meet, and it's unrealistic to expect a child will have equal feelings toward everyone. Let her enjoy her first friends—and treat other kids with respect.

friendships. A friend forms a caring relationship with another person, and this ability is just emerging in young children.

Adults sometimes expect kids to play together before they are ready. Your child goes through stages of play, including observer play and parallel, or side-by-side, play. See Stages of Play, starting on page 143. As her brain development and stages of play advance, your child needs to gain skills that help her join in and play with other children. As with any other social skill, the art of "getting into play" takes practice.

Social skills do have to be learned. Kathy Hirsh-Pasek, a psychologist who advocates for children's play, says many adults assume that social development "just happens." As children learn to interact with peers, they gain social awareness, part of what psychologist Daniel Goleman, author of *Emotional Intelligence* and *Social Intelligence*, calls "social intelligence."

First friendships, which typically start around age three or four, are not usually deep emotional bonds. Kids call each other a friend if they play with the same toy at the same moment. Just as quickly, a friend could be gone. Preschoolers are experimenting with friendship and don't understand if friends are here to stay. Can friends disagree with each other? Do friends always play with the same person? There's a lot kids don't know about friends at this age.

Remember how new all of this is for your child. Many kids have played alongside other children, but never had a friend of their own. By age four or five, the idea of a "best friend" may be tremendously important, but young kids get uneasy about all sorts of relationship questions. *If I play with him, do I have to give up my other friend? Can a person have two best friends at once? If I disagree with her, will she stop being my friend?* There's a lot of basic learning about friendships ahead.

When talking to children about social issues, be honest. Don't sugarcoat. Social relations are rewarding, but rarely easy. Young kids are making their first forays into friendship and just beginning to figure this out. Instead of forcing friendships, adults need to guide all kids in gaining better social skills.

> *You can't force friendship.*

Stages of Play

Mildred Parten first described stages of play in early childhood. Stages of play look like this:

Solo Play

Kids of all ages may choose to play alone, but the youngest ones are not ready for much more. Solo play means the child is absorbed in his own game and is not interested in or aware of kids around him. Kids often use solo play as a respite from too much social interaction.

Onlooker Play

Kids may actively observe play without being part of it. Picture a child watching two other kids build a tower. He might add a comment or two to shape the play but won't actually join in. This is more typical with younger children or kids needing to build up their trust first (either by learning about the activity or the people involved in it). Being an observer is a safe role. Some kids need lots of it.

Parallel Play

Parallel play is about playing side by side. Two-year-olds are great at this. Picture toddlers playing near each other in the sandbox or two kids playing with trains at the same time but not building the track together. Kids in this stage are absorbed in their own game and concerned about safety. *Will I be safe? Will the other kid interfere with what I'm doing?* It takes trust to play next to another child. A child in parallel play is aware of the other child and may imitate what she is doing. This is considered the first stage of group play.

Group Play (Associative and Cooperative)

Starting about age four, children begin to make first friends and advance to complex social play. This group play is often split into associative and cooperative. Associative lacks a true common goal but shares many elements. Cooperative play is often dramatic, pretend play. "Let's play house. I'll be the mommy," or "Sharks! Get away! Come onto my boat, fast!" Games like tag and hide-and-seek are cooperative play, as well as joint projects such as building a tall tower out of blocks together.

Mixing Stages of Play

Children move between stages of play. There's nothing unusual about a five-year-old who wants to play by himself, or a four-year-old who wants to observe for a long time before participating. Kids who are old enough to engage in cooperative play may enjoy being in a group of kids or may prefer the company of a single "best friend."

Getting Into Play

"Will you play with me?"

Some kids seem to sprout instant friendships. Others hang to the side watching, or barge in and scare their potential playmates. It may seem easy, but for many kids the art of getting into play is not simple. It often takes guts, training and practice.

Young kids sometimes try bizarre methods to make friends. For example, my brother, Scott.

Scott was a shy three-year-old who desperately wanted friends. At home, he'd talk to imaginary playmates behind the forsythia bushes that edged our driveway. In Sunday school he jumped kids from behind and strangled them with a half nelson. What was going on? The Sunday school teachers thought he was a violent, antisocial child, and my mother went home in tears.

My brother's story had a happy ending. He started preschool at the School for Young Children, and teachers there viewed Scott's aggression for what it was: a desire to play. Like most three-year-olds, Scott lacked social skills. Like most boys, he used his body to express his feelings. Scott attacked the children he liked the best. Like a puppy jumping wildly, he wanted to play.

Barging into play and launching physical attacks is a fairly common strategy kids use when they don't know how else to join the game. Basic conflict mediation can unravel this type of situation: "Scott, I see you jumped on Ben's back. Ben, did you want to be jumped on? No? Well, tell him. Scott, were you worried about Ben? Did you want to play with him?

Ben, Scott says he wants to play with you. Are you worried he's going to jump on you again? Scott says he won't jump on you. What could you do next time when you want to play?"

Respecting Play in Progress

"Use your words!" That's what we tell kids.

Certainly, asking "Can I play with you?" is a step above barging in and hitting playmates. The trouble is, "Can I play?" doesn't usually work with preschoolers.

Many kids will say no and reject a playmate if faced with uncertainty. The same is true with adults. Adult voters in elections tend to vote no if they feel uncertain about an issue. "Can I play?" is a polite start, but kids need more information.

The key lies in respecting the play in progress and finding an acceptable way to join in. Sometimes this involves setting a limit right away ("Don't knock over my tower"). This sets aside fears and gives everyone a role.

> *"Can I play?" isn't enough. Kids need to learn how to find a role.*

To encourage kids to include a new playmate, respect what they are already doing. Ask, "What are you playing?" "Do you want help with your digging?" "What do you need?" Talk to the newcomer and help him think how to help. Does he need a shovel? A costume? Does he need to become a dog, a monster or a bus driver? Ask: "What could you do? What could you bring?"

Laura Davis and Janis Keyser say one of the most important steps you can take as an adult is to simply acknowledge the ongoing play. Adults who take the time to find out what the game is all about ("Oh, you're playing firefighters") help fears evaporate. The original kids relax; they understand their play will be respected. In an atmosphere of trust, kids are more receptive to a new playmate or new ideas.

Ask questions and help kids come up with a plan to incorporate the newcomer. For example: "Gavin needs someone to get more sand. Can you do that?" or "These kids are playing ghosts. They said you can play if you're a ghost." If it's dramatic play, roles are already established. Ask, "Do you need another animal? Could there be two zebras?" Simply acknowledging the game helps the original kids feel safe and respected. Ask, "Is there a way Mira could fit in your game? What could she do?"

Some kids welcome everybody easily. Others are very picky. Most are scared that the new child will take their toys or otherwise disrupt their play. When kids are nervous about accepting a new child in their play, help them set some ground rules. "Sarah says you can play if you don't crash the trucks."

Try This—Add to Your Toolbox

Adults can guide children into play. Not *how* to play ("This is a restaurant—you're the waiter; take the order"), but how to gain acceptance with another child. This skill is just one of many social skills you already teach your child.

Fostering Friendship

SPOTTING FRIENDS

Help your child notice kids who might be good playmates. Point out similarities and interests. Stay simple: "You're playing with blocks and David is playing with blocks. You both like blocks." Using names and pointing out who's playing nearby can help children develop social awareness. "Mira is pouring sand next to you."

If your child intently observes another child, she might be looking for a friend. "I see you're watching Sarah. Do you want to play with Sarah?

You could ask." Kids sometimes accept new playmates quite easily. For example:

> *Two girls are playing together with a dollhouse. Logan sits nearby and watches them.*
> ADULT: I see Logan is watching. Do you want to play with them?
> *Logan nods.*
> ADULT: Is that OK?
> FIRST GIRL: Sure.
> SECOND GIRL: You can be the brother.

Point out budding friendships: "You've been playing with Pete a lot. I saw you sitting at lunch together and riding bikes together. I wonder if you might be getting a new friend."

OFFER MORAL SUPPORT

"Will you play with me?" is closely linked to "What happens if you won't? Will I be OK?" Just like adults, kids can be frozen by the fear of rejection. You can help out. Offer to stay by her side when she asks to join in.

"Do you want to play with Sarah? You could ask." *(information)*
"She might say yes and she might say no." *(setting expectations)*
"Do you want me to come with you?" *(moral support)*
"Heidi wants to ask you something, Sarah." *(kids talk directly)*
"Is there a way she could fit in your game? What could she do?"
"What does your game need?" *(easing transition)*

Deciphering Friendship

Can someone have more than one friend? Do friends always have to agree? What does being a friend mean?

As friendships develop, you can share information to help kids weather the inevitable ups and downs. For example, explain to a child who feels left out what's going on: "Casey has been playing with you every day, but I see today he's playing with Jack. I know friends can still like each other even if they don't play together all the time."

Kids are so new at friendships that they make lots of mistakes and false assumptions. An adult friendship is based on an emotional bond. A child's friendship is based on playing with another person. It's easy for a child to make the leap and think, *David isn't playing with me right now, so he's not my friend.*

Children also often think a friend is someone who will always agree with them about everything. When a problem comes up, kids say, "You're not my friend anymore!" Kids routinely disagree over play themes and who gets to be the boss. When relationships get rough, kids resort to social rejection: "I don't like you anymore! I won't be your friend! You can't come to my birthday party!"

Give kids basic information. The two biggies they need are: (1) you can still be friends even if you don't always want to play together, and (2) friends don't always agree with each other.

> *At a playdate at Jason's house, Lucas and Jason want to play super-heroes. Jason has the only cape.*
>
> JASON: I'll be Batman.
>
> LUCAS: No, I want to be Batman.
>
> JASON: No, you be Robin. I've got the cape, so I'm Batman.
>
> LUCAS: I'm Batman! I get to be Batman!
>
> JASON: No, you're a poophead. It's my house so I get to decide.
>
> MOM: Jason! Be nice. Lucas is your guest.
>
> LUCAS: You can't be my friend.

This scenario is a conflict like any other, but the underlying issue is how to be a friend. Find out what the friendship problem is. Is it bossiness? Is it name-calling? Is it disagreement over a play theme? Friends can disagree. Friends can negotiate. Friends can set limits on friends. You could help Jason and Lucas learn these lessons like this:

> ADULT: Sounds like there's a problem here. (*Stay neutral.*)
>
> JASON: It's my cape! (*Listen to the problem: sharing a special toy.*)
>
> LUCAS: He won't let me do anything! (*Listen to the problem: a friend being bossy.*)
>
> ADULT: Tell him, "This is my special cape. I don't want you to hurt it." Tell him, "I don't like it when you boss me around." (*Setting limits on a friend*)
>
> ADULT: Friends don't always agree. What can you do? You each have an idea. What's your idea, Lucas? What's yours, Jason? (*Information; listening*)

Kids will gain listening and flexibility skills. They will learn it's OK to change ideas, modify the play and set limits on friends.

Tools for Friendships

LETTERS TO EXPRESS FEELINGS

> *Maya,*
> *I am sad. You wouldn't play with me just alone. Are you still my friend?*
>
> *Lauren*

Lauren, age three, dictated this letter. The two girls had played together the day before, but today Maya was engaged in a game of pirates with two other kids. Reading the letter aloud to Maya helped spark a conversation. She still didn't want to stop playing pirate girls, but she could reassure Lauren. "I don't want to play with her right now," she clarified. "Are you still her friend?" asked the teacher. "Yes," said Maya. The adult then helped Lauren with her sad feelings and reminded her, "You can't make somebody play with you. You really want Maya to play, but Maya is the boss of her own body. She still likes you. Maybe she'll play with you again later."

SIGNS

Making signs is a highly effective tool for setting clear social boundaries. If kids want a clubhouse to themselves, suggest a sign setting out the rules. For example: "Ryan and John and Justin's House, and Brody If He's a Power Ranger." Signs can make preferences, fears and play themes obvious for all to see. Here's another example from four-year-olds: "Only Aliens and Knights in This House. No Calling Bad Names."

PUPPETS

Puppets are an excellent tool for discussing friendships. If Brown Bear has a problem—being scared that his friend Rabbit won't like him anymore—you can safely raise the topic of whether a person can have more than one friend without losing the first one. Involve your child: "Has this ever happened to you?" It can feel safer talking to a puppet about scary topics.

DISCUSS FRIENDSHIP

Ask kids, "What's a friend?" Start a discussion: "How do you get a friend to play your idea?" Brainstorm together and write down their ideas. You can correct any inaccuracies as you talk through it.

MODELING VOCABULARY

Kids learn how to navigate friendships and potential playmates through modeling, just like anything else. Give them specific words to say that can help in friendship conflicts. A child who doesn't understand what friendship is might say, "You're not my friend anymore," when he really means "I'm busy. I'm playing with Sam right now. Maybe we can play later." Say those words yourself, and your child will soon be able to use them, too.

Fostering Friendship Skills

1. **Help kids notice potential friends**

   Describe what other children are doing and point out similar interests.

2. **Offer moral support**

   Go with a child to ask about joining play.

3. **Help kids notice other kids' social goals**

   Describe the ongoing play and encourage your child to think of ways she could contribute. It might involve bringing a prop or adopting a role.

4. **Encourage flexibility**

   "Could there be two babies? How could Jenny fit in your game?"

5. **Remind kids they can set limits on newcomers who enter play**

   Kids often reject a new playmate if they are worried about something. Set the fears aside to help kids say yes. "What are your rules? No knocking the castle down?"

6. **Help kids decipher what friendship means**

   Offer children information: Friends don't always play together. Friends don't always agree. You can still be friends if these things happen. Use a variety of tools (letters, signs, puppets) to explore friendship ideas.

7. **Interpret bizarre or inappropriate behavior**

   If a child attacks when he actually wants to play, redirect and help both kids understand what's going on. "When you run and yell like that, Jacob thinks you're going to hurt him." Bizarre behavior can be a sign the child is hoping to play.

WORDS TO TRY

Getting into play

Do you want to play with Victoria? Let's ask her.

I see you're watching Jack. Do you want to play with him?

What are you playing?

Ben wants to help you build this castle. Do you want help? What are your rules?

Is there a way she could fit into your game? What could she do?

What does your game need? What could he bring? Can you have two bad guys?

Understanding friendship

You don't like that idea. Tell him. Do you have a different idea?

I know friends can still like each other even if they don't play together all the time.

I know kids sometimes like to be alone (or have more than one friend).

I know kids change their minds.

WORDS TO AVOID

We're all friends here.

I see a friend who wants a turn.

Let your friend play with it now.

OUT AND ABOUT

If another adult calls your kids "friends" and they barely know each other, try making an on-the-spot introduction. "I don't think the kids know each other yet. This is Emily." This helps model ways to get to know somebody and keeps the term "friend" in perspective.

You'll find a lot of "friend" comments made by teachers in preschool and kindergarten. Old habits are hard to break, but you can certainly raise the issue. It might open a great conversation about social relationships in the class.

You Can't Play = A-OK

A young boy ran up to his teacher on the playground. "Kevin won't let me play with him!"

"He has to," the teacher answered. Then she recited, "We don't say you can't play."

The boy returned to Kevin, who was busily playing with another child, but a few moments later, he was back.

"He still won't let me play!"

"Kevin!" called out the teacher. "On the bench!"

Renegade Reason

Free play includes the right to choose whom to play with. Let children choose whether to include or reject a playmate.

When exclusionary play crops up among children, we tend to squash it as soon as we see it. "That's not nice," we say. "Let Caroline be a puppy, too."

Adults frantically want children to get along. We see trouble in the world, we've experienced pain in social relationships ourselves, and we want to spare our kids. We wish children could act like superior beings who get along all the time. We tell a group of children they are all friends. We order children to play with another child. While anger scares us and conflict discomforts us, social rejection downright terrifies us.

My childhood preschool is rare in its stance on rejection. The Right to Choose Playmates is considered one of children's fundamental rights. And that right to choose has a flip side—the right to exclude others.

Why is it OK to exclude? The main goal is to meet children's developmental needs by protecting their right to play. Kids are in charge of whom they choose to play with. This means a child can decide to play with one or two friends, play with a selected group or have the privacy to play alone.

Rejection in the Renegade style isn't hurting anyone. It fits the Renegade Golden Rule: It's OK If It's Not Hurting People or Property. Yes, sad feelings often come up when a child isn't welcomed into play, but it's the same frustration a child feels when she wants to play with the blue truck and Danny is still using it. She feels thwarted and mad. The adult's job is to help kids cope with their feelings and help kids care about one another—even if they don't play together. Modeling inclusive and respectful behavior is the best way for kids to learn.

This chapter explains rejection and good reasons why children exclude one another. There are also ways adults can guide kids into play, both to teach friendship skills and to turn around prospects for an oft-rejected child (see Rule 11: We're Not *All* Friends Here, and Rule 14: Take Rejection in Stride).

Simple exclusion is not bullying. It's not mean. Done right, it actually encourages children to be more aware, caring and tolerant of each other. This is what children need to learn:

You don't have to like everyone.
You don't have to play with everyone.
You *do* have to be decent to everyone.

Exclusionary play can be respectful play. When we understand what motivates children to exclude, how little they know about friendships, and how adults can guide children into becoming more accepting and caring toward one another, rejection loses its sting.

Renegade Blessings

Allowing your child to choose her own playmates develops life-long social skills. This includes facing both sides of rejection: respectfully excluding another child and being excluded herself. Kids learn how to take social risks, set limits and cope with negative emotions:

> *I don't have to like everyone. I still have to respect everyone.*
>
> *Even when I like somebody, I don't have to play with him all the time.*
>
> *I can take social risks.*
>
> *I can survive being rejected. I can get over it and do something else.*
>
> *It's OK to play alone sometimes.*
>
> *I know how to stand up for myself without being mean.*
>
> *Adults respect me and my play. I have some control.*

Why It Works

Exclusionary play is routine, not rotten behavior, say Laura Davis and Janis Keyser (*Becoming the Parent You Want to Be*). Although few childhood experts will touch this prickly subject, Davis and Keyser contend it's OK for kids to exclude a child from play, but it's not OK to exclude that child from their listening and caring.

Exclusion happens for many innocent reasons, including trying to maintain a good game already in progress. Kids love the games of pretend they set up. It's a thrill to be the baby birds in the nest or the good guys slaying the *T. rex*. Davis and Keyser explain that this type of exclusion means "I can't figure out how to include another person, and I'm scared we'll lose this play if you join us."

Kids also are experimenting with power in relationships, say Davis and Keyser. What will the other child do if I say, "If you won't be the puppy, then you can't play with us"? Kids also use the wrong vocabulary and say, "You can't play. You're not my friend," when they mean "I want to play with Sam right now."

 Take Off Your Adult Lenses

"She can't play with us" becomes less scary when we view social play for what it is—social learning. Kids ages two to three often can't cope with more than one playmate. Older kids may need help joining play. Experience with both sides of social rejection is valuable for our kids' social and emotional growth. Allowing rejection to happen teaches lifelong social skills about making friends, taking risks and coping with negative feelings. Exclusion can be respectful.

Children need to deal with rejection. It's a reality in life. And so is social risk-taking—whether it's for a grade-school friend, teenage date, job, audition or marriage proposal. We take social risks all our lives, and we all sometimes get rejected. Even from a young age, we can teach our kids how to cope with rejection. Children need to learn how to accept risk and rejection and not be devastated. They can survive and go on. When kids gain practice facing typical rejection early on, they learn both resilience and respect—skills that can help them succeed.

Right to Choose Playmates

In our effort to have kids "all get along," we often hurt play and compound social problems. What happened to Kevin, the boy in the above example? His play got interrupted. He was engaged with one friend when a third child came along. Sometimes kids are worried when another child approaches. *Will he hurt me? Will he change my game? Will he be too loud? Will he take away my friend? Will he do what he did yesterday that scared me? Will he listen to me when I set limits?* These concerns are valid and ought to be listened to.

What about the boy who told the teacher? He lost, too. He didn't succeed in entering the game—the play stopped when Kevin sat on the bench. He missed a chance to learn positive ways of entering play. And his relationship with his peers soured—if he had been feared or disliked before, now he was also resented. Social play involves at least two willing people. The truth is you can't force someone else to play, no matter how much you may want to.

Just as she can keep a toy until she is all done, a child should have the right to keep a playmate. This method fundamentally respects her right to play, prevents interruption and can teach emotional coping skills on both sides of the rejection equation.

Think about rejection as protecting play. Your child has a right to play, and you are supporting her right to play either alone or with one or two chosen children. For the rejected child, it's an opportunity for new social learning and a chance to deal with uncomfortable feelings.

> *It's a child's right to choose her own playmates. It's our job to support that right.*

What We Fear

Rejection scares us. Witnessing social rejection among kids brings back all our own hurts. It hits the heart of so many social fears—not being liked, not having friends, not having the right friends. If you ever felt socially awkward growing up or were the target of teasing, rejection or bullying as a child, you know how hurtful rejection can be. We want to spare our kids this pain.

Let's be clear: Excluding a child is *not* the same as bullying. Bullying is mean and hurtful behavior that is targeted, repeated and fundamentally about power. Kids as young as four and five can bully, but they can also learn to be assertive and respectful. Methods in this chapter actually help prevent bullying.

Rejection will happen. Kids need skills to cope. Whether it's friends now, future recess playmates or dates, rejection is an aspect of social life. Much as we might like to, we can't (and shouldn't) spare our kids every ounce of pain from these situations, but we can teach them coping skills.

You can guide children in respectful rejection (see the Toolbox). For example, when your child says, "You're not my friend" (a common fall-back phrase kids use when they don't know what to say), you can help them figure out the real issue and rephrase it: "I want to play by myself right now." An important part of respectful rejection is leaving the door open for the future: "I still like you," or "After this game we can play," or "Maybe we can play later."

Early childhood is the perfect time to learn skills to deal with rejection. It takes practice to remain confident and respectful. We don't want to raise kids who always give in to social pressure and have a hard time saying no. We don't want excluded kids to become immobilized by their feelings and unable to move on. Social rejection is a simply a conflict like any other.

Children need skills on both sides of social exclusion—how to say no to a playmate without hurting feelings, and how to cope without being devastated when the answer *no* comes. The combination of skills that exclusion involves—assertiveness, social awareness and resilience—are powerful character traits that can be taught, starting with the very young.

Drawbacks of Forced Play

"Come on, be nice. Let Chelsea play with you," says the adult.

Our intentions are good, but insisting that children accept an additional playmate interrupts play and can sour relationships. Play often stagnates or stops. How do the kids feel?

> *Sonja and Tasha, two four-year-olds, are playing house together. Chelsea wants to join in.*
> SONJA: I only like Tasha. You can't come in
> ADULT: That's not nice. Remember our rule, Sonja. You can't say that. Everyone is allowed to play.
> TASHA: All right. You have to be the baby who is sleeping.
> *Chelsea is left sleeping. The other two girls move off to play together again.*

A child like Chelsea may feel:

> They don't like me. They're just playing with me because they have to.
> I don't get to do any of the good parts. They just make me be the baby.
> It's no fun to be here.
> Nobody likes me. I don't have friends.

Kids like Sonja and Tasha may feel:

> What I think doesn't matter. I just have to say yes to please people.
> Adults don't care. What I'm doing is not important.
> I can't cope with another person. I don't know how to include her.
> There goes that game. I was having fun and now it's ruined.
> It's all Chelsea's fault.

Even though we mean well, forcing kids to play together backfires. Often the child we are trying to help is not fully welcomed into the play, which can lead to greater social rejection. We unwittingly make the problem worse. Instead of trying to avoid rejection, view it as a new learning opportunity. Besides, there are plenty of good reasons why children reject other children.

Reasons for Rejection

Kids reject potential playmates for all sorts of valid reasons. When your child says no, stay calm and consider why. Two common reasons—being socially overwhelmed and stages of play (see below)—are part of natural child development.

Reasons for Rejection

1. Socially overwhelmed
2. Stages of play in child development
3. Safety
4. Play interruption
5. Temporary mood

6. Play ideas
7. Experiments
8. Protecting space
9. Protecting a friendship
10. Gender identity

1. Three's a Crowd—Feeling Socially Overwhelmed

When a pair of three-year-olds announce another child can't join their game, they might be right. Three-year-olds have a hard time coping with more than one friend at a time.

Social research shows that young kids can't handle multiple relationships well. Kids naturally choose to limit the number of playmates when they feel socially overwhelmed. Interacting with other children can be taxing work. Listen when your child tells you no. When young kids say no, they may be desperately trying to keep their play alive; they simply don't have the energy to incorporate a new person.

2. Stages of Play

We sometimes assume children can play cooperatively, but this takes time to develop. Younger kids may still be in solo, observer or parallel stages of play (see Stages of Play in Rule 11: We're Not *All* Friends Here). Asking them to play together may be out of the question. Kids may need to watch for a long time or simply play nearby. When kids feel safe and when they are old enough to handle it, they will naturally move to the next level of play. Curb your desire to bring a loner into active play—he may be doing exactly what he needs to do.

3. Rejecting for Safety

When Lily rejected Eric by saying no fiercely, her teacher asked Lily a simple question: "Are you worried about Eric?"

Fear is often the number one reason kids reject kids. Kids say no when they don't feel safe. In Lily and Eric's case, this fear could be anything from a scary picture on Eric's T-shirt to the possibility he might take her toy. Ask the question, "Are you worried?" openly, in front of both children. Eric may be surprised to know that something about him might be causing Lily to say no. An open dialogue gives Eric a chance to clear things up.

As parents, though, we might find it tricky to see the fear behind rejection. We think it's rude. We often fixate on our children's words and forget to ask questions. Instead of feeling indignant when our child says, "Ben can't come in!" we could say, "Hmm. Is there something about Ben you're worried about?" You'll be surprised how often this simple question uncovers the problem. When I was four, I was scared of someone with freckles, because I thought they were measles. Pause. Ask the kids. Listen and deal with the resulting emotions.

> *Fear is often the top reason why kids reject kids. Ask the child: "Is there something you're worried about?"*

Amanda and Mollie built a clubhouse at preschool. They asked for a sign that said "Amanda and Mollie's House. No Boys and No Tigers." It had been a day with lots of dress-up clothes and noisy play. A boy named Ben approached, wearing a tiger suit.

TEACHER: Ben, you have to ask Amanda and Mollie before you go in. Look, here's what the sign says: "Amanda and Mollie's House. No Boys and No Tigers." Do you want to ask? They might say yes and they might say no.

BEN: Can I play with you?

AMANDA: I don't like loud noises!

TEACHER: Are you worried that Ben will make loud noises in your house?

AMANDA: Yeah. Tigers growl.

TEACHER: Ben, will you growl in their house?

Ben shakes his head.

TEACHER: Can Ben come in if he doesn't growl or make loud noises?

GIRLS: Yeah.

MOLLIE: Let's change the sign to say "Friendly Tigers."

TEACHER: OK, here's what it says now: "No Boys and Only Friendly Tigers."

4. Fear of Interruption

Alison and Rachel were having a grand time playing house together. When another girl wanted to join, they felt threatened. What would happen to their game? They already had a mommy and a baby.

Kids often reject new playmates because they are worried the new person will disrupt their play. Adding a new person changes the game. This is a valid concern, but can be overcome if kids are willing. Help kids figure out how to include a newcomer. Acknowledge the play in progress and ask questions. For example: "What are you doing? What's your game? How could Sally fit in your game? Hmm, you already have a mommy and a baby. Could there be two mommies in this game?"

5. Rejecting Based on Mood

Kids' moods change all day. One minute they might jump at the chance to play, and the next be absorbed in something else. Remember, many rejections are temporary.

My son Zach loves to play with his neighbor Tyler. One day Tyler popped by with a grin on his face and asked to play. Zach was immersed in his own game in the sandbox. He said no. "Maybe next time, Tyler!" we called out.

Even well-established buddies like Tyler and Zach don't always want to play. When this happens, kids may get scared that they have lost the friendship. It can help to tell the rejected child, "I know kids change their minds sometimes. Maybe you can try again later." You can also help reassure the rejected child by asking questions—even risky questions like "Do you still like him?" Just hearing the words "Yes, he's still my friend—I just want to keep doing this now" helps friendship fears evaporate.

Of course, with questions like this there is a chance that the other child might reply, "No. He's not my friend anymore." Risk it. At worst you'll uncover a conflict that needs attention. Chances are, it's a misunderstanding. Kids often believe a friend is only someone you are actively playing with, so if no play is going on, the "friend" is gone, too. You can straighten them out. "I know friends don't always play together, but they still like each other."

6. Rejecting an Idea, Not the Person

When one child suggests, "Let's play dinosaurs!" and the other child says, "No, I don't want to play with you," it could be a rejection of the play theme, not the person. You can help your child navigate this one by finding out whether the two children truly want to play together or whether it's the idea that's important. "Do you want to play with Danny? Looks like he doesn't want to play dinosaurs. Is there something else you could do together?" You can also coach the child who says no to add an explanation. "Ruby, I don't think Anna knows why you don't want to play house. Can you tell her?" These conversations help children reach their true goal—the right game or the right person.

7. Rejecting in Order to Experiment

Kids say the darnedest things: "If you won't dig the moat, you can't come to my birthday party." When you hear rejection in the form of threats, likely the child is experimenting with power. Balancing power and decision making is all part of play. Who gets to decide the play theme and set the rules? Who can alter them? Help kids explore these issues. Let them discuss what's fair and lay out different play ideas. Use your authority as an adult to help kids listen to one another.

8. Rejecting to Protect Space

Children's energies are often devoted to protecting their turf. Protecting from what? From intrusions that may disrupt their play.

A group of four-year-olds protected their play by creating a hideout and posting a sign that said, "Kenny, Robert, Sam and Mason. Our Secret Hideout. We Are Good Guys."

Four year-old Bella wanted to play by herself. She dressed up in a zebra suit and asked for a "Zebras Only" sign to be put on her playhouse. Since she was the only zebra, she was safe.

Zebras Only
in This House

Kids like little spaces to crawl into and call their own. Houses, tents, forts, the spot under the chair. Children show their need for privacy by making little houses like this, said Fred Rogers, of *Mister Rogers' Neighborhood*. Sometimes a child just wants to be alone or command a small space all to herself. At the School for Young Children, teachers recognize this need and help kids erect tents and houses with signs that say "Arthur's Tent. Arthur Only" or "Mariah and Rachel's Clubhouse. No One Can Come In." If another kid wants to enter and gets rejected, it's easy to say, "Do you want your own tent?" Once a sense of privacy and ownership is established, kids feel safer. Often they end up playing together by visiting each other.

9. Rejecting to Protect a Friendship

Jayden and Nick, two four-year-olds, huddled together in a corner whispering. Jayden pointed to another boy and said, "Let's not play with him."

Sounds mean, right? Kids often exclude when they are trying to protect a precious friendship. Sometimes kids can't socially handle a newcomer. In this case, Jayden is worried that Nick might play with another child instead of him. He hasn't learned yet that people can have more than one friend. Jayden is experimenting with exclusion to protect the friend he has.

Kids like Jayden can learn that friends sometimes play with other people. Even though he's Nick's friend, he's not Nick's boss. This is a tough lesson, but an important one. He can have fun playing by himself, too, or try playing with a new kid.

10. Rejecting for Gender Identity

Some kids reject the opposite gender in order to explore their own gender identity. It's a big and touchy subject. "No girls" or "no boys" statements bring up the specter of discrimination. See Rule 13: Hang Up a "No Girls" Sign, for more discussion.

Try This—Add to Your Toolbox

There's usually a simple developmental reason why kids reject each other. So although a child's rejection may conjure up terrifying thoughts in your mind, remember it's more likely to be a big deal for you than for your child. Deal with upset feelings first (if there are any). Then help both kids interpret the situation and move on.

Dealing with Exclusionary Play

1. Respect children's right to choose playmates.

2. Consider a child's developmental stage and personal temperament. What is she ready for? Is she able to include others?

3. Acknowledge the social risk and the play that is already in progress. "Looks like they're playing tigers. Do you want to play, too? They might say yes or no. Let's find out."

4. Listen to feelings on both sides. To the excluding child say, "Is there something you're worried about, Ben?" And to the rejected child: "That makes you sad. You wanted to play with Sarah."

5. Guide children into how to say no without hurting feelings. "I want to play by myself right now. I still like you. Maybe we can play later."

6. Make a plan to play later. A big sister doesn't have to play with her little sister all the time, but help kids set a plan to include each other.

7. Help the rejected child move on. "What else could you do? Who else could you play with? Looks like Robbie is playing in the sandbox. Do you want to play in the sandbox, too?"

8. For more in-depth strategies to cope with repeated rejection, see Rule 14: Take Rejection in Stride.

Remind Her of Her Rights

If children aren't forced to play together, there's little reason for teasing or mean rejections. A child often acts that way when she doesn't know any other options. Give her some. When a child's right to choose her own playmates is protected, she will be less likely to use rejection as a weapon that hurts.

"If you don't want to play with Alice, that's OK. Try saying it again like this: No, thanks. I don't want to play right now." If your child speaks in a mean way, remind her that she doesn't have to play with so-and-so, but she still should be kind to her.

Model Respectful Rejection

Model the phrase "I don't want to play with you *right now*." Emphasize the "right now." "I don't want to play that now. I'm busy doing this puzzle. Maybe later." Kids are egocentric and change moods frequently. Help your child give an answer that leaves the door open for the future.

Focus on Feelings

The rejected kid needs support, especially if he just took a big social risk. First, deal with the feelings. Acknowledge them. Bring the hurt feelings out in the open.

"You look sad. How are you feeling? It's hard. You really wanted to play with Nathan but he said no."

Encourage the rejected child to share his feelings: "It makes me feel bad when you won't let me play." For some kids, suggest expressing the feeling in a letter or picture. Write down exactly how he is feeling, even if the words are harsh.

Make a Date

If the rejection is between siblings or involves kids who are often to-gether, consider making a date. This helps brothers and sisters care about each other even as they guard their privacy. If a little brother is always having the door slammed in his face, help him set a time to be together. The older child could explain, "I want to be alone right now. After supper I'll play Legos with you." Or the parent could tell the rejected sibling, "I hear Ruby saying she wants to be with her friend Anna right now. What could you do while she's busy?"

Move On

Be prepared to comfort the rejected child, but don't belabor the point. Some kids get over the hurt of rejection fast. You can ask, "What could you do instead?" Sometimes kids are not in the mood to search out an-other friend. Offer to help, then drop it. An important part of rejection is to move on.

WORDS TO TRY

Finding the issue

I hear you saying Kate can't come in. What would Kate do if she
  came in?

Are you worried about Ben?

Do you want to be with Jeremy, or do you want to do what he's
  doing?

Being rejected

Sarah doesn't want to play with you *right now*. Maybe she'll want
  to play together later.

You're sad. You really wanted to play lions with her.

Are you worried Sarah doesn't like you anymore? Sarah, do you
  still like Fiona?
You can't make someone play with you.
I know kids can be friends even if they don't play together all the
  time.

Protecting the Right to Play
It's OK. You don't have to play with Danny.
You can tell him, "I don't want to play right now, but I still like
  you. Maybe later."
When could you play together?

WORDS TO AVOID
Be nice and let Kathy play.
You don't mean that. Of course she can play.
We don't say, "You can't play."
I don't care, you have to let him play with you.

OUT AND ABOUT
Just as with sharing, most parents will insist that a child accept
another playmate on demand. Simply letting other kids and
adults know it's OK with you if kids don't play together can ease
tensions. "That's all right. It's just fine if Annabelle decides she
wants to keep playing by herself. She can keep right on playing."
Or "It looks as if you hope Brian and Andy will start playing together. It's OK with me if they don't."

Sometimes adults will remain adamant, with words like "Nonsense! Of course he can play." In that case, observe and see where
the forced playing leads. Who knows? Sometimes kids will accept one another. If they don't, you can always move on. If the
culture clash occurs at your house, you can say, "At our house,
kids don't have to play together if they don't want to. I know kids
change their minds sometimes and like playing together later."

Hang Up a "No Girls" Sign

Amelia and Leah set up a pirate house in my mother's class of three-year-olds. "We need a sign!" they cried, and my mother wrote down their exact words. The sign read:

"No Boys Allowed. No Pirate Boys. No Hitting. No Yelling. No Throwing Corn in Our House."

Across the hall in the four-year-olds' classroom, a group of boys made a fort. The words on their sign were:

"The Greatest Good Guy Hideout. Only Boys Who Live in This House Are Allowed. Only Good Guys. No Girls."

These children are exploring several ideas at once and trying to protect all three: friends, rules of play and gender identity.

Renegade Reason
Kids this age often segregate by sex. Rejecting the opposite sex helps kids explore their own gender identity and make friends.

Ages three and up are prime time for children to understand and explore gender roles and identity. Who's a boy and who's a girl? How can you tell? What does it mean to be one? What am I? What kind of things do boys/girls do? Do all girls have long hair? Is that grown-up with short hair a man or a woman? Are all mommies women? When I grow up, will I be a mommy or a daddy? Can a boy turn into a girl?

One way young kids reinforce their own gender identity is by playing exclusively with kids of the same sex. Girls play with girls. Boys play with boys. This same-sex segregation is driven by children themselves and occurs very strongly for many children. When your child shouts, "No boys!" or hangs up a "No Boys—Girls Only" sign on her bedroom door, she may have nothing against boys but simply be establishing herself firmly as a girl.

Renegade Blessings

Support your child's right to play with his chosen playmates. If "no girls" comes up, ask questions and clear up misinformation, but let the play go on. When you allow kids to explore and segregate by sex during play, they can gain many lessons:

> *I know who I am.*
> *Sometimes I like to play with just girls/boys. That's OK.*
> *Boys and girls are different.*
> *Boys and girls also like a lot of the same things.*
> *Adults respect my play. I can play my own way as long as it's not hurting anyone.*

Why It Works

Michael Thompson, child psychologist and coauthor of *Raising Cain* and *It's a Boy!*, explains how children begin to sort their play into girl-only and boy-only soon after they develop the ability to play collaboratively with other children. For many children, same-sex play starts around age three and continues for the next seven to eight years. Thompson says this is normal and natural and occurs throughout the world's cultures. This switch to boy/girl exclusionary play can be a shock for parents, he says, since as toddlers our children played fairly equally with both sexes.

Still, same-sex play alone isn't too troubling. It's when same-sex play is accompanied by exclusion (no boys! no girls!) that we begin to worry. To a preschooler, there's not much difference.

Forming self-identity is a major task of growing up. One way kids define who they are is by being clear about who they're not: "No boys here!" During the preschool years, children start seriously sorting through gender concepts. Your child may do this in many ways—dress-up, imaginary games and exclusionary play.

Exclusion is a powerful way of establishing self-identity. Social groups maintain identity by creating a strong sense of "us" and "them." This doesn't have to be mean—it can be as simple as rallying to an identity symbol, such as a school mascot. When girls are saying "No boys," they are rallying to the "girl" mascot. Nancy Curry and Sara Arnaud, psychologists who study children's play, say sometimes a child can feel defined as part of a group only by excluding someone else.

Many early-childhood teachers discourage children from excluding other children based on any "group" identity, including gender. The School for Young Children's philosophy follows the children's lead in this area. Children this age seem to want to segregate into boy/girl playgroups, and the school allows gender exclusion. Teachers step in only if the gender exclusion hurts someone's feelings.

Take Off Your Adult Lenses

When we see a "No Girls" or "No Boys" sign, we cringe. That's good. We're reacting as adults.

But when your four-year-old builds a clubhouse and announces, "No boys allowed!" remember she's operating in a different world. "No boys" might mean "I'm a girl—I'm figuring out who I am." Gender exclusion at this age is natural social development, and shouldn't be harmful. If someone feels hurt by her statement, use conflict mediation to sort it out.

What matters most is that children get to choose their playmates, and adults support these social decisions. Preschool-age children are engaged in categorizing the world and view many things in black-and-white. As children sort out their own gender identity, they may go through a many-year period of "no boys" or "no girls," just as they may cultivate an excessively feminine pink stage or a masculine superhero stage. Gradations get filled in later. Sometimes children need to take gender ideas to extremes before they can settle into a more balanced, realistic view.

No Harm Done

It's hard for us to set aside our adult views on this one. After centuries of fighting for equal access for the sexes, a "no girls" or "no boys" statement may seem horrific. The key is to understand it through the lens of child development. Your four-year-old has needs to be met. Some of his current needs are exploring gender identity, and he explores his needs through play. If he is saying "No girls," there's a reason for it.

Besides gender identity, "no boys" or "no girls" statements may show a hidden fear. Kids have all sorts of unusual fears based on ignorance. Will boys be loud? Will girls not like trucks? Will playing with a boy make you turn into a boy? If you're wondering what your child might be thinking, just ask. "I see you don't want any girls. Is there something you don't like about girls?" Gender-exclusive play can offer plenty of insights. But don't try to dig too deep. Often it's simply a question of whom your child likes to play with best—and that social preference should be respected.

> *All behavior has meaning.*

Why Children Say "No Boys" or "No Girls"

Excluding the other gender to establish their own identity.

Trying to protect their right to play with one or more chosen playmates.

Exploring differences between boys and girls through play.

Preferring the company or activities of their own sex.

Sending a signal that they are scared about something.

Sending a signal that they are confused about something.

If kids are allowed to explore gender ideas, they often let it go. If the need is suppressed, it goes underground where you can't see it and ideas may get more confused. Like all play ideas, it's best to let gender exclusion play itself out in plain view.

When you look at the child development needs behind children's "no girls"/"no boys" statements, it's easier to let go of discrimination fears. But isn't saying "No girls!" still bad? Won't it hurt somebody? At the preschool age, gender-exclusive play isn't harmful. The Renegade Golden Rule still applies here—It's OK If It's Not Hurting People or Property—which includes hurting feelings. If another child *is* hurt or troubled by the words, then stop and use conflict mediation to work it out.

Going to Extremes

In addition to dividing into two camps, boys and girls often take gender concepts to extremes in early childhood. Children may form rigid ideas about what males and females can and can't do.

It's common for preschool-age children to go through an ultramasculine superhero stage or an ultrafeminine pink princess stage. Gentle, laid-back fathers wonder what's come over their sons. Casual, no-makeup mothers stare in bewilderment as their daughters become pink and lavender girly girls. Exploring extremes helps kids figure out who they are, and this often means excluding the opposite gender.

Kids will even stick to rigid gender stereotypes despite models to the contrary. For example, Benjy, the son of a doctor, liked to play first-aid rescue games. While playing with another three-year-old, he said, "Only boys can be doctors." Benjy's mother was amazed. After all, *she* was the doctor in the family.

You can model and explain until you're blue in the face, but young kids sometimes sort the world into extremes for a while. They are busy categorizing the world and like consistency within these categories. You can bet Benjy won't hold this view when he's a few years older.

Only Child's Play

Finally, don't take gender exclusion too seriously. A five-year-old boy who chooses to play only with boys is not destined to become an adult who discriminates against women. A four-year-old girl who shuns all boys is not likely to turn into a man-hater. Same-sex play is typical through elementary school. Besides, kids often override their own rules. For example, Amanda and Mollie said, "No boys and no tigers," but they let Ben, a boy wearing a tiger costume, enter their playhouse (see Rule 12: You Can't Play = A-OK). Keep it light.

Try This—Add to Your Toolbox

Make Girls/Boys a Nonissue

Kids will do nearly anything to protect their play. Often "no girls"/"no boys" sentiments vanish if you simply reinforce children's right to play—especially their right to choose their own playmates. "Oh, you said 'No boys' because you really want to play with Sophie. That's OK, you can play with just Sophie." See Rule 11: We're Not *All* Friends Here, and Rule 12: You Can't Play = A-OK.

Find the Real Issue

Is it gender identity? Fear someone will crash their carefully constructed fort? Misinformation? Playmate preference? "No girls"/"no boys" statements get adult attention, but they can mask the real issue. Ask questions and find out.

Hang Up a "No Girls" or "No Boys" Sign

Writing signs is a fantastic way to encourage literacy, reinforce rights, and give kids a sense of ownership and control over their play. When you write down your child's exact words, you really let her know that you've heard her idea. Go ahead and write "No Boys Allowed" or "Girls Can't Come In." The paper sign won't last forever, but it gives your child a powerful sense of security and recognition.

PUT ON A POSITIVE SPIN

Although using your child's exact words is usually best, watch out if she singles out an individual for rejection. For example, if your daughter wants you to write "Henry Can't Come In," ask two questions. First:

"Who *do* you want to come in?" Second: "If Henry comes in, what will happen?" Singling out one child, Henry, to exclude can hurt and be too overpowering for him. When naming names, aim for a positive sign. For example: "Secret Clubhouse. Peter Can Come In."

ALTERNATIVE TO A "NO GIRLS" OR "NO BOYS" SIGN

If the idea of a "No Girls Allowed!" sign on a clubhouse makes you truly flinch, write "Robert and Jesse's House" instead. This still meets the goal of allowing the children to choose their playmates, but can be more comfortable for adults. Anyone who wants to enter the house has to get permission from Robert and Jesse first. Names can also be added easily, boy or girl.

Guidelines for Handling "No Girls"/"No Boys"

1. **Let the child initiate**

   No reason to suggest a "no boys" motto. Let your child bring it up on her own.

2. **Don't overreact**

   Remember, you are dealing with a very young child. Her needs are not yours. Her need to explore gender exclusion is part of her development.

3. **Use her own words**

   Repeat your child's words back to her verbatim. If writing a sign, use her exact words as much as possible. This helps her know you've heard, and helps you both explore the idea behind the words.

4. **Ask probing questions**

   Find out what is prompting a "no girls"/"no boys" statement. Is it self-identity? Fear? Protection of friendship? Misunderstanding?

5. **Reinforce what's right**

Reinforce gender identity: "Yes, you're a girl and Sophie is a girl." Reinforce your child's right to select her own playmates: "If you want to play just with Sophie, you can."

6. **Clear up what's wrong**

Offer information to clear up gender confusion: "You're worried boys will be too loud. I know boys can be quiet, too." "I know girls can play baseball."

7. **Clarify the real issue**

After your discussion, rephrase her original message ("No boys") to convey her real meaning ("I'm a girl and I like playing with other girls best"). This reinforces the true message and helps a child understand her thoughts clearly. Together, you might decide to modify an earlier sign you wrote. For example, "No Boys Allowed" becomes "Megan's House. Only Quiet Kids Can Come In."

Discrimination

What about exclusion for other reasons? When rejection rears its head, we get scared of discrimination. If we allow "No Girls" or "No Boys" signs, will we also be faced with signs that say "No Blacks" or "No Spanish Speakers" or "No Muslims" or "No Jews"?

Racial discrimination and exclusion based on looks, special needs, and so on are serious social issues, but more relevant to older kids and adults. Young children group themselves primarily by sex and play interests. Sometimes they simply seek information.

When I was six, I wanted to be friends with a little girl named Liz. She was building a tower and I wanted to play blocks with her, but I was scared to touch her hand. She was African-American and I was white. I thought my skin would change colors when I touched her. "It won't," said my mother. That was all I needed. It was a relief to me to know skin color didn't work that way. Liz and I played together the rest of the year. My mother also asked me a follow-up question: "Why do you care what color your skin is?" "I want to look like you," I told her. My fear of touching Liz had been a fear of difference and a fear of losing connection to my own family.

Children hold all sorts of odd ideas and fears; they are curious and ignorant. Race is no different from a young child's point of view, but it can be a lightning rod for adults. Children's comments about race, body type or disability typically fall into two categories: name-calling and ignorance.

Dealing with Difference

Children innately notice differences. It's how they learn. Sorting, classifying and recognizing patterns is vital for learning language, culture, reading and science. Kids are bound to notice differences in race and appearance as their world expands.

Under age three, kids focus on self and family. They assume the whole world looks and acts the way their family does. As kids edge close to four, they start to really notice differences and classify. A chief fear of three- and four-year-olds is people who look different (beard, skin color or disability) from their own family.

If your family is multiracial, your child has already sorted people of different skin colors into the category of "friends and family." If your child moves in a homogeneous world, she's going to notice differences but lack information. Give her information, very basic information. For example: "I know that Teresa is a girl and you're a girl. I know you both like to play house," or "Yes, her skin color is lighter/darker than yours." Dispel any fear by asking: "Is there something about that little girl you're worried about?"

Children have to be taught to hate or disdain people based on race or other factors. Family values have an enormous influence on a child's moral development, so model your views and speak out against stereotypes and discrimination. When it comes to exclusionary play, race and religion rarely factor in for the six-and-under crowd unless adults have trained kids to segregate. Gender, however, matters to this age group. Kids begin to sort themselves into boys and girls and care about playing with children who share their interests.

WORDS TO TRY

Gender identity and fears

You're a boy. Right now you want to play with just boys.

If a girl comes in, what will happen?

You're worried girls will wreck your fort.

I know boys can have fun playing house, too.

Protecting the Right to Play

If you want to play just with Sophie, you can.

You can play with whoever you want.

Who you play with is up to you.

WORDS TO AVOID

That's not nice.

You can't say that.

Of course, boys/girls can come in.

You have to let everyone play.

OUT AND ABOUT

When other adults shoot down "no girls"/"no boys" statements from children, you can follow up with a question. "I heard you say, 'No boys allowed.' If a boy plays in the sandbox, what will happen?" If another parent isn't comfortable with direct gender exclusion, just acknowledge that fact. "I know we make signs like that at home, but Mr. Jeffers isn't comfortable with that. He's worried someone will feel hurt."

"Why is that woman so fat?" When questions about race and body differences come up in public, you can quietly acknowledge your child's comment on the spot, but it's OK to defer a full explanation until you're home. As with other sensitive topics (see Section 7: Sensitive Subjects), every situation is different, and these questions deserve time and honesty.

Take Rejection in Stride

Nobody wanted to play with Adam. Time after time, other children paired up or played in groups, while four-year-old Adam hung around the edges of the game.

Brianna, age five, had a habit of bossing other kids. Soon the other girls in the class avoided her.

Hunter stuck by himself. When other kindergarten-age children came up and invited him to play, he ignored them. Eventually they stopped asking.

Occasional playmate rejection is unremarkable. Children frequently reject each other because of mood, worries, fear of play interruption, child development stage and other common reasons (see Rule 12: You Can't Play = A-OK). Repeated rejection is different. Be on the lookout for an oft-rejected child.

Renegade Reason
Even chronic rejection can be turned around. Step in to help your child.

There are times when rejection seriously hurts. Kids who are repeatedly rejected frequently need adult help to turn the pattern around.

Don't despair if your child is late in making friends and developing social skills. Being rejected by peers in preschool and kindergarten is certainly not an all-defining social sentence for your child. Andrew, for example, did not make friends with kids his age as a four- or five-year-old, but in first grade he blossomed and made several close friends.

The preschool years are prime play years. Sometimes a little help is all your child needs to "get into play" and be successful with peers.

Renegade Blessings

You can help a chronically rejected child improve her social skills. She can learn:

> *I can be adaptable. I can change my behavior if other kids don't like the way I do things.*
> *I can take more social risks. I can recover if things don't work out.*

Why It Works

Most kids will be fine when excluded from time to time, but in about 10 percent of cases, adults have to take a proactive approach, says Michael Thompson, coauthor of *Best Friends, Worst Enemies: Understanding the Social Lives of Children*. Children who are repeatedly rejected in the early years often have a tougher time in school later and are more likely to be bullied, get in trouble and suffer from depression. With these kids, we need to step in when rejection is chronic and help them overcome their social challenges.

Young kids get many of their social needs met through family in the early years, but peers become increasingly important in a child's life as the years go on. Peer rejection is hard for children to shake once it becomes established. Researchers like Dr. Karen Bierman have found that chronic rejection follows children even if they change schools and peer groups. She says the main difference between rejected kids and well-liked kids is social savvy. Kids who know how to "get into play" do well. Kids who don't understand social cues don't. This includes children who don't take turns, act aggressively and can't control their impulses.

 Take Off Your Adult Lenses

"She'll grow out of it." Sometimes we don't take children's social issues seriously. "It's just kids' play," we tell ourselves. Mostly it is. But when a child faces repeated rejection or other social isolation from her age-mates, the situation needs our adult attention. Observe carefully. Take concrete steps to break the cycle. Your help might make all the difference.

Sometimes intervention is fairly basic. It can include teaching particular social skills, modeling appropriate behavior or helping kids understand what's going on. For example, "Gavin said hello. When someone says hello, people usually say hello back."

Other times we may need to call in additional help. Children with a whole range of social challenges, including kids on the autism spectrum, can gain so much from early action.

Try This—Add to Your Toolbox

When a child is occasionally rebuffed from play, she may need help with her sad feelings. When a child is repeatedly rejected, she needs our help. Isolated and ostracized children are at risk.

Spot Repeated Rejection

Notice when rejection is typical and when it's chronic. Allowing kids to choose their own playmates helps adults spot repeated rejection early on. The right to choose playmates (which includes being able to exclude another child) makes it easier to see which children are truly being rejected—and rejected repeatedly. When adults insist that kids accept every child into their play, these destructive social patterns can take longer to catch. See more about the benefits of exclusionary play in Rule 12: You Can't Play = A-OK.

Also notice the opposite. Which children are ignoring their playmates' attempts to involve them in play? When a child makes an overture, does your four-year-old rebuff their invitations to play? Children who fail to respond appropriately to their peers are showing signs they may need extra help—whether it's with high social anxiety, attention to social cues or other issues.

Teach Friendship Skills

Making friends is not natural to every child. See Rule 11: We're Not *All* Friends Here for ideas to help children join play.

Change a Reputation

Oliver wanted to play so badly. He was an only child and, at age four, still thought the best way to play was to shove or hit other children. Everyone avoided him.

When a child gets a reputation, it can be hard to shake. If a child does reform and mature, point that change out to the other children. In Oliver's case, he stopped shoving and hitting kids midway through the preschool year, and he learned how to join dramatic play games. His teachers could announce, "You'll be safe playing with Oliver. He plays without hitting now. Do you want to ask to make sure? Oliver, will you hit Lydia? No? OK."

Asking "Are you going to hit me?" or "Are you going to take my shovel?" is a simple technique that helps both kids. It reassures the fearful child that he will be OK. And it puts the other child on notice that he had better keep that behavior in check if he wants to maintain his playmates.

Team Up

Adam was a four-year-old nobody wanted to play with. When the other boys played exciting playground games, Adam hung around and watched, but he wasn't wanted. When his teacher, Darren, saw the pattern, he made sure to include Adam. "I like having Adam on my team," he said when they played outdoor games. "Adam is fun to play with." After the other kids saw Darren enjoying Adam, they stopped rejecting him. Darren had demonstrated that Adam was fun to be with.

Kids categorize their peers. A child can be considered someone who's fun to play with or someone to avoid. You can show kids how fun a rejected child can be. Be his buddy. Laugh a lot. Demonstrate that each child you encounter is valued and accepted. How you treat people matters. Your kids are always watching.

Showcase Strong Ideas

Sometimes kids can attract playmates by coming up with a cool play theme. At preschool, Noah was left out of group games. One day he turned the climber into a giant "nest" and announced a new game. "I'm an owl. I eat mice!" he called out. Noah's play idea became an exciting chase game, and other children loved it. After that day, Noah had no problem making friends. His peers viewed him as a leader, someone with good ideas for games. If your child has great ideas but no friends, help him showcase his strong play ideas.

Bring the Right Prop

Gaining acceptance in the preschool years can be as simple as adding the right prop. "What does this game need? What could you bring?" You can help a child notice what props are being used and what new props a game might need. If there's a game of "good guy, bad guy" going on, what about a helmet or a cape? If kids are digging a tunnel, maybe a good shovel? Kids this age may be interested in another child if he brings something interesting with him. This could be a cool toy, or it could be his dog from home. The rejected child gains social currency by being the gatekeeper to the object. Just as in adult life, social control often involves control of resources.

Improve Social Skills

Brianna was often left out of games because she acted too bossy. "You have to do it my way," she'd say. Other kids reacted by saying, "I don't want to play anymore," and walking away. That left Brianna stranded. Her mom and teachers worked to help Brianna recognize what was bossy behavior and how to take turns with play ideas. It helped to have an adult stand by to coach social skills.

One day Brianna was playing with Ava in a toy kitchen. She ordered Ava around and told her to do it "my way." Ava was getting tired of being bossed around.

AVA: I don't want to play anymore. I want to play kitty.

BRIANNA: You have to do it my way.

AVA: I don't want to play with you anymore.

ADULT: Ava doesn't want to play this game anymore. She wants to play kitty.

BRIANNA: What's kitty?

ADULT: You can ask her.

The adult's role was simply reinforcement of Ava's words, but it helped Brianna listen to what her playmate was saying. Brianna asked Ava how to play kitty. At that point there was a shift of power. Kitty was Ava's game, so she was naturally in charge. Brianna listened to Ava during the game and checked her impulse to be bossy.

Seek Outside Help

Some kids need more help with social skills than you can give. If your child has extreme difficulty reading social cues or is struggling with sensory integration, high anxiety or other issues, the wisest step is to seek an outside evaluation. Early intervention in a variety of social skills can make a tremendous difference in your child's life.

WORDS TO TRY

You'll be safe playing with Oliver. He plays without hitting now.

Do you want to ask to make sure? Oliver, will you hit Lydia? He said no.

Adam is fun to play with. I like having him on my team.

What does this game need? What could you bring?

I notice that Ava doesn't like it when you don't listen to her ideas.

A lot of kids don't like it when someone's bossy. Do you know what being bossy means? Let's talk about it.

WORDS TO AVOID

Come on, don't be shy.

What's wrong with you?

You're going to get along and that's that.

You're too bossy/shy/rough, that's your problem.

OUT AND ABOUT

Sometimes other people can see things that we miss about our own child. Do your best to be open to comments from other adults you respect, perhaps a close family member or your child's preschool teacher. Most early-childhood educators aren't qualified to make a diagnosis of autism or other social issues, but they can share observations, such as, "I don't see Ryan making eye contact. Have you noticed that about him, too?"

You can also share with other adults what you're working on with your child. "Layla is trying to understand when she's being bossy, so if you see a time when she's bossing Grace, it would be helpful to us if you pointed it out." Gather allies who have your child's true interests at heart.

Running Room: Kids, Power and Action

Childhood decides.

—Jean-Paul Sartre

Ban Chairs—
Not Tag

The best room at my childhood preschool was called the "Running Room." Apart from a few mats on the floor, a climber and a hook for a swing, the room was nearly empty. Just wide-open space. Here you could jump, climb, run, wrestle, crash things and yell. A kid's paradise. Almost anything was possible in the Running Room.

As a parent, I remember buying a child-size chair for my son when he was three. He loved to draw, and I thought he would use it with the table we'd placed in his room. But the chair was only a nuisance. Myles far preferred to draw standing up, lying down, sprawled out, or on the move with a clipboard. He did put the chair to use eventually: building blanket forts.

Young kids don't need chairs (except when they're eating). They do need to move. Children—especially boys—need plenty of room for action.

Renegade Reason
Children need to move—run, jump, climb, scream and wrestle. Boisterous play is an essential part of childhood.

Tyler was an active five-year-old. He was expelled from his private preschool on the grounds that he wouldn't sit still and do class activities.

The School for Young Children welcomed him. Tyler spent most of his time in the Running Room jumping, climbing, playing chase games with other kids and riding trikes outside. He made friends and fit right in.

Misbehavior is usually a sign that our expectations are not right. Young children are not being "bad" when they wiggle and playfully pummel the child next to them (see Rule 17: Only Punch Friends). Their needs are not being met. Either our expectations or the environment is wrong. So chuck the chairs and let kids *move*.

Renegade Blessings

When your child's need for movement is met, you will both feel saner and safer. Boisterous play helps kids develop physical, mental and social skills and learn these lessons:

I can be who I am.

I'm not bad just because I like to move.

The world is not off-limits. The outdoors is great to explore.

Running and yelling are OK, but not everywhere. I can find the right place for them.

I'm beginning to know my limits. The world does have dangers, and I can't expect someone else to save me.

Feeling my body grow strong and gain new skills feels terrific.

Why It Works

Kids are wired to move. All children need action and frequently get in trouble when they do move. Many "misbehaviors" simply stem from a lack of space and opportunity for active movement.

Take Off Your Adult Lenses

"He's not paying attention to me!" Kinesthetic learners need to move in order to learn. If your child has ants in his pants, accommodate his need to move. Many boys are kinesthetic learners, and chances are, he'll be able to pay attention to you better when his body is in motion. We ask kids to sit still so much. Think what a child needs and change the environment to accommodate big, loud and fast movement. Remember, a child's misbehavior most often stems from inaccurate adult expectations.

Biologically, boys are in motion more than girls. Studies by psychologist Warren Eaton show boys are consistently more physically active, starting at age two and peaking at ages seven to eight.

After years of worrying about boys being favored over girls, today there is increased awareness that we perform a cultural disservice to boys, particularly in early childhood. Three-, four- and five-year-olds are expected to sit still for long periods and ignore their natural physical instincts. Michael Thompson, author of *Raising Cain* and *It's a Boy!*, says normal child behavior gets demonized in homes and preschools.

"Many women cannot stand that boy energy," says Stephanie Rottmayer, director of the School for Young Children. "They don't understand it. They find it disruptive. They don't value it. They try to make boys behave like girls."

In the preschool years, boys are much less verbal than girls and much more physically active. A study from the Yale Child Study Center shows that boys are expelled from preschool at a rate five times higher than girls. Boys learn through action and need to have their physical energy valued.

Physical activity is important for *all* children, and adults who make life more "boy friendly" help girls, too.

Active Energy Is Not Misbehavior

Elementary schools in many parts of the United States are reducing recess time, and (gasp) even eliminating it altogether. Some schools have

> *Make room for
> action. Kids need
> space for loud, fast,
> daring and rough-
> and-tumble play.*

banned games adults perceive as too rough, such
as tag. This shows adults don't value and understand kids' intense need for motion. It also shows
an unnecessary fear of rough play.

What's the matter with high-energy play?
Women. Yes, that's an extreme statement and cer-
tainly not always true, but it can help to frame the issue. Despite more
stay-at-home dads and involved fathers, young kids' lives are still domi-
nated by women: mothers, teachers, grandmothers and babysitters. Many
women find high energy (often boy energy) disturbing. It's too wild. Too
loud. Too scary. Too rough and prone to break things. The adult females
in a young child's world seek to control that energy. Across the United
States, you hear a constant litany: "Stop running! . . . Get down from that
tree, you'll fall. . . . Put that stick down! . . . Get your hands off each
other. . . . Don't get dirty. . . . Be careful. . . . Inside voice. . . . Stop fooling
around and just *sit still*!"

When kids enter preschool and kindergarten, they typically encounter
a fleet of tables and chairs. Some children can adapt, but in-motion kids
frequently get labeled as troublemakers. Very few early-childhood programs have a big-muscle room like the Running Room that is constantly
available. Running is relegated to specific recess time. But kids' bodies
don't work that way. They don't need to move only from 11:25 to 11:45
a.m. Motion is part of their very being. For most kids, it bursts out every
waking hour.

Brains on the Move

"Learning" is considered something you do only sitting down. But the mind of a young child is always learning—whether she's whacking a stick or throwing ice chunks across a pond. In fact, some children absorb information best when their bodies are moving. These kids are called "kinesthetic learners." This is especially true for many boys, whose brains need action.

Girl or boy, adult or child, when we move we boost our brain power. John Medina, author of *Brain Rules*, says the human brain evolved while humans were in near constant motion, and motion is the optimal way for our brains to process information. When we move, the brain gets more oxygen. It's also been known for many years that movement that crosses the midline of the body (going from left to right across the body) develops connections between the brain's left and right hemispheres. Movement activates the brain. Brain researchers are finding that movement helps new neurons to grow and neutral pathways to develop. All this boosts learning, memory and focus.

For some highly active kids, occasional motion isn't enough. They need to be on the move nearly every waking minute. Logan, age five, couldn't sit still in kindergarten. Luckily, his teacher understood. She pointed out Logan's need to move to his parents, and allowed him to pace the back of the room. He was a bright boy. With his need for motion met, Logan was able to thrive in class.

Try This—Add to Your Toolbox

Young kids need space, power and action. Accommodate this fundamental need as often as you can.

Make Space for Action

Young kids need big space for physical play. Space to move, and move fast. Space to yell and be loud. Space to be rough and wild. Suppressing physical energy does no one any good. Give kids the space they need every day as often as you can. For most families, that's outside, either in the backyard or a local park. It could be the basement, porch or other designated space.

Read to Kids As They Move

At age three, Gabe loved books, but he couldn't sit still long enough to listen to them. His mother read aloud to Gabe as he walked around the living room. Find ways to include movement with traditional sit-down activities like stories and art. Get kids engaged through motion.

Put Safety Second

"Jackson! Put that stick down right now! You'll put someone's eye out."

We worry about the wrong things. Our children are far more likely to be killed in a car accident than anything else, yet we drive them about in cars constantly from infancy on. Unless it's violating the Golden Renegade Rule—"Is it hurting people or property?"—encourage children to play outdoors in nature and take reasonable physical risks. That means saying yes to tree climbing, wall walking, stick playing, puddle jumping, rock scaling and the like. Teach kids how to fall properly (rolling) and help kids stay away from real dangers (busy streets, cliffs). Children become safer as they gain experience using their bodies to jump, balance and climb. They learn what they can do, develop improved coordination and begin to understand their limits.

Drop "Be Careful"

"Be careful" is one of the empty phrases we say to our children. It adds general anxiety without offering any specific help. Too many warnings to "Watch out!" and "Be careful!" cause some kids to avoid risks and stop trying new things. Instead of saying "Be careful," either don't say anything or offer information, such as: "You're near the edge"—"Look at your feet"—"Someone is behind you." Or ask a basic question: "Do you feel safe?"

Ask: Do You Feel Safe?

Next time your child starts to climb too high, bring it to her attention. Ask her a simple question: "Do you feel safe?"

This question serves as a great reality check for children. It forces children to take stock of the situation. A typical response might be: *Oh, I didn't realize I was so high up on the climber. How am I going to get down?* It helps kids listen to their own internal warning signals.

Cameron, age six, was ready for a snack. He climbed up on the kitchen counter, stretching on tiptoes to reach cookies on a high shelf. His mom asked if he felt safe up there. "No, not really," he admitted, and climbed down while his mother handed the cookies down to him.

Of course, children's reactions will vary by their temperament; some will never think to slow down or climb down. If a child exceeds your safety tolerance, say, "It's my job to keep you safe," and put a stop to it. Decide in advance whether you will let the child make her own safety decision. Ask yourself: Is the situation safe enough? Would you be willing to let her risk a short fall or a bumped knee? Sometimes the answer is a definite no (for example, a ten-foot-high wall with concrete to land on). In general, hold back on your urge to protect. Ask yourself, "What would it hurt?" Let her take a few risks and knocks.

Be Direct and Clear

If your three-year-old is screeching in play, be direct about what you don't like. "That is too loud for my ears!" Most young kids are lousy at volume regulation. Telling a child to use an "inside voice" doesn't offer much information. Tell her directly it's too loud, make it visually clear by covering your ears, then find a space where she can be noisy if she wants. Being loud or fast is a vital part of play for kids, so set limits but make room for it. If kids are running wild through the kitchen, don't say, "Stop running," or "Remember, walking feet!" Give them specifics: "This room is not for running. Go outside if you want to run."

Let Kids Climb Trees—and Don't Help Them Down

Morgan loved to climb trees. But whenever she got up too high, she called for her mom to help her down. Don't rescue kids. Don't lift them out of a tree. It's typical for kids to climb past their ability to cope and then call for help, but don't reinforce this habit. Whether it's a tree or a playground climber, tell kids, "If you climb up, you have to be able to climb down again." This is an early lesson in appropriate risk-taking. Go ahead and stand nearby if your child gets stuck. Reassure him and coach him with your voice. "I won't do it for you, but I'll stand right here. Where could you put your foot next?" This method promotes body awareness and helps kids learn their limits and become partners in their own safety.

Create a Running Room

Make one part of your house into a "Running Room." If you have the space, give your kids a playroom or basement room where you let them ride bikes and throw balls. Protect windows and lightbulbs with a screen so kids don't have to worry about hurting anything in the room. Leave out furniture, but add balls, tumbling mats and items like a mini-trampoline or a large cardboard box. Creating a big-muscle space is a lifesaver for everyone, especially during the winter. If space is limited, and you don't have a room to offer, designate one chair or sofa as OK for roughhousing and climbing.

Find Welcoming Spaces

Find a preschool that welcomes motion. Do chairs dominate the room? Is there an indoor big-muscle space? How often and how long do children get to play outdoors? Ideally, children should be able to move freely between indoor and outdoor play areas.

Get Kids Outside, Even in the Rain

Kids sit so much of the time—in car seats, on plastic chairs at preschool, at home. Get them outside. Don't mind the rain. Send them out barefoot or invest in a pair of rubber rain boots. Join generations of parents who knew this truth. Outdoors is truly the best room in the house.

WORDS TO TRY
Movement
Go outside if you want to run.
You need more room for this game. Go to the basement.
You can jump on the old basement sofa.
This is not a place for climbing.
If you want to scream, you can do it outside.
That's too loud. It hurts my ears.

Risks and safety
You're close to the edge.
Look at your feet.

Use both hands.

Someone's behind you.

Do you feel safe?

My job is to keep you safe.

If you climb up, you have to climb down again.

WORDS TO AVOID

Be careful.

Stop running.

Walking feet.

Inside voice.

Put that stick down!

Don't climb up there; you'll break your neck.

You'll get hurt.

Don't get dirty.

Watch out, you'll get wet.

Sit down. Be quiet. Behave!

OUT AND ABOUT

Even at the park, you'll find parents who disapprove of physical play. Julie, a mother of two, gets the "look" whenever she lets her children climb low walls. Decide what you think is safe and follow the Renegade Golden Rule. Is your child's physical play hurting people or property? If not, then it's OK. A great place to allow physical daring is on a nature hike. Here people are less likely to be judgmental, and the kids can run, leap over streams and balance on logs. Nature, after all, is the original playground.

Rule 16 Give Kids Power

My nephew, Robin, gave himself a powerful name when he was two. He answered to Robin Johnson Track Excavator Scoop Pinball.

Stella, age five, loved to play teacher. She would line up her stuffed animals after kindergarten, ring a bell and tell them what to do.

Diego, age six, ran everywhere he had to go. He delighted in throwing things, and could send a ripe walnut spinning through the air so it split against a tree trunk with a powerful smash.

Renegade Reason

Kids thrive in powerful roles and actions. Give kids lots of time for superhero and tough physical play.

My three-year-old, Zach, cannot play with a train peaceably for even a minute.

"Oh no! Crash!" he yells, and derails the engine.

Every truck, train, boat and baby doll in Zach's world has instant accidents. Cars crash. Trains topple off cliffs. Boats capsize and the Lego sailors get eaten by sharks. *Tyrannosaurus rex* comes along and eats the baby. "Oh no! Big dinosaur! Save the baby!" he cries. Then he springs into action mode: Zach will save them from the crisis. The Hero Is Here to Save the Day.

We don't even have a TV in our house, so Zach's interest in disasters and Good Guy hero themes doesn't come from movies. Zach is simply displaying what many preschool-age kids enjoy—high drama and the feeling of being powerful.

Power play is a central part of preschoolers' play. Playing in powerful ways—whether it's crashing trains, swooping in as a superhero or whacking a stick against a tree—gives kids a chance to feel strong and important. Games of being boss, like playing house or teacher, likewise give children the chance to experience power and be in charge. Whatever form it takes, kids need plenty of chances to feel powerful.

Renegade Blessings

When children find opportunities to experience power in their play, they gain in many ways:

> *I'm strong. I'm a person who can do many things.*
> *It feels great to help people or save people.*
> *I'm figuring out right and wrong.*
> *I can confront my fears.*
> *I know what it feels like to be both powerful and powerless.*
> *I can be boss in my own games, but my parents are really in charge.*

Why It Works

Ever wonder why some children love dump trucks, diggers and all construction vehicles? Or role-playing Spider-Man, firefighter or mommy? What about dinosaurs? The reasons are diverse and complex (and scientists are still digging into evolutionary and social reasons as the kids keep on playing), but one aspect these games all share is power.

"I hate those superhero costumes with the fake muscle chests," said one mother. "It's like they're on steroids. I don't want my kids to think that's what 'real' men should look like." Children's play is not always to our taste. To a child, however, those fake foam muscles convey power.

Being "big" is important to little kids, and being powerful comes with it. As they grow out of toddlerhood, children gain new independence. They experiment with being in control, making decisions in play and trying on powerful roles for size. Preschoolers dare to try out new physical and social skills, and strive to understand social roles.

Adults are powerful creatures in a child's world. Big legs walking around, grown-up voices telling them what they can't do. Adults even have arms so strong they can scoop up a preschooler's entire body. Children have little power in their daily lives, yet they yearn to feel strong and important. Play is where kids experience power and can practice being strong and in charge.

The world is often confusing and scary to a young child. Sometimes power play helps kids confront fears. Here's an example of how young kids experiment with power and then retreat for safety. Liam and Kyle, both age three, are dressed up in tiger suits.

KYLE: I'm a tiger! Grrr!
LIAM: I'm a tiger, too! Grrrowl! Roar!
They playfully paw each other. Then both boys pick up toy baby bottles, sit down and suck on them.

Young children are all balancing their needs for power and security like this: they need times to fight like a tiger and also times to suck on a baby bottle.

Morality in Superhero Power Play

Ruby and Elizabeth wanted to play in the block area. A group of four- and five-year-old boys was already there, dominating the area with superhero play. Ruby held up a doll and announced, "Someone is kidnapping this baby!" The boys instantly took the bait; they rushed to save the baby and abandoned the blocks. The girls moved in and started their own game. These girls recognized what parents, preschool teachers and psychologists have witnessed for years: many boys find superhero games irresistibly fun.

Play for many kids this age, especially boys, often involves fantasy action, including violence and aggression. This kind of dramatic play is actually pro-social, a term psychologists use to describe behavior that is positive, helpful and promotes social acceptance and friendship. Not only does it involve saving people, but it typically involves cooperative social play among children. As kids battle the bad guys or kill the imaginary monster, they engage with peers in complex problem-solving skills that involve negotiation and compromise. "Good guy, bad guy" play is tremendously rewarding and exciting for children, so they do everything they can to work out their differences to keep the game flowing.

Superhero play is fascinating to kids since it requires a bad guy. Kids have to take turns being good and bad: being the protecting hero and the aggressor, and also being the victim and the vanquished. Sometimes in a group game, no one wants to be the bad guy, so they create an imaginary one, but kids often enjoy the turnabout in roles. Imaginary play is "real" to young kids because they intensely feel the real emotions. Being able to take different perspectives like this is a fundamental step in developing moral values like empathy. A child can think, *This was good for the hunter, but bad for the bear.*

Behind all the bang and bluster, superhero play helps children make sense of the world and develop moral values. Dramatic play full of fights, disasters and evil adversaries gives kids the chance to rescue and help people. Michael Thompson, coauthor of *Raising Cain*, observes that violent superhero play serves a deep purpose: it allows kids to develop empathy and courage and become their most compassionate. "It's about courage, loyalty, risking all to save friends in the face of powerful foes," he says.

> *What does it feel like to be the bad guy? Taking different perspectives in play helps children develop empathy.*

When kids take on magic or superhuman roles they gain real-life confidence:

I can be a hero.
I'm someone with good ideas. I can be a leader.
I will stick up for what is right.

As they play out "good guy, bad guy" games, children are exploring their emerging ideas of right and wrong. Kids this age are interested in concepts of good and evil. "Good guy, bad guy" play may be action packed and violent, but if you look closely, you'll see it is often fundamentally hero play. The good guys win. The world is safe for friends and family.

Take Off Your Adult Lenses

Fantasy and aggressive play are *not* a recipe for future violence. If your child favors games with disasters, explosions and powerful bad guys, welcome his imagination. Fantasy ideas are creative. Fantasy play is typically cooperative and social. Fantasy violence is an age-old way for kids to feel powerful. Keep a limit on kids' actions (no hurting people or property), but let play ideas run free.

Author Brian Edmiston calls superhero and war play "mythic play." An education professor at Ohio State University, Edmiston spent six years studying his son's play. At first he was squeamish about what he viewed as violence. Now he says mythic play is about stories of power that help form a child's ethical identity. As a three-year-old, Edmiston's son loved war play; as a thirteen-year-old, the boy spoke out against the Iraq War to his congresswoman.

Confronting Children's Fears of Reality

Battling an imaginary monster is one way children fight their own fears. Within play, children can confront fears, explore these scary ideas and vanquish these fears again and again.

Fears may be something straightforward, such as a scary image your child has seen. Tigers are scary. Will I get eaten by a tiger? Are there tigers in the backyard? Will they hurt me? One thing young kids fear is pain. They try to avoid it and may play out games to cope with this topic. Children also fear their own impulses and aggressive feelings. For older preschoolers, ages four to six, it's common for kids to play games involving death as they confront their first fears of mortality (see Rule 27: Be Buddies with Dead Birds).

Remember that every play theme a child chooses is based on her own needs. If a child is engaged in lots of powerful play, including powerful play with violent themes, then that type of play is serving her present needs. Peter Gray, a psychologist who does research on children's play, says we expect children's play to be sweet and innocent even though the world is not. "It is wrong to think that somehow we can reform the world, for the future, by controlling children's play," he writes. Children will always play what fascinates them and what matters to them right now.

Confronting Adult Fears of Fantasy

As adults, we are sometimes scared by fantasy play. When kids make shooting noises with their tongues, we envision future terrorists. When we see kids playing *Star Wars*, we worry about the fighting and miss the universal struggle for good. We even worry that a child who thwacks a tree with a stick will grow up uncaring and won't respect nature. We fear this type of child's play and react by trying to control it. We see the chosen play as wrong because of a future threat of unkindness. After all, this strikes at one of our deepest fears as parents: that the child we raise will someday grow up to be a callous, uncaring and potentially violent adult.

It's OK to relax and enjoy your child's childhood. If you find yourself thinking about some *future* harm (a future murderer), stop and take stock. Chances are, there is nothing to worry about. Concentrate on *present* harm instead. Ask yourself: Is this creative play hurting real life people or property? Is the game hurting any living thing right now?

> *No interference: children have a right to choose their own play themes.*

Early-childhood educator Jane Katch, author of *Under Deadman's Skin: Discovering the Meaning of Children's Violent Play* and others say kids aren't violent when they play imaginary games like these. The games may have pretend aggression and violence in them, but the game is full of cooperation, and the kids understand it's fantasy.

We worry that kids can't tell the difference between fantasy and reality, but actually we are the ones who mix it up. It may help to think about your reaction to authors of exciting murder mysteries. Do you fear these people? Is the person who imagines these stories somehow dangerous? No. Most of the time, we applaud authors' imaginations, find their stories thrilling and line up at book signings.

If you are worried about your child's play themes, think about cutting down their media exposure. Whether it's G-rated movies or the nightly news, media images are often inappropriate for young children. Cut their screen time, not their play.

Kids need us to be in charge and stop real people from getting hurt. They also need no interference from adults when it comes to play themes. When we do this, the division between fantasy and reality becomes clear to everyone, kids and adults alike.

Try This—Add to Your Toolbox

All young kids need a chance to try out power, and some kids have a huge need to engage in powerful activities regularly. If your child has high energy or shows inappropriate aggression, she might need more acceptable outlets for experiencing power. Fill the need. You can give kids plenty of opportunities to experience power through powerful actions and powerful roles.

What's Powerful

Power Actions

Powerful actions get out a lot of energy. They challenge kids physically, and help develop body strength and spatial awareness. Powerful actions satisfy kids' intense need for movement (See Rule 15: Ban Chairs—Not Tag), make them feel strong and important, and are simply a lot of fun. Power actions include anything from playing chase and lifting heavy logs to wild dancing and pounding play-dough with a hammer.

Power Roles and Actions

Running and Rough Action

Running and games of chase

Roughhousing

Kicking (balls, boxes . . .)

Punching (balled-up newspaper, punching bag . . .)

Karate chopping sticks or paper

Hitting trees with sticks

Arm wrestling

Wrestling or boxing

Standing up on swings

Climbing up a slide

Throwing, Jumping and Climbing

Climbing trees

Climbing anything (ladders, walls . . .)

Jumping from a height

Jumping in a leaf pile or on Bubble Wrap

Hanging on a rope and crashing into a stack of boxes

Launching backyard rockets

Throwing balls (or snowballs)

Throwing rocks in water

Throwing mud so it splats

Making big splashes

Fast and Loud

Using loud voices

Blowing loud horns or whistles

Riding bikes fast

Swinging high

Muscle Strength and Construction
>   Pounding play-dough
>   Using a workbench with real tools
>   Lifting heavy objects (logs, bricks)
>   Moving big objects
>   Building
>   Digging (especially with sturdy metal shovels)
>   Playing with hoses

Fantasy play
>   Superhero play (good guy, bad guy)
>   Fantasy play and dress-up (tigers, monsters, witches, pirates)
>   Playing with swords, lasers or other toy weapons
>   Crashing toy cars and trains
>   Role-playing powerful people (mommy, daddy, teacher)
>   Hero play (doctor, soldier, firefighter)

Creativity
>   Any free artwork
>   Painting big things
>   Standing up to paint
>   Storytelling—dictating a story and acting it out
>   Being a leader—creating an idea that others follow
>   Dancing

Power Roles

Powerful roles put the child in charge through fantasy play. Kids step into the role of powerful figures, whether it's rescue and hero play (doctors, police, firefighters), powerful animals (bears, tigers, dinosaurs or sharks) or exciting fantasy and superhero play (pirates, Batman, Spider-

Man, *Star Wars*). Pretend power roles also include games of house or school, where the child gets to experience being the boss as mommy, daddy or teacher.

Creative Power

Creativity is another type of power. It's easy to see the power in super-hero play and physical action, but creating something also conveys feelings of power. This could be anything from storytelling to artwork or coming up with original ideas. For example, William, age four, felt the combined power of leadership and creativity when he invented a "bird of prey" game and seven other kids joined in. His idea was so compelling that others wanted to follow it. Young kids also feel a sense of power and importance from the act of writing their own names.

It's important to recognize all these forms of play as power play. And not to be scared by any of it. When children play, they explore ideas that matter to them. The more we limit children's access to powerful experiences, the more they may try to get power.

Give your child plenty of opportunities to feel powerful. Create physical space that allows power actions. Encourage fantasy role-playing of all types. Provide materials for creativity. A little bit of real-life power helps, too. Recruit your child to help you do a job—build something or move something heavy. If your child is having behavior issues or is often angry, try giving her more opportunities to feel powerful. It just might be the outlet she needs.

Parents and the Balance of Power

A powerful child is not an out-of-control child. You are still in charge. Letting your child feel powerful during play fulfills a deep developmental need. But so does keeping the true power with the parent.

Some of us are nervous about letting go. The idea of a powerful child frightens us. Letting *my* kid have a taste of power? Letting a whole class of four-year-olds engage in power actions? Hoo, boy. We spend all our time trying to control our children's behavior. Simply try it: encourage powerful play. At the very least, your child will have glorious fun. And you might be surprised at the results: all-around behavior improves for most kids when their desire for power is not squelched.

Allowing your child chances for power does not mean giving up adult limits and authority. If children get too much power in family life, they become insecure and anxious. Parents need to be the ones who set consistent household rules: safety rules, bedtimes and so on. Although kids are eager to experiment with power, kids feel most secure when they know their parents are in charge. Give children appropriate power by giving them power in their play.

WORDS TO TRY

What do you need for your game?

Who are you?

Are you a fierce lion or a friendly lion?

You're really using your muscles.

WORDS TO AVOID

That's not a nice game.

No superhero costumes allowed here.

Why not have the *T. rex* be friends with the other dinosaurs?

Don't pick up that log.

No snowballs.

OUT AND ABOUT

Some schools ban superhero play. Adults you meet may try to get your child to change her play theme or express disapproval.

If fantasy power play is central to your child's life, do your best to surround her with people who accept it. You might have to change preschools or find a different child-care arrangement. Let folks who care for your child know that any play theme is all right with you: "As long as she's not actually hurting anything, we encourage all her dramatic play." If your child must censor her play at preschool, make sure she has plenty of chances for unhindered power play at home.

Only Punch Friends

Dan punches Leo, and Leo punches right back.

Nearby, an adult looks on, but doesn't interrupt. These two four-year-olds are having fun. Dan and Leo are both wearing pint-size boxing gloves, purple and red, and standing barefoot on a tumbling mat. They are giggling and having a marvelous time.

Renegade Reason

Roughhousing—even play boxing—is social and healthy. But it has no place if someone's angry.

When I told a fellow mother that I was writing a book that included boxing at preschool, she was shocked. "Boxing? You've got to be kidding me. I spend my time trying to keep their hands *off* each other!"

That can be a problem. Young kids are physical creatures. They like body contact and have a deep need for touch. Especially since verbal skills are still developing, one of the ways children show interest in a friend is through physical contact, sometimes hugs, sometimes play fights.

Lee and Janet, the founders of my childhood preschool, noticed this. They watched kids play and saw how much young kids liked to wrestle.

Children would roll around together like little lions or puppies. Lee and Janet thought: If kids want to play that way there must be a reason. Well, *why not*? Lee and Janet equipped rooms with wrestling mats and boxing gloves. Roughhousing games blossomed into a forty-year tradition at the School for Young Children.

Roughhousing games, like boxing and wrestling, give kids outlets for high energy and boost friendships—but only when everyone is having fun. If someone's angry, it's not a game. Roughhousing is not a way to settle a conflict. Games should be between willing partners who are in a playful mood.

> *Roughhousing should be between willing partners in a playful mood. It's a game, not a way to solve conflicts.*

What's more, it turns out that boisterous play like preschool boxing not only is a legitimate way to have fun, but also has a positive, important role in child development.

Renegade Blessings

Rough-and-tumble play helps our kids grow on many levels. A child can learn:

I'm strong and powerful.

It feels good to use my body actively.

I can make friends and take on new challenges.

I can set limits on other people and stop something I don't like.

I can listen to my friends and know when to stop.

I can cope, even if I get hurt a little bit.

If someone gets hurt, we can make new rules so it doesn't happen again.

Why It Works

Whether it's called rough-and-tumble play, boisterous play, horseplay, puppy play or roughhousing, this kind of play is a vital part of childhood. Dr. Anthony DeBenedet, coauthor of *The Art of Roughhousing*, calls rough-and-tumble play the "holy grail" of children's play.

Rowdy puppy play helps bodies and brains develop. When two kids tussle on the floor, or roll around together, they are showing the need to wrestle. If we say no to rough play, we are thwarting this need. Instead of issuing a ban (Get your hands off him! Quit hitting your brother. I don't want to see any bodies touching), think how you can best meet this age-old need.

Horseplay may look like out-of-control goofing off, but it serves a deeper purpose. Studies by Dr. Jaak Panksepp show that rough-and-tumble play helps to develop the brain's frontal lobe, including the prefrontal cortex. This is the key brain region for executive function, the most complex human abilities. These include self-control, resisting temptation, reasoning, focused attention, working memory, problem solving and cognitive flexibility. The prefrontal cortext can be strengthened, much as exercising improves your muscles. The better this area is developed, the better kids do in all areas of life, whether it's social, emotional or academic. Ongoing research by Adele Diamond and others suggests that having strong executive function is the top predictor of kids' success.

Since this part of the brain is so important, is it really any surprise that kids develop it by simply doing what kids do best, rolling about the floor and tussling with squawks of high excitement? Rough-and-tumble play must be welcomed.

As early-childhood educator Dan Hodgins puts it, "It's just as important to roughhouse with kids as to read them a story."

Take Off Your Adult Lenses

Most mock battles between kids are joyful, and so is roughhousing between kids and adults. Don't automatically break up "fights" when you see them. Ask first: "Are you both having fun?" Physical puppy play is natural and healthy. It does not lead to real fights and does not make kids more aggressive. On the contrary, rough-and-tumble play helps kids boost friendships and brain function. Its many benefits include understanding boundaries, reading emotions, developing empathy and practicing impulse control.

Time and Location

Of course, not all daily life should be devoted to wild wrestling matches. As with everything in parenting, it's up to you to place limits. Kids need to learn that roughhousing is good play, but not all the time and not everywhere. It all comes down to time and place.

When you curtail rough play for good reasons, make sure kids understand there are options. For example: "You can't play that game here, but you can do it outside." "It's not time to wrestle right now. It's time to go to the grocery store. There'll be time to wrestle when we get home."

Wrestling games often start spontaneously. If kids start jumping on one another, check and make sure no one is angry. Then move the game to a more appropriate location. For example: "It looks like you two want to wrestle. Let's go downstairs and get out the exercise mat."

Pro-social Play

Teachers at five-year-old Sarah's school, a Montessori preschool in California, are so worried that roughhousing will make kids more aggressive that they promote banning it at home. They teach parents to "refrain from wrestling and other aggressive play" with their children.

But doesn't this type of play promote aggression among kids? The opposite actually appears to be true. Daniel Goleman, author of *Emotional Intelligence*, says playful fights help kids learn impulse and anger control, and this helps stop real fights from happening. Professor of child development David Fernie says parents mistakenly worry that rough play, including playful hitting and fun fights, will create more aggression in kids. His research shows that children ages three to six who roughhouse become less aggressive and display more appropriate social skills. Play fights remain playful, and the more they play, the better kids get at reading social signals.

Roughhousing is necessarily social. Other physical activities, like doing somersaults, swinging, or punching a punching bag, also release physical energy, but they remain individual activities. Kids need a partner to box, wrestle or pummel. The very act of engaging another child in play is a social act, and roughhousing is a great friendship booster. When two kids roughhouse, they share physical activity together and also enter into a relationship with their partner.

Physical Friendship

"Arrgghh!" Jack yells and falls on Milo.

"I got you now!"

Pushing and play punching can be a sign of friendship, not aggression. Jack and Milo are four-year-olds who love to tussle together. Their physical interaction is entirely appropriate. Verbal skills are still developing in preschoolers, and girls typically outshine boys in speech and relationships. Almost all kids crave body-to-body contact, but for boys it can be a social lifeline. Boys can connect with other kids through physical play, so roughhousing gives boys the chance to develop friendships.

Many mothers and female teachers dislike the physicality of boys' play. But William Pollack, author of *Real Boys*, says boys rely on exuberant, rough play to meet their emotional needs. While rough-and-tumble play is also good for girls, boys especially need it to form healthy relationships.

Reading Emotions

Simple games of chase and wrestling contain complex social skills. Whether it's getting hurt, monitoring whether a friend is still having fun, or setting boundaries, rough-and-tumble play gives kids intense practice with reading emotions.

Is my friend still having fun? Am I hitting too hard to keep the play going? How can I change my behavior so my friend will still have fun and stay in the game? What about me—did I like what he just did? Frances Carlson, author of *Big Body Play: Why Boisterous, Vigorous, and Very Physical Play Is Essential to Children's Development and Learning*, says it's so much more than just physical exercise.

Children who are allowed to play rough-and-tumble games learn to manage peer relationships. They watch body language and listen to one another to keep the play going. With a little coaching, kids can learn to assert themselves, set limits on a friend and react in turn when the other child says "Stop."

Winners and Losers

No one is vanquished in child wrestling games. It's an activity, not a competition. Kids get out of breath and have fun with a friend; then they're finished. Most often, both kids come off feeling strong. "I've got powerful arms!" cries out four-year-old Lucas. "I've got powerful arms, too!" calls his boxing partner, Katie.

Benefits of Roughhousing

Friendship

Energy outlet

Chance to experience power

Impulse control

Risk taking

Building brain power

Body and spatial awareness

Need for motion

Need for physical touch

Practice setting limits on peers

Negotiating skills

Building trust with peers

Self-esteem

Reading emotions

Showing empathy

Joy

Benefits of Risk

Roughhousing is delightfully fun for kids partly because it involves risk. As parents, we do our best to eliminate risk from our children's lives. But risk assessment and some level of risk taking are good for kids. Early-childhood educators, such as Bev Bos, believe children need the chance to take risks in order to gain self-confidence and grow. "Risk propels us forward," she says, "and helps us trust ourselves." Games like boxing and wrestling give kids a safe place to practice risk taking. The physical intensity challenges children to their limits and helps them realize, *Gee, I can do this!*

Getting Hurt

When kids play active games, they sometimes get hurt. No matter whether it's tag or roughhousing, minor bonks are part of play.

As adults, we have different attitudes toward safety. If you're the kind who can't bear to see any pain, it's hard to stop saying "No running. Be careful!" let alone "Go ahead and wrestle." But do your best to stop your worries. Do you see smiles? Giggles and laughter? If roughhousing kids are having fun, let them take the risk. It's OK if kids get mildly hurt. Remind yourself (and the kids) that getting hurt is not the end of the world. Set expectations when they start rough play: "You might get hurt a little bit. You might get some bumps. You can always say 'Stop' or take a break if you don't like it."

Getting hurt actually helps develop skills on many levels. If both kids are willing partners and the roughhousing match is in a safe spot, don't worry too much. Let the kids decide when enough is enough. Children learn to take a few risks, to cope with getting hurt, and to problem solve to minimize their risk of getting hurt again. These are important skills that kids can start to learn through play. When a roughhousing partner gets hurt, kids learn to read emotional cues and take care of each other. Ask them: "What can you do so you don't get hurt?"

Four-year-old Mason got hurt several times boxing with his friend Jake. "Ow!" he'd cry, but then get back in the game. Then Jake shoved Mason hard enough that he hit his head. Mason cried, but still wasn't done playing. He told Jake not to shove him again and they both continued playing and laughing together. "That was fun!" Mason exclaimed.

It can be scary to give up control and let kids play rough games if you're not used to it. But the benefits are enormous. Take the risk yourself and watch your child bloom.

Try This—Add to Your Toolbox

Rough-and-tumble play brings so many benefits—including a chance for a literacy lesson that's meaningful to kids. Here are some ideas on how to welcome it.

Renegade Guide to Rough-and-Tumble Play

1. Check in. "Are you both having fun?"
2. Stop if it's anger. Deal with upset feelings through conflict mediation.
3. Redirect. Move the game to the right time and location.
4. Set a ground rule. "Stop when someone says 'Stop.'"
5. Set kids' rules. "Do you want to make any rules?"
6. Decide what to do when kids get hurt. "Do you want to make up a new rule now?"
7. Check in. "Is this still fun for both of you?"

Assume the Best

When you see kids wrestling, don't automatically break it up. Check in and make sure the fight is play, not anger. Ask, "Is this fun for both of you?" This simple question helps you assume the best and opens the door to positive puppy play. Hint: Make sure each kid answers. Sometimes one child thinks it's a game and the other does not. If there's anger or it's not fun for both, unravel the situation with conflict mediation.

Stop When Someone Says "Stop!"

Even wild play can be guided by a simple rule: Stop when the other person says "Stop."

This is really the only rule you need to set. What's most important during roughhousing is that kids listen to each other's limits. Each child needs to stop when someone says "Stop" and know she has the power to get out if the game's no longer fun.

Roughhousing Limits

1. The Renegade Golden Rule applies: It's OK If It's Not Hurting People or Property."
2. Stop when someone says "Stop."
3. Choose the right place.
4. Choose the right time.
5. Follow your partner's rules.
6. The adult is the final boss.

Make Kid-Based Rules

Once you've directed roughhousing to the right time and location and everyone knows when to stop, let kids create any additional rules. Some parents like to spell out a long list of safety rules (no shoes, no pulling hair, open-hands touching only . . .) but kids learn much more if you invite them to make their own rules. Listening and rule making are part of roughhousing's many benefits.

Rule making is pretty straightforward. Here's how it unfolded for two five-year-olds:

ADULT: This is where you can wrestle. The rule is: You have to stop if someone says "Stop!" Do you want to make up any rules? No? OK.

Ryan and Jameson grin and begin to wrestle.

RYAN: Stop!

ADULT: Jameson, I heard Ryan say "Stop." You need to stop when he says "Stop."

After another bout of friendly wrestling, Jameson starts to frown.

JAMESON: Hey!

ADULT: Ryan, did you like it when Jameson grabbed your shirt? No? Do you want to make a new rule now?

JAMESON: Yeah. No grabbing clothes.

ADULT: OK, Ryan, if you want to wrestle Jameson, you have to follow his rule: No grabbing clothes. Do you want to keep wrestling? Yes? OK.

Write the rules down as the kids come up with them. It's usually a growing list.

The list makes the rules clear and visible and reinforces the power of the children's personal rules. Besides, what could be better? A rule list developed by kids integrates meaningful literacy into their lives (see Rule 7: Take Dictation from Your Tot).

Here's an example of rules developed by two four-year-olds as they were playing:

Boxing Rules—Max and Oliver
1. *No punching in the face*
2. *No kicking*
3. *Say "Stop" or get off the mat if you want to stop*
4. *No shoes*
5. *Take a break and drink water*

When a new rule comes up, each child has to agree to abide by the other child's rules. "If you want to play with Hannah, that's her rule." Wait and get a verbal yes. If a child won't agree, the game stops.

Allowing children to set the rules achieves the job of keeping everyone safe. It also empowers kids and makes your job easier—you don't have to think of every little thing that might go wrong. What's important will come up. If kids forget, remind them of their own rules: "Is that OK with you? Because I heard you say 'No punching.'" Rule making combined with roughhousing is a powerful combination for learning.

When Smiles Stop

Play is over when smiles stop. Kids are still learning to read each other's emotions, so they might miss a change from laughter to fear. Step in and sort out a game that has gone too far.

For example, Jason was playing rough games in the park with three other boys. It started out as fun, but suddenly Jason's face showed he was scared. He started to karate kick and lash out, and then burst into tears when his mom came up. The other boys stopped instantly. "We thought he was still having fun," they said.

You can tell kids, "Look at his face. It looks scared. He's not smiling anymore." It might just be time to take a break—"Everyone stop and get a drink of water." No matter how wild it gets, you are still in charge. You can put an end to it. You can stop a wrestling match if one child's face shows that the game is too rough.

Depending on your kids' ages and temperaments, you don't have to be in the same room when they box and wrestle. Younger kids especially may learn more when you're there watching, but you don't need to hover. Kids will yell or leave if the play gets too rough.

Observing and Feeling Safe

Some kids prefer to observe high-action games. Don't ever force participation. Let kids observe as long as they want. It can help to set up a
"Safety Corner" nearby where children can watch and still feel safe. The
Safety Corner I've used is just paper with a Red Cross symbol drawn on
it. Designate a spot, and let everyone know that no boxing, wrestling or
chasing can go on there. Some children love having a Safety Corner and
go in and out of it at will.

Cautious children are often fascinated by rough play. Alexandria, a
four-year-old who liked to dress up as a princess and carry her blankie,
watched kids boxing from the sideline. "I don't like boxing," she said.
"Blankie likes boxing, but I always have to help him." Then one day she
tried it and had so much fun she went through two partners. "Ready, set,
box!" she cried. "I *love* to box!" Because of all the power involved, roughhousing games can be great self-esteem builders, especially for kids who
tend to be shy.

Younger Siblings and Uneven Partners

Kids come in all shapes and sizes, so putting two five-year-olds together
may still be an uneven match. But boxing and wrestling games are fun
and viable for kids of different body sizes and ages. Games like this develop awareness of the other person and bond kids together. Maybe your
five-year-old and your three-year-old can't both play Candy Land, but
they can both wrestle.

> *Kacy, age four, is eager to box. She's a special-needs child. Her partner,*
> *five-year-old Carson, is tall for his age and often roughhouses. Kacy*
> *dances around the mat, waving her boxing gloves.*
> CARSON: Knock me down, Kacy! Come on, push me!
> *Kacy grins and pushes at him with her gloves.*

CARSON: Yeah! Push me again, come on, knock me down! Oh, you got me! (*He falls down dramatically.*)
Kacy is delighted. She puts her arms in the air with a big smile.

Like Carson, bigger, tougher kids often scale down their actions to match a younger partner. Play like this develops excellent impulse control. Physical games with a mix of ages and abilities help develop body control and social awareness. If a younger child is interested in the game, let her play. Setting rules and limits is the same, and you can issue reminders. Check in: "Is this still fun for both of you? Remember, you can always say 'Stop' if it gets too rough."

Of course, older and stronger kids don't always know their own strength, and can't always control their bodies. If a child is too rough, say, "It looks like it's too hard for you to wrestle without hurting Sam, so I can't let you wrestle now." Children often self-police this and reject a partner when things get too rough. Chances are, the rejected child will be so keen to roughhouse again that he will work hard to control his body next time to become an appealing partner.

Adult Roughhousing

As soon as my three-year-old spies his dad he shouts out, "Let's wrestle!"

Dads often bond with their kids through roughhousing. Kids love the thrill of tackling a bigger person, but it's not every grown-up's cup of tea. "I just couldn't wrestle with my kids," said one mother. "It's just not me."

If you're not comfortable roughhousing, don't force it. But if you're willing to try something new, your kids will love it. Lie on the bed (or on the ground outside) and fend off attackers. Or kneel on a carpet or other soft surface and invite your preschooler to try to push you down. You might prefer to play a game of chase.

Important: Don't get carried away. Adults need to check in with a child frequently and pause the action. This allows kids to get out of the game if they're not having fun. Adults are so much bigger and can be psychologically overpowering. Children sometimes react by giggling hysterically when actually they are overwhelmed and want to stop. Read emotions carefully and take breaks.

WORDS TO TRY

Welcoming rough-and-tumble play

What's going on? Are you both having fun?

It looks as if you two want to wrestle.

Do you have any rules?

My rule is: Stop if someone says "Stop!"

You can play that game, but not here. You can do it outside.

Getting hurt

Sometimes you get bumps when you roughhouse.

Is there a problem? I see your face looks worried.

Do you want to take a break?

That looks like it really hurt.

What can you do next time so you won't get hurt?

Setting limits

Are you both still having fun?

Did you like that?

Remember, you can say "Stop!" if you don't like it.

Do you want him to pull your shirt? You can make a new rule.

If you want to play with James, you have to follow his rule: No pulling shirts.

Stopping rough play

Look at his face. He looks scared. He's not smiling anymore.

I need to stop you. I'm worried you're going to hurt his body.

It looks like it's too hard for you to wrestle without hurting Sam, so I can't let you wrestle right now.

WORDS TO AVOID

Stop fighting!

Be nice.

Keep your hands off each other!

Quit that. Behave!

I don't want to see your bodies touching.

I won't have any fighting here.

OK. That's it. Game's over.

Why can't you play quietly like Natalie?

OUT AND ABOUT

When you meet up with another family, chances are, the other parents will shy away from rough play. "No, no, boys! Stop that. Come away from each other. Brook, you play over here." You may find yourself in situations where another parent breaks up healthy puppy play when you (and the kids) wish it could continue.

If it's a stranger at the park or someone you don't know well, you might let it go. Or say, "I'm OK with that sort of play, if it's OK with you. Looks as if the kids are having fun." Often on hearing those words, the other parent will visibly relax.

If a friend comes over to play, it's easier to talk about. You can do this ahead of time: "At our house, we let kids play roughhousing games. We have a mat we bring out and the kids usually have a lot of fun. Do you mind if Carter wants to join in that kind of play?" Or after the fact: "We loved having Carter over. They played in the sandbox a long time and then they did some roughhousing. Carter had so much fun and really listened when Jacob said 'Stop.'"

If another parent truly feels uncomfortable, respect his or her wishes. Tell your child, "Carter's family doesn't like that game. You'll have to save it for later. No wrestling now."

Bombs, Guns and Bad Guys Allowed

Max lived in a household where toy guns were banned. He charged around the backyard wielding the toilet plunger and yelling, "Bang! Bang! Bang!" Gabe wanted to play *Star Wars*, but his preschool didn't allow games like that. His teacher made him turn his laser gun into a magic wand.

Lasers, lightsabers, guns, swords. Weapon play scares adults so much that many families and classrooms ban it. But for kids who yearn for weapon play, shooting and swashbuckling is an unstoppable energy that needs to be respected—and played out.

Renegade Reason
Playing with toy weapons will not make a child violent. Respect a child's right to play.

When we see a child dressed up as a pirate, we smile. How cute. A skull-and-crossbones hat. A small voice growling out, "Arrrr, matey!" Somehow as adults we don't mind it when kids play pirate. Why is pirate play tolerated and considered benign? Pirates are actually violent, murderous, thieving thugs. And although we romanticize them, pirates are still active today on modern seas, waylaying boats off the shores of Asia and Africa. But no U.S. preschool parent worries that his child is going to grow up and become a pirate. We recognize pirate play as fantasy play.

The same should be true of "Bang! Bang!" weapon play. Wielding a toy gun or sword as a preschooler is not going to cause our child to grow up to be a violent criminal. It is social, appropriate fantasy play. Some kids need it more than others, but just because your four-year-old is fascinated with shooting his friends now doesn't mean he will become an antisocial, violent teenager. In fact, just the opposite may be true. By welcoming your child's needs and allowing him to explore his unique ideas with playmates, you set the stage for understanding, cooperation and community.

Renegade Blessings

Weapon play is simply one more type of dramatic play. If we make room for it, children feel welcome and understood:

> *I can be who I am.*
> *Adults respect my play.*
> *I can have fun with my friends.*
> *Not all people like toy weapons pointed at them. I have to ask first.*
> *Toy weapons are not the same as real ones. Real ones are dangerous.*

Why It Works

The sight of a three-year-old toting a gun can be chilling. Even if it's a bright blue plastic toy with an orange safety tip. It can be hard to view weapon play among tots as anything but repulsive. And with school shootings and terrorists in the news, it's perfectly understandable that many of us feel this way.

We abhor the idea that our child might grow up to be violent. These are the three things we fear:

1. War play will make our children violent.
2. War play will confuse our children about real weapons.
3. War play just isn't nice.

But just like any other action-oriented power games, toy weapon play does not mean the same thing to children as it does to adults. More than with any other imaginary play, we need to take off our adult lenses when we view children's weapon play.

When a child says "Bang! Bang!" or grabs a sword, remember to invoke the Renegade Golden Rule: It's OK If It's Not Hurting People or Property. Look at the situation. Is anyone actually getting hurt by this play, or are the children engaged, happy and laughing? Dramatic sword play or laser fights are usually high-energy fun for children. It's one more type of power play and a great way for kids to forge friendships. The play is OK. Trust it.

What we worry about as adults, though, is potential future violence. Won't weapon play lead to violent behavior later? The simple answer is no. Violent people display warning signs, which include cruelty to animals, extreme isolation and rejection, and a feeling of being persecuted and misunderstood. Pretend play brings the opposite. The play is often social, and involves complex give-and-take as children develop play ideas. Play ideas may be overly dramatic (exploding laser beams, poisonous cannonballs), but children display empathy when a playmate gets hurt in real life. Many kids forge tight friendships through this play. The effects are exactly the opposite in the case of true violence.

Take Off Your Adult Lenses

War play is as legitimate as playing house. When a preschooler says "Bang! Bang!" it's a game, not violence. Don't be fooled because the topic may be violent—this play is typically highly social and cooperative, teaching your child skills in friendship and even early morality. If we fear weapon play and ban it, children may still pursue their fascination with power and weapons—often in places we can't see it. Playing with toy swords and guns is not harmful, but your reaction to it might be. Trust your child to choose her own play themes.

Think about your own childhood. Most of us grew up in an era of cap guns, water pistols and *Star Wars*. As a five-year-old, my brother, Scott, loved playing Daniel Boone and even slept with his toy rifle. Now he's a stay-at-home dad and activist for human rights through his church. I loved games with squirt guns and water-balloon bombs. And the way he tells it, my husband spent most of his childhood playing at blowing things up. I hear this refrain echoed time after time when parents agonize over their three-year-old's new love of bombs and swords. *We* played these games as kids and grew up into responsible parents. Isn't it OK?

Yes. When it comes to pretend play, it's not the topic or toy that's wrong, it's how kids act in real life. For it's real life that counts. What's important is that kids learn: (1) peaceful ways to resolve real conflicts, and (2) coping strategies for strong emotions. It's about how they treat one another.

It's also important how we treat children. What happens when a child like Gabe is told to change his laser gun into a magic wand? Most kids in such situations feel thwarted, bad and misunderstood. *They never let me have any fun*, he might grumble, or *I'm a bad kid—the games I like are bad*. Since Gabe was in a preschool classroom, he might also think, *They like girls best*, or *School is no good. I don't fit in here*.

Every time we ban weapon play, a child like Gabe can learn:

> My ideas are bad.
> Grown-ups don't like the kind of person I am.
> They don't care about what I'm really interested in; they want to change it.
> I'm a bad kid.
> It's better to lie. I can tell them it's a magic wand, but it's really still a gun to me.
> School is not a place where I fit in.
> My parents won't let me have fun with my friends. They only try to stop fun.
> When I play with weapons, I have to hide it.

These are not lessons we want our child to learn. They erode trust and damage relationships. If interest in weapons is driven underground, there can be serious safety issues.

It's OK to change your mind and change your policy. Many a family has started out with a "no weapons in this house" rule and abandoned it midcourse. "I was very strict about no toy weapons when my first son was little," one mother told me, "but by the time the second and third boys came along, it was obvious that wasn't going to work. They had all sorts of pop guns." For Max's mom, that point came when she looked out the window and saw her son joyously engaged with a friend who had a toy gun. Max was shooting with the toilet plunger. "I began to realize that Max had a very different view of toy guns than I did. I had been looking at things in an adult, sociopolitical way."

After watching numerous parents go through this transformation from a "no weapons" parent to one who accepts such play, I'm convinced that a parent's attitude toward weapon play depends on the individual child. Some kids have a strong interest in and desire for weapon play and some don't. We follow our child's lead. For many parents, no amount of scientific argument will sway us, but if one of our children deeply needs this play, we will begin to value it.

Props for Play

Kids need props when they play. Perhaps because of the evolutionary need to be toolmakers, kids need to move and manipulate objects when they play and learn. This seems to be particularly true for boys, who tend to be more spatially oriented. David Geary, a psychologist who wrote the book *Male, Female*, says boys play with objects more than girls do. Of course, kids can shape their fingers into a gun or laser beam, but they usually prefer to use a toy or pick up a stick. "We don't deny children props in other types of play," says Jan Waters, of the School for Young Children. "We give a child a doll—why shouldn't we give a child a toy weapon as a prop?"

When we limit kids' access to toy weapons, they often sidestep our rule and find another way. Children who need a weapon will bite their crackers into the shape of a gun, use spoons or Legos, or even the toilet plunger, as four-year-old Max did. The list of objects that have been used as weapons by kids who are denied them verge on the ridiculous. Benjamin, a four-year-old whose parents prohibited guns, said, "This is not a gun," before picking up a toy gun and shooting. Even if a child is coloring quietly with crayons, the urge doesn't go away: "This is a witch. This is her purple moustache. A big, bad, purple moustache that shoots! *Pow!*"

For some kids, there is simply a deep need to play this way. Whether their play themes are respected or not, kids will find a way. With a need so deep, isn't it better to allow children a chance to explore and grow in an atmosphere of acceptance?

Objects Kids Have Used as Toy Guns (A Partial List)

Candy cane	Hobby horse
Toilet plunger	Stick
Fingers	Kitchen spoon
Pretzel or cracker	Legos
Broomstick	Bubble wand
Mop	Snow scraper
Slide whistle	Swimming noodle
Icicle	

Fears and Safety

Riley, age four, was quiet around kids his age. He liked to carry six plastic swords stuffed in his belt and hands at all times. Carrying these weapons made him feel safe. As the months went on, Riley began carrying fewer swords. Eventually, he was able to play with other children without any swords at all.

Just as they use superhero or other power play, some kids use toy weapons to help them master fears and feel strong. A plastic sword may be a security object, as it was for Riley, or it may be wielded ferociously in a game involving Darth Vader. Four-year-old Sam, for example, walked down the hall holding a sword and calling out, "I'll save you! I'll save you!" to his classmates. Gerard Jones, author of *Killing Monsters: Why Children Need Fantasy, Super Heroes and Make-Believe Violence*, has interviewed children of all ages about what they love about fantasy violence. Time and again, Jones says, children play out games with shooting and weapons to master their own fears and to experiment with feeling strong.

"Weapon play is not always aggressive, not at all," says Stephanie Rottmayer, director at the School for Young Children. "Especially for three-year-olds, playing with weapons is a way for kids to feel safe and a little more powerful." (Rule 16: Give Kids Power.)

If you are concerned about aggression, recognize that fear, anger and emotional immaturity spark most aggression in young children. Common fears that appear as aggression are:

Fear of getting hurt

Fear someone is trying to take something away *(sharing)*

Fear of scary things *(monsters, the dark, dogs, strangers, loud noises)*

Social fears *(unsure how to make or keep friends)*

Separation fears *(missing mother or father, blankie or teddy)*

Weapon Play as Moral Play

Kids use weapon play to explore deep human themes of right and wrong, virtue and evil, safety and danger, and power and protection. Weapon play also helps kids explore ideas about life and death and their own mortality.

Early-childhood expert Vivian Paley says all imaginative play—including war play—helps kids learn and create a base for moral development. Weapon play gives kids a chance to practice being compassionate and courageous, as psychologist Michael Thompson says, stepping in to save their friends in feats of derring-do. If you listen to children's imaginary scenarios, they're often about clearing the world of monsters and bad guys to make it safe for their friends and family. Developmentally, this is where your child is now. Shades of gray will come later. (What about the monster's feelings? Are there really any bad guys in the world or just bad circumstances?) As long as her play doesn't violate the Renegade Golden Rule (It's OK If It's Not Hurting People or Property), then allow her play to unfold.

With all this talk about morals, what if your child isn't interested in war play? No worries. She'll get her moral development and need for power met in other ways.

Fantasy Versus Reality

But what about mixing fantasy and reality? The truth is, very young kids understand the beauty of pretend play. In pretend play you can do anything you want. You can be anybody you want. And no one's supposed to get hurt.

One way kids show they understand the difference between make-believe injuries and real life is by squawking the moment they get hurt in real life. The line's been crossed. Once when Zach and my husband were bopping Nerf swords, Zach protested when my husband playfully hit his belly. "Hit on swords," Zach corrected. "Don't hit my body. It hurts." Even though real swords are tools designed to hurt or kill, both of them understood this was a game of pretend.

Kids understand play. It's what they know best. It's clearly a game, since they intend to have fun. Kids can easily play cowboy fights or *Star Wars* for hours, but will rush over in empathy if a playmate gets hurt. It's all harmless play to them.

War Play and Violence

Violent story lines and toy-weapon play don't create violent children in real life. No long-term study has found a link between kids who play with pretend weapons as children and future violent behavior when they grow up. Despite the controversy over toy weapons, there have been very few research studies *at all* on the topic of weapon play. Dr. Steven Kirsh, author of *Children, Adolescents and Media Violence: A Critical Look at the Research*, reviewed existing research and found only fifteen papers published in the last fifty years, most of which focused on cases of aggressive make-believe play. However, there are plenty of examples of people who committed violent attacks in their youth or adulthood who struggled socially and emotionally in childhood. Imaginative weapon play is not a path to violence; it is most often pro-social play that helps kids face a range of emotions.

What helps stop violence? Kids who understand how to cope with their emotions. Kids who can set limits and listen to others. Kids who develop impulse control and skills for making friends. Kids who know how to say "Stop!" and when to get adult help. This is the work of play and conflict mediation.

War Play and Aggression

Even if kids don't become violent, won't sword and gun play make them more aggressive? Jan Waters has observed war play in classrooms of four- and five-year-olds for thirty-five years at the School for Young Children. She sees the opposite. When kids are allowed to follow their play themes, they feel accepted and understood. High-energy games like war play channel aggressive energy appropriately so kids don't lash out so much at other times. Penny Holland, a teacher and researcher in England, strongly agrees. She used to insist on zero tolerance of war play, but discovered the classroom became more peaceful when fantasy war play was allowed. When adults repeatedly pounced on kids to stop war play, these kids considered themselves "bad," withdrew from the social group and became more disruptive.

Children will play what they need to play. As psychologist Peter Gray points out, "Some people think that violent play creates violent adults; but in reality the opposite is true. Violence in the adult world leads children, quite properly, to play at violence. . . . If we want to reform the world, we have to reform the world; and children will follow suit."

A classic 1961 study by psychologist Albert Bandura showed how watching violent action made kids more aggressive. The "Bobo doll" study exposed children to film footage of an adult attacking an inflatable clown with a mallet. Children punched and attacked the clown more after watching. This isn't surprising, since children learn lots through modeling, but of course the clown wasn't real and couldn't get hurt. Media violence, whether it's cartoons or the news, can certainly influence children's play. But violent plots in pretend play don't necessarily equal increased aggression. Kids may reenact *Star Wars* and other war stories, but still behave kindly to each other. Scientists are still trying to figure out if there is a link to bad behavior. Current research is contradictory, with several studies showing no significant change in aggressive behavior. Recent research by psychologist Jamie Ostrov indicates that even watching violent movies or video games is not so bad. His findings suggest that what makes children more aggressive (behaving badly to one another) is watching people insult each other, either in person or on the screen. Children's TV is full of insults. A study by psychologist Cyndy Scheibe found that nearly every children's show contained insults, even educational ones, and most insults were rewarded by canned laughter.

When you watch your child's war play, look for this: Is she treating her real playmates well? In other words, is she following the Golden Renegade Rule: It's OK If It's Not Hurting People or Property?

Try This—Add to Your Toolbox

Kids are different. Myles preferred to read books and never picked up a toy gun. Zach came out of the womb shooting and making exploding noises. If your child is one who loves gun and sword play, then don't try to stop him. Suppressing play isn't the answer. And chances are, you can't suppress desire this strong. Instead, find a way to make this kind of play comfortable in your house.

Reinforce "No Hurting" Policy

No matter how violent kids' make-believe play becomes, make sure they know that "people are not for hurting." Kids get this. They understand they can do anything they want in make-believe land, but real people can't be hurt. When a problem comes up, help kids talk about it with conflict mediation.

Set Limits with Respect

"I going to bang you," said Zach, my three-year-old. He was holding the mop and cradling it like a gun. "You want to get banged?"

"Sure, you can bang me," I told him.

"Bang! Bang!" he cried out, wielding his mop gun. "You're dead!"

"Ahh!" I cried, and pretended to be hit. Next he turned to his older brother.

"You want to be shooted, Myles?"

"No," answered Myles, who was coloring.

"OK," said Zach, taking off his sun hat and putting it on the ground. "I bang my hat. Bang! Bang!"

The child who needs to explore weapon play deserves our respect. So do the people around him. This comes about just like any normal courtesy and limit setting. For example, if kids are playing in a leaf pile and one child tosses leaves in another's hair, there might need to be a limit. "Do you want him to throw leaves in your face? She said no. You can throw leaves at me, but not at Sonja." In the same manner, explain to kids that it's OK to make shooting noises, but not everyone likes to be shot. Tell kids, "You have to ask first."

Warm Up to Weapon Play

If you're still feeling tentative about weapon play, try setting a limit you can be comfortable with, rather than an outright ban. You'll be in good company. Even *Mothering* magazine—that bastion of breast-feeding, baby wearing and all things wholesome—featured an in-depth story about welcoming toy weapons in fantasy play.

It's perfectly OK for your kids to understand you don't like some kinds of play. But as Michael Thompson, coauthor of *It's a Boy!*, says, "If you are going to be the parent of a boy [or any child who likes weapon play] you have to learn to trust his childhood fantasies . . . even if they are not to your taste." If a child has a deep need for this kind of play, chances are, she will adhere to your rules so she can continue her pretend play. War play is exciting and powerful, and kids long to join in the drama. The box below includes an array of different levels of limit setting some parents use.

Setting Family Limits on Weapon Play

Please remember these limits are to *make adults feel more comfortable*. Kids would almost universally choose option number 8.

1. Swords are OK, but not guns.
2. Swords are fine, but no touching swords. (Takes a lot of impulse control!)
3. Gun play is OK, but only with found objects (like sticks or fingers).
4. Toy guns are all right, but not realistic-looking ones.
5. Pretend gun play is OK, but no pointing toy guns at people. (Hard to do, since the play demands it.)
6. Pretend gun play is OK, but no pointing at someone's head.

(Kids can do this. Can make gun play seem less scary and re-inforces the lesson that real guns are dangerous.)

7. Weapon play is allowed, but only in certain places. (Only at home, since many adults don't like it; only outside.)

8. Any type of pretend weapon play is fine. Kids need to listen to one another's limits (for example, "Don't shoot me!").

Parents often feel most nervous about toy guns, and don't worry as much about toy swords or lightsabers. It's actually easier for kids to play safely with toy guns. Guns never touch another child; kids hold them at a distance and just say "Bang!" Toy sword play, on the other hand, brings kids close together and invites more unintentional injuries as kids cross swords.

Help Kids Feel Safe

Young kids are most often worried about getting hurt. Am I going to get hurt? Is my friend going to get hurt? Address these fears. Say to the kids with toy weapons, "Heidi is feeling scared. Are you going to hurt her?" Usually the kids who are playing react with surprise, thinking, *No, of course not. We're just playing. We didn't even know she was there.*

A worried child might be wondering if the play fight is a real fight, or if the play weapon is a real one. Again, involve the children who are playing to allay these fears. "Robert is worried about your gun. Is it a toy gun or a real gun?" or "Ava wants to know if you're mad at each other. Are you having a real fight? Oh, they said it was just a game." Repeat these words out loud, even if it's obvious to you. It's much more powerful if the answer comes directly from the children. By involving both sets of kids, you help children sort out what's real and what's not, and help them develop the ability to read others' emotions.

Just as in any play conflict, you might have to teach kids how to stand up for themselves. One day Zach made a sandbox shovel into a pretend gun and tried to play with his neighbor, Tyler. Tyler, age two and a half, raced away, shouting, "Don't! No!"

"Say, 'Don't shoot me!'" I said, demonstrating a stop signal with my hand. Tyler copied my motion with a powerful stance and said, "Don't shoot me!"

Zach obligingly shot someone else, which caused Tyler to change his mind.

"Shoot me," he said, and smiled.

"Bang!" said Zach. Tyler fell down dramatically and giggled on the ground. Then he hopped up and begged Zach to do it again.

Sometimes just the knowledge that they can set limits on other kids and have control makes kids comfortable enough to engage in a game.

Some children won't like weapon play. They might have been taught "We don't play with toy weapons," or they might have private concerns. If the neighbor kid is playing a loud shooting game with your oldest child and your younger one starts cowering, find out what's going on and give him a way to feel safe. Set a limit or find a separate place to play. Tell the child, "I will keep you safe." If a child says, "Guns are bad," agree with

---

When Kids Don't Feel Safe Around Weapon Play

1. Agree with their fears. "Yes, real weapons are dangerous."
2. Explain what's going on. "This is a toy. These kids are playing a game and having fun."
3. Address fears directly. "Are you worried you might get hurt?"
4. Get reassurance from the kids who are playing: "We won't hurt you."
5. Set limits. Make a safety zone or set a kid-based rule: "Don't shoot me."

him. "You may have heard your mom say guns are bad. She's right. *Real* guns are dangerous. This is a toy. It's not real."

Teach Real Gun Safety

Every year in the news, there are tragic stories of children who accidentally shoot their sister or brother. A child is always in danger if she encounters a real gun—no matter whether she plays with toy weapons or not.

Where I live, in Michigan, nearly 40 percent of households own at least one gun. In some states that number runs as high as 50 to 60 percent. No matter where you live, gun ownership is an issue. Even if you don't own a gun yourself, someone you know might. Banning toy-weapon play can't protect your child. You must teach your family real gun safety.

Real guns are a real danger. But this danger has nothing to do with toy weapon play. Parents worry that if children play with toy guns, they won't be able to tell them apart from *real* guns. The fact is, kids are *always* in danger if they encounter a real gun—whether they play with toy weapons or not. Even if children say they know a gun is real, they simply can't grasp its incredible power.

Kids and Real Guns

Guns are in one-third of U.S. households, and in some states even more (as high as 60 percent). Even if your family doesn't own one, your child might encounter a real firearm at a playmate's house. And sadly, too many adults don't store guns properly. Preventing gun accidents is 100 percent adults' responsibility.

Safety Lessons for Children

Teach children that real guns are dangerous. Bring up this basic safety lesson by the time your child is three or as soon as he takes an interest in toy weapons.

1. STOP!
2. Don't touch. Never touch a real gun.
3. If your friend wants to show you a real gun, say no!
4. Leave the area. Get away from the gun *right away*.
5. Tell an adult.

Essential Gun Safety (What Every Caregiver of Young Children Should Know)

1. Never, never point a real gun at a person (including yourself).
2. Store real guns locked and unloaded.
3. Store ammunition in a separate, locked location.
4. If you don't know whether a gun is loaded or not, assume it is. Leave it alone.
5. Teach your children gun safety. If you own a gun, it's not enough to say, "Never touch the gun closet." Kids are curious and attracted to banned items. Give a thorough safety lesson.
6. Before your child goes to visit a new friend's house, always ask, "Do you have any guns in your house?" Say, "We are teaching Kate about gun safety. How many guns do you have? How are they stored?" Cancel the visit if you are not satisfied.

Teaching gun safety can seem daunting, but look around and you'll find good resources. You might try the Eddie Eagle video on YouTube. This cartoon clearly conveys the major safety points and is appropriate for preschoolers.

When it comes to playdates, it can seem awkward at first to ask the "gun question" of four-year-old Susie's parents. I still remember arriving with my son for his first-ever playdate. The first thing I saw was a rifle slung over the garage wall. "Uh, I see you have a gun," I said. So instead of "hi-how-are-you's?" we stumbled through a talk about locking up ammunition. Better to broach the subject over the phone or e-mail. It gets easier over time, and this is one conversation you don't want to skip.

It's a child's job to play. It's the adults' job to keep real guns away from children at all times.

WORDS TO TRY

Ava is worried about your game. Is that a real sword?

Are you worried you might get hurt? Let's ask the kids: "Are you going to hurt him?"

This is a toy sword, not a real sword.

Not everybody likes to be shot. You have to ask first.

Say, "Don't shoot me!"

Remember, if you want to play with the gun, you can't point it at people's heads.

Remember, swords can't hit bodies.

This is a game we play at home, not at Aunt Jennifer's.

Some people don't like this kind of game.

What can we do so everyone feels safe?

Yes, real weapons are dangerous.

WORDS TO AVOID

We don't play with toy guns here.

That's not a gun, it's a magic wand.

That's not a nice game.

Don't go near the gun closet. (Invites curiosity)

OUT AND ABOUT

If you decide to allow weapon play, know that some parents you meet will *not* be happy. It's an incredibly touchy topic. If you allow weapon play in a child-care or preschool setting, you are guaranteed to lose some families over this topic. Don't back down—let them go. And be gracious: you are both trying to do what's best for the children.

To avoid culture clash, some families make a rule to keep weapon play at home. This gives kids lots of room for free expression, but makes them aware that the playground and classroom have different rules. "That's a game we play at home, remember? Not everybody likes sword play."

If you feel strongly about sticking up for weapon play wherever you are, be prepared to problem solve. Be candid with adults you encounter who disapprove of your child's joyful shooting game. Simply acknowledge their discomfort. "I see that game makes you uncomfortable. Are you worried their play will lead to real violence?" Don't try to convert another adult to share your views on the spot, but go ahead and share your story. For example: "My sister and I used to play these exact same games as a kid, and she's such a pacifist now . . ." or "We used to have a 'no weapons' policy at our house, but Connor made me change my mind. I've realized it's such creative play." You might find sharing the example of pirate play useful.

When cultures clash with neighbors, friends or strangers, you'll have to explain it to your child, too. Present it as an issue of consideration and safety. Try saying, "I know you're having a good time, but some people don't like shooting games. They get scared because real guns can kill. What can we do so everyone feels safe?"

It's hard not to bow to adult social pressure. We falter under the judgment of other adults, whether it's the unknown parent at the playground or your sister-in-law at a family get-together. Take confidence. When you stand up for your child's right to play, you gain her respect and meet her needs, and that's a tremendous good.

Boys Can Wear Tutus

My son Zach likes to be Cinderella. He puts on dress-up clothes and pretends to lose his fleecy bedroom slipper. "Oh no! Midnight. Bong, bong, bong . . ." Other days he's Dorothy and clutches his pug-nosed stuffed dog in his arms as Toto. "I Dorothy," he tells me, "and you the wicked old witch."

When Zach runs through the living room in a lace-frilled dress and flopping wig, my husband just smiles.

"I'm glad you don't mind," I say to him.

"Mind? Why would I mind?" replies my husband. "He's just a kid playing."

That's true, but gender-bender play can startle us. A boy in a dress? Heck, even a boy playing with dolls? Our culture currently lets little girls try out both sides of gender play, but imposes strict masculine roles on boys. Even by age three, many boys stop freely playing and don't dare cross those lines.

Renegade Reason

Play that crosses gender roles is creative and harmless. Let kids play. It won't change who they are.

Connor pretended to be pregnant. He shoved a pillow up his shirt. "I'm a mom having a baby," he said.

Mateo and Gabe liked to put on panty hose. When they were all dressed up, they put on plays for their moms.

Grace, age four, loved dinosaurs. She refused to have bows in her hair, and wouldn't wear the dresses her mother bought for her. Year after year, she asked for a dinosaur birthday cake.

If your five-year-old boy dons a girl's wig, or your girl wants to wear a fake moustache and put on a tie—there's no harm in it. Kids are trying out ideas and roles. This play is like any other exploratory or make-believe play. A preschooler's job is play and exploration. We need to encourage creative play, especially at this young age, not squelch it.

Renegade Blessings

All kids can benefit from a supportive environment when it comes to gender-based play:

I can try new things.

I can see life from the perspective of others.

I can play freely following my own ideas.

I can be quiet and gentle sometimes and rough and loud sometimes.

I can get to know girls and boys—through play.

> *I can be who I am. When I grow up, I can be whatever I want to be.*
>
> *I can do things that interest me. I don't have to worry about what other people think.*
>
> *I trust myself.*
>
> *My parents like who I am. They support me.*

Why It Works

When Zach arrives at his babysitter's house, she doesn't say, "How are you?" The first thing she asks Zach is "Who are you?" because it changes nearly every day. One day Zach arrives in a bear suit; the next day he's an elephant, firefighter or pirate king. Sometimes he's a mermaid. Not long ago, Zach fell in love with the story of Snow White. For two weeks, he wore a princess dress and serenaded everyone—from ladies at church to clerks at the grocery store—with the song "Some Day My Prince Will Come."

At age three, Zach is quite clear he's a boy. He spent much of one year proclaiming, "I a man! Papa a man! Big man!" He's into all things loud, fast and fierce and loves trucks, tigers, dinosaurs and diggers. But most of all, Zach loves games of pretend. If a story strikes his imagination, Zach jumps up to act it out. And being an egocentric three-year-old, Zach always likes to be the main character. So sometimes he's Robin Hood and sometimes he's Snow White. Donning a wig and skirt is simply another way for him to explore life and try on different roles. Pretending to be a girl is just part of the fun. "I not Zach," he'll say. "Zach not here. I Little Red Riding Hood. See my basket? No, no, now I the wolf! Grrrrowl!"

This ability to take different roles in play helps kids develop awareness of others. What does it feel like to be someone else? What does life look like from another's perspective? Psychologist William Damon says taking another's perspective is an important step in developing empathy and morality. Ellen Galinsky, author of *Mind in the Making*, says perspective taking helps kids avert aggression and learn to solve problems peacefully.

> *Playing different roles helps a child develop empathy.*

Looking at life from another perspective is a marvelous human trait. It helps teachers, social workers, negotiators, actors, ministers, writers and many others. Just think of a fiction writer, for example. When a male author writes from the point of view of a female character, we don't stop to wonder if the author is "male" enough. We don't think it's odd. If the book is good, it shows the author is observant and imaginative. He understands what life might be like as a woman and transports us into her world.

That's exactly what your preschooler is doing, too. Trying out roles in life. Exploring. Playing. Imagining new ideas and bringing them to life. Denying children the full range of play experiences means denying their ideas and denying part of who they are.

Freedom to Play

The kids in Cindy's preschool class were listening to music from *The Nutcracker*, dancing and acting it out. First Jenna was Clara, then Nate wanted a turn. "But Clara's a girl," protested one four-year-old. "Nate can't be Clara. I'm a girl—let me be Clara." Nate stretched his hand out to hold the nutcracker. "Anyone can be Clara," said the teacher. "It's Nate's turn now. You can be Clara next." With a big grin on his face, Nate leaped across the room with the nutcracker in his arms.

Children are universally curious. They want to sample and explore everything—whether it's what Mom is doing in the garden or what Dad is doing in the kitchen. If their play involves storytelling, they want to take the lead role.

Meanwhile, in Myles's preschool class, it was Valentine's Day. The teacher passed out two crafts: one for the boys and one for the girls.

Take Off Your Adult Lenses

Children's play cannot harm anything. If a boy wants to wear a dress, or a girl wants to wrestle, don't spend time worrying about their well-being. A child whose play ideas are honored will be well. Stand up for a child's right to choose his or her own play themes—kids benefit from our acceptance. If teasing comes up, deal with hurt feelings directly through conflict mediation.

Myles reached for the "girl craft," which included a cutout bear. Myles liked bears. "You can't have that," he was told. "That's just for the girls."

Part of giving children the right to choose their own play themes is allowing them to play games that cross traditional gender lines. A five-year-old boy should feel free to try *any* dress-up, play with *any* toy and explore any role. The same is true for girls. A short time ago, it was unthinkable for a young girl to climb a tree or even wear pants (unladylike!). Now girls enjoy tremendous freedom as children. A girl can play princess one minute and dress in camouflage the next. Girls are encouraged to try sports and art, dance and tae kwon do. But their brothers and male peers are more restricted. Even by age three or four, boys' play gets inhibited by the Boy Code.

The Boy Code

The "Boy Code" term was coined by Harvard psychologist William Pollack, but we all know what it means. Boys aren't supposed to like pink. Boys can't play with dolls. Boys don't sing. Boys are supposed to be good at sports. Boys can't cry. Boys have to be tough all the time and hide their feelings. Being caring is a sign of weakness. If you do girly things or have friends who are girls, you're not male enough.

Boys get this message from their fathers, mothers, the media and other kids. By the age of five, many boys already hide their feelings, says Pollack, author of *Real Boys: Rescuing Our Sons from the Myths of Boyhood*. "Weak" (girly) feelings like fear and sadness get masked as anger. Preschool-age boys censor themselves and limit their imagination and curiosity.

> *A child's play is not the problem. It's our reaction to it.*

Even as we expand girls' options and tell them they can do anything boys can do, we send boys a firm message: Don't cry like a girl, don't throw like a girl, don't try on girls' clothes; basically, don't be a girl. What's a young boy to think? *Girls are somehow bad—the worst thing I can do is to be like one.* At the same time we tell girls: You can be anything you want to be. It's a mixed message. And kids get hurt because of it. When boys get the message that being a girl is the worst thing they can be, girls pick up that message, too.

Dividing Boys and Girls

When I was growing up, families were expanding gender roles for both sides. Boys in the 1970s sported long hair. Many girls had butch haircuts. Everyone wore pants. Toy trucks were mostly marketed to boys and doll-houses to girls, but many toys had pictures of both sexes on the box.

Now it's hard to find even a gender-neutral toothbrush in the stores. Girls' toothbrushes are princess pink and boys' toothbrushes come only in tough colors—like red and black—with pictures of Spider-Man and cars. Nothing is neutral any longer. The boy-girl divide is ruthlessly strong, locking children into strict roles. That makes it even harder for kids who push back against these imposed gender roles and try to experience life on their own terms.

At age three, Myles admired the red, blue and pink nail polish his babysitters wore. He liked the pretty colors and wanted to try some toe-nail polish, too. I'm not a nail painter myself, so I didn't have a single bottle in the house. I called a friend. "What color?" she asked. "Red and pink," said Myles. We met down at the beach and painted Myles's toenails bright colors. When two-year-old Jacob saw what we were doing, he wanted to paint his nails, too. "OK," my friend said with a sigh. "I just hope his dad is OK with this."

Not long ago, a J.Crew ad shocked many families by showing a mother and her five-year-old son laughing together while she applied nail polish to his toes. The caption read, "Lucky for me I ended up with a boy whose favorite color is pink. Toenail painting is way more fun in neon." Meanwhile, across the country in Seattle, five-year-old Dyson of *My Princess Boy* fame made a media splash with his love of wearing pink princess clothes and glittery jewelry.

Something irks many of us deep inside when a boy crosses the line. We doubt his masculinity. We worry he's all mixed up. We get scared about what people will say—will he get bullied? Many parents try to silence the small voice that asks, *Does this mean he's gay?* Yet in this parenting age, we don't mind if a girl dons a pirate hat and pretends to be Captain Hook, or scales the monkey bars, laughing, with the boys. Only two or three generations ago, this would have been unthinkable. Times change. Our own ideas change. Dyson's mother at first tried to redirect him toward trucks, but then accepted her son's deep love of all things bling and wrote the book *My Princess Boy.* As Dyson's father says, it's not contagious.

Here and Now

Some kids try out gender-bender play for a day. Others may take an intense interest, and take things to extremes during the preschool years. Whatever the case, your child's play is all about the present. Let her play, and don't project onto the future.

For example, day after day, four-year-old Alexander wore princess underwear, barrettes in his hair, and a princess nightgown. As a teenager, Alexander couldn't even remember dressing up in girls' clothes. If his play had been stopped and forbidden, however, it's likely he would have remembered his parents' prohibitions starkly. *Something's wrong with me. My ideas for playing are bad. There's something bad about being a girl.*

Three-year-old Felix envied his older sister's dress-up evening gown. He wanted one of his own. His mom took him to the thrift store, and Felix chose a silk prom dress, emerald green with hot-pink lining. They cut it to the right length for him, and Felix wore it with rhinestone ear-rings plus a yellow hard hat. He lost interest a short while later. Today Felix is a twenty-something who wears regular guy clothes. "Green is still his favorite color," says his mom.

A teacher once said, "Just because your child likes to play with trucks doesn't mean he's going to grow up to be a truck driver." In the same vein, just because your child likes to wear a girl's dress as a preschooler doesn't mean he's going to grow up to be a cross-dresser.

We tend to jump to conclusions as adults. We forget how much explo-ration and fantasy exists in young kids' minds. It's not about the future for young kids. It's about the here and now.

Is My Preschooler Gay?

Maybe. It's simply too early to know. Preschool-age children are far too young to be classified at all. But we do know that children's play cannot "make" someone gay. According to current thinking by psychologists and other researchers, homosexuality develops from a complex combina-tion of genetic, hormonal and environmental factors. Your parenting makes little or no difference in the matter; sexual orientation is largely based in biology.

When a child is born, we do not gaze into his newborn eyes and say, "I will love you only if you grow up straight. I will love you only if you be-come an engineer, take over the family business and give me grandchil-dren." We just plain love them.

This is our most important role as parents: unconditional love. Children and youth who are respected and supported by their families tend to thrive. Gay and transgender youth who lack their family's support suffer dreadfully high rates of depression and suicide.

We can't change who somebody is. We can only guess who a child will become. Will a child like Dyson grow up to be an adult who cross-dresses? No one knows yet. He's five. His interest in dresses may drop off, or it may not. Some kids do sustain a deep interest in opposite-gender behavior, but researchers like Dr. Edgardo Menvielle say gender-bender kids at age five are not necessarily gender benders at age ten or fifteen.

Whoever your child grows up to be, it's your job to love her and support her on her journey to adulthood.

Try This—Add to Your Toolbox

Watch Your Reaction

As a girl, I remember wanting to be a boy. I even called myself Timothy for a while. If your daughter says she wants to be a boy or your son says he wants to be a girl, don't be shocked. Go ahead and talk about it. "So you want to be a boy. I wonder what you like about boys that makes you want to be one?" If anyone asked me, I had the answer: Boys had more fun because they could take off their shirts when it was hot, and girls couldn't.

When your son tries a "girl" activity or wants to wear girls' clothes, think about it as what it is: play. Make a calm statement: "You're playing with dolls today" or "I see you've got on a feather boa and glittery shoes." Statements like these lets boys know it's safe for them to try new things.

Watch what you say to girls, too. Gender researchers say we tend to praise girls for their looks and praise boys for what they can do. "Oh, you look so pretty!" We say this all the time to little girls. The comment tumbles out of our mouths before we notice it. If your four-year-old daughter looks adorable, it's OK to say so, but try to acknowledge what she is doing, rather than how she looks. "You put on a fancy dress today." You can also ask her to tell you what she likes about it ("It feels good when I twirl"). If a girl is trying something rough, or traditionally male, let her explore. Keep a check on saying, "Be nice," "Keep clean," and "Be careful."

Watch Peer Comments

"Girls can't be pirates."

"That's a girl color. You can't have pink."

"Boys can't wear tutus. Ballet is for girls."

Kids themselves are some of the fiercest enforcers of gender roles. When a child announces, "Girls can't do that," or "Boys don't do that," go ahead and speak up. You'll be doing kids everywhere a favor when you do. Remember, kids don't need a lecture on gender equity, but one sentence said with authority does wonders. It clears up misinformation, it lets kids know there are many ways to be male and female, and it offers your obvious support for the risk takers. "I know both girls and boys can be pirates if they want to." "Lots of girls like pink, but I know boys can like pink, too. It's just a color." "Dancing is very athletic. There are boy dancers and girl dancers." "Dress-up clothes are for everyone to play with. Boys can wear dresses if they want to. It's OK with me." Children don't police one another to be mean. At this age, they are still sorting out in their minds what it means to be male or female.

If the boy/girl comment stings, address it as you would any conflict mediation. "I'm worried that boy hurt your feelings when he said that. Did he?" Help the children talk it out. With your support, kids can make their worlds bigger, rather than smaller. You may even find that the teasing child feels comfortable enough to cross the gender divide herself.

Create Safe Places

At the School for Young Children, all children are welcome to try on dress-ups and push their limits in nontraditional play. Boys scoot across the floor wearing red, glittery Dorothy shoes. Girls don boxing gloves and wrestle. Boys play house and try on tutus. It's a safe place.

Find safe places for your child to explore. Maybe they include a friend's house or grandparent's house. The safest place for your kids to expand their play beyond gender stereotypes is usually at home, so think what new props you might bring in. Keep a doll on hand for a houseful of boys, and add a fancy skirt or two to the dress-up bin. Try adding dinosaurs, pirate hats or toy tools if you have only girls. Young kids of both sexes enjoy toy kitchens, necklaces and funny hats. Having a mix of toys offers options and sends a welcoming message.

Don't go overboard, though. You don't want toys that will just grow dusty. Studies of play behavior consistently show that girls prefer dolls and boys prefer trucks. Some families load their daughter's toy boxes with dump trucks and train tracks in an effort to raise a child free of gender stereotypes. The key is to give your child options, but don't force it. Your child will surely take the lead in showing you what she's interested in.

WORDS TO TRY

I know girls can wrestle, too. I know boys can cook.

Pink is just a color. I know a lot of boys who like pink.

It's OK with me if you want to wear that dress.

The costumes are for everybody to play with.

You can pretend to be anyone you want to.

You can play with anything here.

At this house it's OK to try on girls' clothes.

That's a fancy dress.

I see you have sparkly shoes today.

Different places have different rules. You can wear that dress at
  home.
I'm worried she hurt your feelings when she said that.

WORDS TO AVOID
Boys can't do that. Girls can't do that.
That's only for girls.
Why would a big boy like you want to wear a dress?
You're a boy. Act like one.

OUT AND ABOUT
Myles has always liked green and purple. When he chose the
purple crayon at preschool, sometimes kids would laugh and tell
him purple was a girl's color. Cultural norms are strong out
there. If you think your child might walk into a social trap, you
can prepare him. Arm your child with a few phrases to say when
gender issues come up. "Boys can play however they want," or
"Purple is the color of kings."

Speak up. Let adults and kids know your preferences. If you're
fine with boys wearing the girls' dress-up clothes, say so. This
lets everyone know your home is a safe place to play and try new
things. "At this house, boys can wear tutus if they want to. It's
fine with me. Kids can try on whatever they want."

Sometimes one parent in a family will be OK with play that
crosses gender lines and one will worry. Read up on the subject
and share it with your partner. If that doesn't bring you to agreement, it's OK for a child to know that Mommy or Daddy is uncomfortable with some kinds of play. See if you can set up family
rules and create space and time where nontraditional play is safe
and allowed.

When it comes to public places and social visits, you'll have to
decide what you're comfortable with and what's best for your
family. It's part of our job to teach kids cultural expectations. A

friend told me that her aunt closed the door on her friend when her son arrived in a dress for Thanksgiving. "Go home and change his clothes," she told his mom. "I'm not having a boy dressed like that at my table."

Kids can learn that different places have different rules. Some families might decide to keep the boy's dress at all costs and break the friendship. Others would follow the host's request. Still others might allow greater freedom at home, but follow cultural norms in public. It may not be a big deal to your child—or then again it may be. Use your judgment.

Creativity, Persistence and Empty Praise

*Every child is an artist. The problem is how
to remain an artist once he grows up.*

—Pablo Picasso

Pictures Don't Have to Be Pretty

Three-year-old Sam concentrates hard and finishes painting a picture. "Oh, what a pretty picture!" says his mom. Sam walks away. "I'm done with it," he says.

Two-year-old Kara is sponge painting. Her dad steers her to make her art project more beautiful. "How about some more red? That would be pretty. You haven't used any blue yet. Let's put that up here."

Kids these ages are busy experimenting with color. They may create something beautiful to your eyes, and smear it into a gray mess the next minute. Let them. Art for toddlers and preschoolers is rarely about beauty. It's all about exploration and personal expression. In fact, young kids rarely care about the end product at all. Art is action.

Renegade Reason
It's the process, not the product. For young kids, art is doing.

After a child works hard on a picture, it's tempting to say, "Oh, what a nice picture! How pretty!" and hang it on the refrigerator. Before you say, "How pretty," think about what art might mean to your child.

Not all children's art is pretty. Some of it is an ooey-gooey, brownish mess. Some of it is scribbles or blobs. Your child might be trying to draw a scary picture, not a pretty one at all. Even asking "What is it?" can cause trouble for young artists. That question assumes the picture must represent something. Whatever your child's creation looks like, what's most important is what it means to your child.

As a three-year-old, my son Myles liked to experiment with mixing colors when he painted. The more he mixed, the browner it got. Sometimes he'd mix so much he'd make a hole in the paper. If anyone asked him what the picture was, he had no answer. But if you asked him, "How did you do that?" he happily shared elaborate details about his process.

Many young kids don't care what happens to the final painting. When the activity is done, they are done, too. Hanging a picture on the fridge is just fine, but be aware you are probably doing it for yourself, not your child.

Renegade Blessings

Help kids explore process and true creativity rather than praising the product. Here's what they can learn:

> *Art lets me explore ideas and express my feelings. It feels good.*
> *I don't have to follow what everyone else does.*
> *I can take risks and try new things.*
> *I have faith in my ideas and abilities.*
> *I can think on my feet.*
> *Adults care enough to ask me about my pictures. I know the answers because it's my creation.*

Why It Works

Creativity is much more than just art. Creative people think on their feet, try new ways and aren't afraid to question. Especially when it comes to "creative arts," children should be encouraged to explore and take risks.

Fredelle Maynard, author of *Guiding Your Child to a More Creative Life*, says that most young children start out with faith in their ideas but end up limiting their creativity because of criticism. Too often, fear of making mistakes, disapproval and humiliation can stifle children's interest in taking risks and exploration, and ultimately learning.

Janet Stocker, cofounder of the School for Young Children, believes that how adults react to children's efforts matters tremendously, and that too many crafts can blunt creativity. Crafts create a specific object. She says free-form exploration with materials is more important. Early-childhood educator Bev Bos agrees: Crafts can be fun, especially at holiday times, but shouldn't be confused with art. Creative artwork occurs when kids engage with media independently, and the role for adults is to hand out supplies.

For young kids, there is little difference between art and science. Every new color and material is cause for new experimentation. Young kids need to touch, squeeze and sometimes even taste everything. Some art experts say all children need time to explore and play with art materials before they can begin to express ideas through art. For example, children ages two to three in Reggio Emilia preschools are encouraged simply to play and experience the feel of clay or paint. Once young children have had enough time to become familiar with paints and other materials, they turn to them to express ideas.

Take Off Your Adult Lenses

A messy, globby picture may be your child's way of exploring color and texture. Follow your child's lead and don't focus on the finished product. It may not be important. Young kids are fascinated by the process of art, but may not care what happens to their picture when they're done. Art is action.

Crafts and Creativity

Madison came home from kindergarten one day. Since it was Art Day, her mother asked if she'd done any art. "Well," said Madison, "the teacher said it was art." "Oh," said her mother. "What was it?" "I don't know," Madison replied. "But it wasn't art." They talked about what art was, and five-year-old Madison came up with this definition: "Art is when you decide what you want to make, and make it the way you want it to be."

Madison's class was doing a craft.

Crafts can be fun, but think of them as a structured game, like playing Candy Land. It's just fine to play a board game or do a craft project at home—sometimes—but keep it in perspective. Crafts are not the same as art, and they should make up a small percentage of a child's experience with art materials. True art, like true free play, is all about experimentation and creativity. Creativity comes from inside the child and can't be forced.

Why do we expect children to do so many crafts? Well, for one thing, many of us adults enjoy crafts and like sharing the activity with kids. Crafts are big at holiday times. Since craft projects usually look better than most children's art attempts, we may introduce a craft in hopes of producing a cute homemade present for Grandma's birthday. And, of course, a craft can be a good way to keep kids busy. These are all legitimate reasons. However, we need to go easy on crafts. Crafts typically have an end product in mind: a rainbow, a tree or a snowman, for example. For young kids, process—the gluing, coloring or painting—is more important.

If you enjoy crafts yourself and want to share the fun with your child, make sure you leave room for new ideas. Try not to show a model. And if your three-year-old takes the project in a different direction, allow him to explore. Don't stick with a set notion. For example, you might intend to make a colorful paper chain for the holidays, so you get out construction paper and glue. If your child prefers to glue the paper strips together in her own way, let her go. You can make the chain yourself.

A home setting makes exploration easier than a school one. In group settings, group pressure is strong. The teacher shows a model, and kids are usually expected to toe the line and make an identical finished product.

Avoiding Models

"Class, today we're going to make a clown. Everyone gets a paper plate, two round eyes, one square nose and a big triangle for the hat. . . ." Up and down the hallways of preschools and kindergartens, you can see the results of identical art projects. The teacher demonstrates with a model, and the children reproduce it.

Imagine if *you* were trying to copy a Renoir scene. How would you feel? Inadequate. Copying a model can make a child feel bad about art. When four-year-old fingers try to replicate a project an adult did, they usually slip and spill. The lines aren't straight, the nose comes out crooked. Crafts and models often serve the adult's interest, not the child's. They impose ideas, rather than allowing new ideas to flow.

Brendan was a boy who didn't want to make a clown like everybody else. When the teacher passed out the paper plates and glue, he hid under a chair. His teacher made him come out and participate. Heidi, another four-year-old, was happy to do the craft project but wanted to change it.

She tucked some construction-paper hair under the clown's hat, but made it small and on the sly so the teacher wouldn't see it.

What kids like Brendan and Heidi learned:

There is a right way and a wrong way to do art.
The teacher's model is perfect. I can't do it exactly right.
You have to do things just like everyone else.
Art is something grown-ups make you do.
My ideas don't matter.

The song "Flowers Are Red" by Harry Chapin sums it up well. The lyrics tell the tale of a young boy who is bursting with creativity. At school, the teacher tells him, flowers are red, green leaves are green. Everyone must color the same way following the teacher's model. The little boy protests: *There are so many colors in the rainbow, so many colors in the morning sun, so many colors in the flower, and I see every one.* By the time he meets a teacher who accepts his creativity, it's too late. The little boy colors all his flowers red and recites: *Flowers are red, and green leaves are green . . .*

> Models impose a fixed idea and create an expectation of perfection.

In contrast, here's how one three-year-old expanded an art project and made a bit of a mess. Kacy began painting canvas bags with the other children. After a while, she put down her paintbrush and dipped her fingers in the paint. First she painted with her fingertips, then her hands. Soon Kacy expanded to painting with her arms all the way up to her elbows. The paint was washable and Kacy had a glorious time experimenting.

Allow Scary Subjects

As a five-year-old, my dad drew pictures of airplanes dropping bombs. It was the 1940s and he was living through World War II. Bombs and warplanes were on his mind. Even in peaceful times, many young kids are attracted to the power and excitement of explosions, car wrecks and other disasters. So they draw them. Bad guys and bombs are on their minds.

Seeing violent themes in your child's artwork can be unsettling. But free expression through art and stories is essential. It's no different from allowing free expression of play themes in imaginary play. Art is just one more way to express emotions and ideas.

Pictures of death, bombs or fight scenes may be exciting. Young kids like power. Maybe death is something your child is struggling to understand (see Rule 27: Be Buddies with Dead Birds), or he's illustrating a favorite story line. In any case, something about it interests him. Art is an excellent (and safe) way to explore ideas. Far better to let your child express the idea than keep it buried inside. If a child draws a picture of something, that means he wants to explore it. It's on his mind.

Encourage Creative Struggle

Creativity is all about problem-solving, risk taking and experimenting. Let kids struggle a bit. If a child says, "I can't draw a house. You do it for me," be firm. You can say, "I will help you, but I won't do it for you." Helping a child draw could mean staying close by and offering moral support. "If I draw it, then it's my house. What does *your* house look like?"

As parents we sometimes leap in and solve problems, or even direct our child's style. If a child is painting all in one corner of a piece of paper, that's just fine. There's no reason to tell her to spread out. If a child has covered every inch of the paper, you could make an observation: "I see you're painting all over the paper." Or offer information—"If you want more paper, it's on the counter"—rather than swooping to the rescue with a fresh sheet. The point of your child's painting may be to layer all the colors on top of one another.

Before you say, "What a nice bird!" or "What pretty mountains!" find out what the picture means to your child. It may not be a bird or a mountain. React to your child's art by making observations and asking a few key questions. Ask, "Do you want to tell me something about your picture?" The answer might be no.

When you allow art to develop unhindered and invite your child to tell you what's important about her artwork, someday she may use art to express her innermost ideas.

Try This—Add to Your Toolbox

Try unhindered art. Provide materials and give your child space to explore. Children may experiment with texture or color and have little interest in a finished product. Kids will often "expand" an art idea and take things in a new direction. Respect kids' creativity.

For example, you might introduce the idea of splatter paint—splattering paint around an object, maybe a maple leaf. If your daughter fetches other leaves, sticks and bark, she is fully engaged in the idea and expanding on it. Maybe next she'll start blowing paint with a straw or rolling leaves in the paint. You can always curb your young artist's creativity if it threatens to hurt people or property.

Make Room for Art

Keep the basics out and available (markers, crayons, play-dough, glue, paint).

Designate a messy space for art—kitchen, porch, bathtub, art table, outside.

See more tips on mess in the next chapter, Rule 21: Paint off the Paper.

Keep Focused on the Process

Ask "How?" questions.

Let kids stray from your plan.

WORDS TO TRY

Do you want to tell me something about your picture?

How did you do that?

You used a lot of red.

You worked on that picture a long time.

It was tricky to make those boxes stick together. You did it.

I see you covered the whole paper.

If you want more paper, there's some on the counter.

I'll help you, but I won't do it for you.

If I draw it, then it's my house. What does *your* house look like?

What do you want to do with your picture now?

WORDS TO AVOID

What a pretty picture!

What is it?

That's a nice dog you drew.

OK, here's a house for you.

You need more paper. Here's a clean sheet.

Oh, that's not nice. You shouldn't draw pictures like that.

Oh, good job! You're so good at painting.

OUT AND ABOUT

Models, rows of identical artwork and prescribed crafts are most likely to appear in kindergarten and preschools. Look for a program that allows free art, if you can. When you visit a school, it's easy to discover. Just stroll along the hallways and see how many copycat pictures line the walls. If your child's school is big on crafts, you can balance that by giving him lots of opportunities for free-form art at home.

Paint off the Paper

There weren't many rules at my childhood preschool, but this one stands out: "Don't paint other kids, unless they say so."

That's because paint doesn't always stay on the paper there. Children experiment with painting their fingers, bellies, knees and noses. Sometimes a child will paint her entire body green. Or paint her friend's arms purple—but only if she agrees first.

Renegade Reason
Some kids shun art unless you engage their large muscles. Think big. Take art outside.

Neat and tidy art appeals to only some kids. The very nature of typical art projects—stay indoors, sit down, wear a smock and keep clean—can be a turnoff. Sometimes active kids show no interest or get left out. But experiences with art should be something active kids can enjoy, too.

There's no need for art to stay at the table. Expand the environment. Take art outside. What about painting a giant cardboard box? Dan, a five-year-old, was always outside. He disliked sitting at a table and painting primly on a piece of paper. When Dan's teacher brought paints outdoors— into Dan's territory—he painted for a long time. He painted huge stripes. He loved experimenting at the outdoor easel, and jumped at the chance to decorate the bicycle-shed door. Kids like Dan may display zero interest in indoor art activities, but will happily paint something BIG.

Renegade Blessings

Making art big and taking art outside can bring new joy to your child's creative explorations:

> *Art can be for me, too.*
> *My ideas might be different, but we can find a place for them.*
> *I know there are places to be messy and places to be clean.*
> *I can create and discover new things. That's exciting.*

Why It Works

Big is better for young kids' art experiences because it matches their developmental needs. Many children, especially boys, don't have fine-motor control. Projects involving scissors and small paintbrushes can frustrate them. Children must gain strength and coordination with their large muscles before they can control their smaller muscles.

Also, some young kids can't stay on the paper because they haven't yet developed spatial boundaries. Above all, kids' bodies need to move.

Dan Hodgins worked for years doing art with kids at a preschool based at the Mott Community College in Flint, Michigan. He found boys love art that is big and projects they can make using their whole bodies. Introducing *big* brushes—enormous bottle brushes and horse-grooming brushes—makes art more accessible and enjoyable for boys. Hodgins's all-time favorite art tool is painting with a toilet plunger. It's big, it makes neat patterns, and prying off the suction takes power.

When kids get in the habit of doing art when they are young (even before they can control their small muscles), art can become part of their self-identity. A child who likes to run and can't hold a pen yet may see himself as "a kid who does art." Then, when small-motor skills do emerge later, he may continue to enjoy art.

Creativity comes alive for preschoolers when they fully engage their bodies. Using large and small muscles, and as many senses as possible—touch, sound and smell, as well as sight—makes art interesting to kids. Engaging children's emotions makes it meaningful—is it fun? Ticklish? Delightful? Scary? For young kids, art is a full-body experience.

"Art" for young kids is about exploring materials and being creative. It doesn't always look like what we consider art. For example, Jessica played with shaving cream squirted into a tub. First she buried toys in it. Then she wiped it on her body. It tickled. She covered her bellybutton, then her shoulders, arms, legs, toes and hair until every inch was foamy white. As Jessica explored shaving cream, she was engaged in art.

Take Off Your Adult Lenses

Art doesn't have to be a quiet activity where children sit with crayons and glue. Art can be loud and joyous. Add action to art. Paint outside. Color something big: murals, boxes, large paper or wood. Art for a young child is any creative exploration of materials. When we confine art projects to a table, active kids sometimes show no interest. Expand art experiences and help every child discover how wonderful and powerful creativity feels.

Action-oriented art lets kids revel in the process, and helps prevent adult from focusing on the end product.

Expanding Art

At my childhood preschool, kids paint trees purple. They squirt colored dyes at paper hung up on a fence. They walk in paint barefoot and decorate playground equipment. You may not wish to have your trees painted purple, but it's possible to designate one outdoor creative space. What if the kids could paint a climber, a clubhouse or the back of the toolshed?

One mother let her kids paint old window shutters. The children used finger paints and hosed the driveway off afterward. Jacob, age five, loved the cleanup as much as the painting. Isabella, age two, stuck with the shutter painting for a long time, much longer than she usually did with indoor painting. The next day she asked to paint the shutters again.

Adding action to art draws more kids in. Active kids, especially ones who like power games, can discover new joy. Creating something is a powerful activity.

Accommodating Mess

Mess is inevitable. If you allow kids to expand—maybe painting their feet—you'll have even more mess. Give kids some space to be messy—it could be an art table, the porch, the kitchen (with lots of washable surfaces) or even the bathtub. Outside is always great. Expect mess. If an activity gets too messy, change the location, not the idea.

For example, one minute Dylan had a paintbrush and was swirling colors on paper. The next minute, he was dipping his brush in the paint jar and purposefully dripping the paint on the floor. It made a splatter of color as it fell. Dylan watched, fascinated.

What would you say to a child like Dylan? You could ignore the mess, perhaps applaud his creative spirit, and watch the paint pool around the chair and ooze under the fridge. You could stop his dripping the paint on the floor and say, "Keep the paint on the paper! If you can't paint properly, I'm taking the paint away."

There is another way. Set a clear limit, change the location, but let your child continue his idea, if possible. For example: "If you want to drip paint, you need to move outside. The kitchen's not the right place." Dylan will learn, *Oh, I can't do that here. But there's a place for my ideas. I can experiment.* Once outside (maybe on the patio, where it's easy to hose off the mess), you might say: "Wow! Look at those red spots your drips are making!" Most kids' paint is washable. Get your child to help hose off the mess; that's part of the process, and usually a whole lot of fun.

Don't worry if you feel squeamish about mess. I do. All families have different tolerances for mess. Decide where it's OK and where it's not OK. Set expectations. If kids expand beyond what's acceptable, step in and redirect. "You can paint your body, but not here. Only in the bathtub." Or, "I see you're squeezing colors on the floor. If you want to do that, you have to go outside."

Not up to any mess? Maybe your child can be messy at day care or at her cousin's or friend's house instead. Different families have varying tolerance for disorder.

Keeping Artistic Mess in Check

Put paints in trays or dishpans.

Go outside.

Locate projects on washable surfaces (kitchen).

Use the bathtub for messy projects.

Put down an old shower curtain, sheet or tablecloth.

Buy playclothes at the thrift store.

Make great painting smocks out of old adult-size T-shirts.

Materials

Creative experiences do not have to be expensive. Water and mud work well. Items from the recycling bin are great for art projects. Back sides of paper. Old boxes. There's no need to buy pricey art supplies at the store.

Exploring texture is important, as well as color. Let kids try rough and smooth things, thick and soupy things, and sticky and slippery things.

Bev Bos at the Roseville Community School suggests visiting the hardware store to find art supplies and ask: Could children paint with this? Almost anything could work. She uses dog toys, massage rollers and old spindle table legs to roll paint. One of her most active art ideas is to fill nylon stockings with sand, dip them in paint and drop them from a height.

Kids always want *more*. More glue, big piles of beads. Some early-childhood experts urge unlimited access to art materials, especially in a school setting. That's not always possible or desirable. We live on a planet with finite resources. Some materials—sand, mud, water—may be plentiful, but kids can also learn about finite resources. As a five-year-old, I remember drawing on the back of my dad's old lesson plans and learning to reuse paper. Creativity also kicks in when kids have less rather than more. Oh, no more beads? What happens if I add pinecones?

Try This—Add to Your Toolbox

Add action to kids' art. Take materials outside and see what creativity appears. Go to the hardware store for supplies. Raid the recycling bin; use materials from nature. Add on to the traditional lineup of crayons, paints, clay and markers.

Action-Oriented Art

Paint standing up

Paint outside

Zoom toy cars through paint

Run through paint barefoot

Push combs, brushes or other objects through paint

Blow paint using straws or a hairdryer

Paint with rollers

Color something unusual—a pumpkin, seashells, leaves

Paint trees or clubhouses

Decorate large cardboard boxes

Use big brushes: house-painting brushes, scrub brushes or bottle brushes

Spray colored water or paints at paper outside

Drop color bombs (sand inside a stocking, dipped in paint) from a ladder or wall

Throw sand or cornstarch and see what patterns it makes

Finger paint, nose paint or elbow paint

Draw or paint while listening to music or a story

Draw big pictures with sidewalk chalk

Color on large pieces of whiteboard from the hardware store

Use a range of supplies: real wood and nails, recycling items, wire, mud and water

Build something up (taping boxes together or carpentry)

Take something away (carve soap or packaging foam)

WORDS TO TRY
Where could you do that?
If you want to drip paint, you need to move outside.
What would happen if . . . ?

WORDS TO AVOID
Art stays at the table.
You can't do that.

OUT AND ABOUT
Your tree-painting, color bomb–throwing young artist won't be welcome everywhere. Nor should she be. Kids need to learn where mess is OK and where it isn't. That's all part of setting limits. Set expectations as you go. If your daughter is enjoying painting her arms outside, tell her, "That's something we do at home." When you go to the library later that day and they have craft supplies, tell her what's expected in that space: "Paper and glue stay on the table at the library." Set limits and expand art when you can.

Stop Saying "Good Job!"

This is a hard one. "Good job!" dominates our speech as much as "How are you? Have a nice day." Yet phrases like "Good job," "You're so smart" or "That's pretty!" echo with a hollow sound. Kids don't need empty praise. They need meaningful attention and a chance to develop persistence, self-motivation and inner self worth.

Renegade Reason
Acknowledgment is better than praise. Inner satisfaction is better than outside approval.

Why? Showering kids with praise is *not* the same as building healthy self-confidence. Kids need to feel capable in life, to believe they can do many things and take on challenges, and they also need to feel lovable and worthwhile for just being who they are. We can help a child develop that confident outlook, but heaping on praise isn't the answer. In fact, it can backfire. Compare the different feedback two five-year-olds heard at the playground:

"Look at me!" called Bianca, swinging on the monkey bars. She made it halfway across and then fell. "Good job!" said her mother. "Oh, good job, Bianca!"

Natalie started climbing the playground climber, but stopped partway up, nervous about the height. "I'll be right here," said her grandma. "I'm not going to hold you, but I'll stay close so you won't fall." Natalie climbed higher, eventually reaching the top. "You did it. You worked hard to climb up there," said her grandmother. "Wow, you're really up high!"

What did Bianca and Natalie learn?

Bianca learned that swinging on the monkey bars pleased her mother. She didn't need to take a risk or try harder; what was important was pleasing others. Next time, she would seek her mother's approval.

Natalie learned that her grandmother noticed how important getting to the top of the climber was to her. She learned to rely on herself and figure it out on her own. She felt a rush of good feelings—the glow of her own accomplishment plus her grandmother's interest and caring. Next time, she would be ready to try something new even if it was hard. She would keep trying until she got the new skill.

It's hard not to praise our kids. They're cute. They try so hard. We want them to feel good about themselves. It's tempting to reward young kids with stickers and attaboys all day long. But developing persistence and inner confidence is more important than praise. Praise-seeking habits can become destructive, whereas lifelong patterns of self-confidence and persistence lead to success. Tell your child "I love you," but pare down the praise. When children have confidence paired with inner motivation they can meet challenges again and again.

Renegade Blessings

I like a challenge.

I stick to things. If I can't do something at first, I'll keep on trying.

Usually I get better when I work at something.

> *I don't have to seek praise all the time. Stickers and rewards aren't so important.*
> *Adults are interested in what I do: they respect me.*
> *I know I'm loved.*

Why It Works

"Lookit, Dad! Lookit me! Lookit me! Loooook!"

The litany of "lookits" we hear in a day can be brain numbing. Our kids seem to need some sort of answer, so we say, "Good job!" or "Great!" Try counting how many times a day you say, "Good job!" or other praise words to your child. It may surprise you.

Kids are not automatically looking for praise when they beg for our attention. They want to share something they did; they want acknowledgment. A "Lookit me!" doesn't need a "Great!" or "Good job!" to follow it; you can simply say, "I see you!" When we praise too much, we condition ourselves and our children. It's natural for children to share with the adults they love, but when they constantly ask, "Do you like my dress?" "Am I pretty?" "Do you like my picture?" kids are seeking outside praise and approval. By age three or four, some kids have already become praise seekers, a habit that can haunt them throughout life. As teens, they may be desperate for peer approval. As adults, they may doubt their own ideas, lean too heavily on others' opinions (media, friends, spouse), and constantly need rewards from the boss.

Alfie Kohn, author of *Punished by Rewards*, *Unconditional Parenting* and other books, says children and adults often perform below their potential when praise is involved. This happens because people grow to depend on praise and fear taking risks in case they lose outside approval.

> *Limit vague praise words like: great, nice, pretty, smart, good.*

Dr. Carol Dweck's research on persistence shows that children succeed when they develop a "growth" mind-set. These kids face challenges with persistence because they understand they can get better at something by practicing. Saying "You're smart," or "You're pretty," or "You're so good at sports," builds ideas that all these traits are unfalteringly fixed. She found that children who believed they couldn't change the outcome backed away from challenges, didn't take risks and gave up. Don't be afraid to tell children something is hard. Kids actually enjoy a challenge and may try harder when something is deemed difficult.

Helpful praise comes in two parts, Haim Ginott said. First, adults describe what they see or feel ("You got all the way to the top. You're really high up") and then the child reacts to the description and praises herself internally ("I'm pretty good at climbing"). Descriptive praise helps children develop healthy self-confidence. You can find multiple examples of this method in Adele Faber and Elaine Mazlish's book *How to Talk So Kids Will Listen and Listen So Kids Will Talk*.

There's no need to reject all words of praise (you can certainly still say, "Good catch!" when your child catches a ball). It's a question of moderation and specificity. Kids need acknowledgment and descriptive feedback more than they need a string of Good, Great, Awesome!

👓 Take Off Your Adult Lenses

It seems as if our kids are constantly looking for praise. So we supply it: "Good job!"

What children actually crave is our attention and acknowledgment. This helps kids realize they are loved for simply being who they are and lets them discover the inner glow that comes from challenge and effort. Try slicing the empty praise from your vocabulary and offering descriptive words instead. Observations can do more good than judgments.

Process, Not Praise

Hailey was a four-year-old who sought adult approval all the time. She painted pictures of people using two triangles to make the body, trying to make them look like the ones her older sisters made. Nearly every day she painted a figure identical to the one before, and would ask an adult, "Do you like it?"

"What's important is that *you* like it," said her teacher. "Do you?"

Instead of praise—which bestows outside approval—focus on the child's own feelings and her process. Just the way young kids care more about the act of drawing than the final picture, young kids are all about *process* in their play. Talk to kids about how they did something. For example: "How did you make that oven?" "I wonder how you made those Legos so tall?" or turn the question around: "What do you think? Do you like it?"

A process approach also means letting the child see herself stretching into the future. She knows she can get better at something. If we say, "You're so good at drawing!" then the message can be taken as *I'm already good at drawing. I don't have to work harder to be good at it.* Saying "You're good at" something is a stagnant statement that labels the child ("You have brown hair"). Instead, try a comment about process. "You put a lot of details in that picture. I see you worked a long time on it." Process words help kids stretch and grow.

Try This—Add to Your Toolbox

Observe, Don't Judge

When we say "Oh, good girl! That's so nice! Good job!" the praise is vague. Young kids don't always understand what they did that was "nice" or "good" or "pretty." For example, if Danny puts his coloring away and is told, "Good boy," he may have no idea what he did that was good. But when his dad says, "You know how to put caps back on the markers," Danny knows exactly what he did right. Chances are, he also feels the warm glow that comes from being competent, knowledgeable and independent.

Instead of praising, make observations. Observations are specific. It's easy once you get the hang of it. Just state what you see.

INSTEAD OF . . .	STATE WHAT YOU SEE
Good job, Nicky!	You're pumping on the swing by yourself.
You're so good at that!	You got to the top of the climber!
You're so smart.	You know a lot of numbers now. You can count to twelve.
You're so pretty!	I see you put a fancy hat on your head.
Good girl!	Thank you. You picked up your toys.
You're such a good boy.	You know how to put caps back on the markers.
That's a beautiful picture!	You used lots of colors.
That's so nice!	You gave Bobby a turn with the airplane.
That's great!	You did it.

At young ages, children aren't looking for praise, they simply want acknowledgment: Look at me! Look what I did! The simplest is an honest acknowledgment: "You did it," or "Look at you!" "I see you." "You know how to do that." Allow the child to tell you more.

Focus on Persistence

Persistence—taking risks and keeping at it—is another part of process. Don't focus your comments exclusively on your child's accomplishments (praise), but rather notice the struggles. When your child grapples with a jigsaw puzzle, or attempts to zip her jacket, offer encouragement and acknowledgment that the task is challenging. "Zippers can be tricky. I see you are really working at it." Kids often enjoy a challenge and appreciate knowing they are working on something hard. Your acknowledgment—not praise—helps kids develop persistence.

You can reinforce this by telling stories about when your child was "little." For example: "I remember when you couldn't pedal a tricycle. Now you can pedal fast!" Remember, young children are constantly facing new challenges—gaining language, tying their shoes, pumping a swing. It can be comforting for kids to realize that things that once were hard for them (walking, chewing) now come easily. My son Myles loves to hear about how he tried to say my name: "First you said Mully, then you tried Munny, and finally you got it right!" Storytelling is fun and helps reinforce positive traits of persistence.

Avoid False Praise

You know you're diving into the realm of false praise when, as Alfie Kohn says, the words come out in a "squeaky, saccharine voice that slides up and down the scale and bears little resemblance to the way we converse with our friends." Teachers and parents often use false praise manipulatively by saying things like "I like the way my friend Maria is picking up toys." Maria is being used as a tool, not actually being praised. And remember how you used to feel when adults singled out a "good" kid? Chances are, several children are shooting Maria dirty looks and the praise certainly doesn't improve her social standing. "It's snide and indirect," explains Jan Waters, of the School for Young Children. "I like how Maria is picking up means I *don't* like the way anyone else is doing it. Just be direct." Far better to say, "I see toys still on the floor. It's cleanup time."

A Final Word on Praise

"But isn't it good to tell my child she's smart or beautiful once in a while?"

Not really. It's better for your child to *feel* smart and beautiful. A child gains that feeling through your constant affection and your simple interest in who she is: in her thoughts, dreams, actions and unique personality. What does "You're smart" mean? Usually there's another way of saying it: "You figured it out"—"You got that right"—"You really know a lot about dinosaurs." When it comes to looks, especially for little girls, the less said, the better in the early years. Concentrate on noticing their thoughts, actions and ideas instead. (See more in Rule 19: Boys Can Wear Tutus.)

So do your best to cut back on vague praise like "Good job!" and start adding descriptions of what you notice. But when it comes to direct labeling (smart, pretty, athletic)—give those phrases the boot.

□– –□

WORDS TO TRY
Acknowledgment
You did it.
Look at you!
You know how to do that.
You hung up your coat on the peg all by yourself.
You put all the trucks in a row.
You're wearing a fancy dress.
You gave everyone a turn.

Persistence, process and effort

You worked hard at solving that problem.

I see you spent a long time building blocks.

Wow! That looks tricky. You're trying to make a tall tower and
 it's not easy.

I wonder how you built such a tall tower.

How did you do that?

What do you like about it?

WORDS TO AVOID

Good job! That's great! (avoid at least most of the time)

What a nice picture! That's so pretty.

That's so nice.

You're pretty/beautiful.

You're such a good girl/good boy.

You're so smart!

You're so good at jumping/drawing . . . (makes the child's talent
 seem fixed)

I really like how Maria is picking up.

OUT AND ABOUT

You can improve on vague "Good job!" praise when someone
else says it by simply adding a descriptive observation after it.
"Good job, Leah!" then becomes "Good job, Leah! You put your
shoes away in the closet. You know how to be responsible." This
works well for yourself, too, when you're trying to break the
"good job" habit. Focus on adding descriptive sentences about
process and effort first, and pretty soon the number of "good
jobs!" will dwindle away. Remember to be gracious; often the
best response to well-intended praise is "Thank you."

Bad Words, Polite Words and Lies

Moral principles are like measles. They have to be caught.

—Aldous Huxley

Kids Don't Have to Say "Sorry"

Two-year-old Danny crashes into another child at the playground and knocks her down. Aghast, his mother rushes up. "Say 'Sorry!'" she commands. "Sorry," repeats Danny. Then he ignores the girl and continues his game.

Renegade Reason
Saying "Sorry" is a cop-out. Take action instead to set things right.

Young kids love the word "sorry." Like magic, it lets them off the hook. Push someone? Elbow someone? Step on a picture? Just say "Sorry" and you're scot-free. It's a little like teaching kids to be hit-and-run drivers.

What we want to teach kids is to stick around the scene, to take responsibility for their actions, and understand that their words, arms and legs can impact other people.

First, kids must realize what they did. What's obvious to you—your son knocked somebody down—needs to be pointed out. To young kids, cause and effect often remain mysterious. Your child thinks, *Really? The way I jumped (or drove my trike, or swung a toy) caused an accident? Oh. I was just playing.* Tell them the facts: "You swung your lunch box and hurt Lucy's arm. Look—it hurts. She's crying."

Sticking around the scene also helps kids develop empathy for the child who got hurt. Ask, "Are you OK?" Take the time together to look at the other child's tear-stained face. Examine the red mark. You might say, "Look—that's where the owie is. She's really crying. It must hurt a lot." Then take steps to help.

Once the child who caused the problem fully understands what happened, it's time to take action. "Sarah is still sad you bumped her. Can you get her a tissue?" Often kids are grateful to have something tangible to do. *A rescue mission! I can't make Sarah's leg stop hurting, but I can make it better.* Young kids are good at taking action and often delight in running to get a towel, a tissue, an ice pack, a teddy bear or somebody's mommy or daddy.

Renegade Blessings

Eventually, your child will say "Sorry" and really mean it. For now, action and observation teach deeper skills. Here's what she can learn by not being forced to say "Sorry":

> *My actions have consequences. Sometimes what I do hurts somebody else.*
> *I can understand how someone else might be feeling.*
> *I can do something to make it better.*
> *I have time to understand and feel remorse.*
> *When I do say "Sorry," I really mean it. I feel bad for what I did.*

Take Off Your Adult Lenses

Young kids are rarely sorry. Many haven't even reached a stage of moral development to feel sorry yet. Don't force apologies. Instead, help kids set things right by getting a tissue or an ice pack. Learning to say "Sorry" lets kids off the hook, but saying "I won't knock your bike over again" offers meaningful safety. Model manners, but don't demand them prematurely.

Why It Works

Young kids sometimes fool us. They can mimic "Sorry" and even cry when another child cries, but most children are not capable of being sorry yet. Children differ—you may have an early bloomer—but most children simply lack the emotional and cognitive development to feel remorse. Remorse requires the ability to take another person's perspective and fully understand cause and effect. These skills are still emerging in young children. Expecting young kids to say "Sorry" teaches them nothing more than a misguided lesson in sequence: kick, say "Sorry," move on.

As parents we want to raise caring kids. Unfortunately, "Sorry" gets in the way of teaching empathy. William Damon, renowned researcher on child moral development and author of *The Moral Child*, says moral awareness in children needs to be guided but it cannot be imposed. When parents demonstrate empathy, it helps children develop moral compassion.

Compassion will evolve naturally, agree early childhood experts Janis Keyser and Laura Davis, authors of *Becoming the Parent You Want to Be*. We worry it won't and insist our kids say "Sorry" to teach them to be compassionate, but Keyser and Davis say compassion only needs to be supported. Bring children together to communicate, model respect for feelings, and kids will have a chance to show their caring. They write: "Children who are given the opportunity to participate in helping the other child feel better often do amazing things."

Action, Not Words

My son Zach was visiting his grandmother's class of three-year-olds at the School for Young Children. He joined in a fast running game with five other boys, including Charlie, a tall and awkward child. When Charlie runs, he tends to crash into playmates in his excitement. It was inevitable when Charlie collided with Zach head-on. Zach howled in pain and climbed into my lap. The next thing we knew, three ice packs arrived, thrust forward by eager little fingers. Charlie and two other three-year-olds had run to take action. Charlie stayed at the scene and asked Zach, "Are you OK?"

These children have learned how important it is to take action, and how good it feels to help someone. Charlie took responsibility and didn't run away (nobody got mad at him, either). He went back to the game only once Zach was up and feeling better.

"Young kids aren't sorry," says Jan Waters of the School for Young Children. "They can't be sorry, but they are good at taking action."

Young kids are always getting banged or bonked—on purpose or by accident. This gives us lots of chances to help kids practice skills of empathy and responsibility. Most childhood bruises are not serious. Comfort the hurt child, but remember, the child who can learn most from the situation is usually the one who caused it.

Make a Guarantee

"Sorry" pleases adults, but is not meaningful to young kids.

When two kids collide, emotions are sure to burst out, but remorse is not likely to be one of them. Young kids are rarely sorry.

The kid who caused the collision may be scared—afraid a grown-up will get mad at him—or embarrassed or even mad at himself for hurting someone. The child who gets hurt is also sad, mad and scared. Sad because it hurts, mad because she didn't like being pushed, and scared because of the shock and surprise. Chances are, she's especially scared about getting hurt again. *This kid just pushed me. Will she do it again?* "Sorry" doesn't make it better.

What the hurt child finds much more meaningful is a guarantee that she won't be pushed/kicked/hit again. Instead of extracting a "Sorry," try reestablishing trust. For example: "Tell him, 'I won't hit you again!'" or "Tell him, 'I won't hurt your body.'" Boldly ask, "Are you going to hit him again?" Make sure both kids hear the answer. Repeat it in a big voice for them if there's any doubt: "Rachel, Jack says he won't push you against the wall anymore." If it truly is an accident, kids can offer a guarantee like this: "I'll watch out for you so we don't crash again." Reassurance that it won't happen again means something. "Sorry" does not.

> A guarantee—"I won't push you again"—is more meaningful than "sorry."

What happens if a child refuses or answers "Yes!" when you ask, "Are you going to hit him again?" Step in with a firm limit. You can empathize, "You still feel like hitting, but it's not OK to hurt Parker. I will help your body stop." Reassure the other child, "I will keep you safe. I won't let him hit you." See more on limits in Rule 2: It's OK If It's Not Hurting People or Property.

Accident or Not?

"Oh, it was an accident. I know she didn't mean to do that."

Maybe. Maybe not. Don't assume you know a child's intentions. Saying these words seems innocent, but the truth is, we often don't know. The goal is to teach children responsibility for their actions. Dismissing an event as "just an accident" lets kids off the hook, too.

Kids sometimes do aggressive acts on purpose, and kids age four and up can get sneaky about it. It could be they're retaliating for a past conflict that hasn't been resolved. Whatever the reason, don't assume you know it, or that your child is always innocent. Responsibility for action is important—whether the act is intentional or not.

Modeling "Sorry"

Of course, eventually we do want to hear our kids say "Sorry." It's a cultural norm. But teaching manners works best through modeling manners. Young kids can be trained to parrot "I'm sorry" without meaning it, but the phrase becomes meaningful when you demonstrate. T. Berry Brazelton, author of *Touchpoints* and other books on child development, says modeling works because it introduces children to what's appropriate but lets them discover their own social rewards. So go ahead and say "Sorry" yourself, but don't insist they say it.

When you model making apologies, say "Sorry" and include a plan to do better. For example: "I'm sorry I ruined your picture. I didn't realize it was important to you. I'll ask next time before I recycle it." Or "Oh, I'm sorry! I promised to bring your bike and I forgot. What can we do to help me remember?"

Raising Myles this way, I began to wonder if he even knew *how* to say "Sorry." Was this modeling method really working? Then, at age five, he stepped hard on my foot. "I'm sorry. I didn't mean to do that," he said with genuine care in his voice. I never prompted him to say "Sorry," yet the lesson had sunk in. Now he pulls it out whenever he needs it.

Try This—Add to Your Toolbox

Try these steps for everyday accidents. If the action is purposeful (Eva shoves Jesse, and it's no accident), then unravel the situation using conflict mediation. See Rule 3: Kids Need Conflict.

When involved in an accident, some children instinctively run. Bring them back. Put an arm around the child and say, "You need to come back here. Ben got hurt. Maybe you didn't mean to do it, but Ben got hurt."

For Everyday Accidents

1. Bring the children together.
2. Tell the child who caused the accident what happened—be specific: "Your bike knocked into her body."
3. Describe what you see: "She's crying. Her leg is bleeding."
4. Model empathy for the hurt child: "Are you OK?"
5. Take action. "Go get a tissue! Here, bring her this Band-Aid."
6. Give a guarantee: "James says he won't crash into you again. He'll bike on the sidewalk."
7. Model saying "Sorry" in your own life.

For Other Conflicts

1. Ask the child who got hurt, "Did you like it when he pushed you? Tell him!"
2. Bring the children together and follow conflict-mediation steps.

3. Extract a promise: "Tell him you won't push him again." Repeat it in a loud voice so both kids are clear: "Jack says he won't push you."

4. If a child refuses, make the promise yourself: "I will keep you safe." Then set a firm limit.

Watching compassion unfold in your child is beautiful. Kids who aren't forced to say "Sorry" often open their arms in a hug or spontaneously offer their food or blankie. Explain the situation clearly, suggest something your child can *do*, and you'll be surprised to see how genuinely caring and compassionate your child can be.

WORDS TO TRY

Responsibility and Action

You need to come back. This girl got hurt.

Maybe you didn't mean to, but she got hurt. We need to check and see if she's OK.

When you were running fast, you knocked her down.

Are you OK?

Look—she's crying. It hurts.

Run and get a tissue (ice pack, teddy bear, pillow, Band-Aid).

Thank you. That might help her feel better.

Child-to-child guarantees

Saying "Sorry" isn't enough. You need to tell Jesse you won't push him again.

Are you going to push him again?

Eva, if you want to play with Jesse, you have to follow his rule: No pushing.

WORDS TO AVOID
Tell him you're sorry.
Say "Sorry!"
Where are your manners?
It was an accident.
She didn't mean that.

OUT AND ABOUT
You won't be able to stem the tide of "Sorry" out there. Parents are quick to rebuke perceived rudeness, even in two-year-olds. The other day at the library, I saw a mother drag along a tot who seemed to be about twenty months old. "That was rude," she said. "Do you understand Mama? You can't be rude to other people like that. You have to say 'Sorry' to the other boy."

If another child trots up and says, "Sorry," you can simply say "Thank you" and tell your child, "He was checking to see if you were OK." If the situation allows, you can always go deeper. If it's your child who caused a problem, bring her back to the scene. Help her take caring action and make a guarantee that means more than "Sorry."

Let Your Kid Swear

Jillian was five years old. She knew her mother didn't like hearing the word "stupid." So she said it.

"That's not a word we use in our family," her mother said.

Jillian looked her mother in the face.

"Stupid Mommy," she replied.

No matter what word is "bad" in your family, many kids savor the shock value. They like to see you jump. Bad words are powerful words, and young kids want to experience power. Help your child learn social conventions and learn to use power wisely. You can save your ears and give kids freedom of speech—by changing the timing and location.

Renegade Reason
Most kids love to say banned words, so let them—in the bathroom.

Bad words vary by family. Some make a sailor blush. Some are potty talk. In other homes, words like "stupid," "dummy," "shut up" or "boring" are banned. No matter what your tastes, you have the right to set limits on words you don't want to hear. But be wary. Complete censorship usually backfires.

"Poop!" said Ben, a five-year-old. All his friends dissolved into giggles, and their teacher reacted spectacularly. Nearby, Emma got a mischievous glint in her eye: "Poop—poop—poop—poop—poop," she chanted.

Censoring speech has two major problems. One is practical: You can't control spoken words. Just as you can't force your child to sleep, you can't truly stop her from saying something. The other is human nature: Banning anything creates an illicit thrill. Kids gain an extra jolt of delight when they use a forbidden word. It's just too tempting. Besides, your reaction is bound to be exciting.

Instead, say yes to bad words. Keep your face calm. Try to give no reaction. Then offer your tot information: "That's a word grown-ups use when they're very angry. If you want to say that word, you need to do it in the bathroom." When you give kids a place for free expression, you diminish the thrill of censorship.

Renegade Blessings

By allowing free speech—within limits—you can teach your child how to explore the power of speech and use it wisely:

I can say bad words, but it's not that exciting. Nobody watches me.

I know what the bad words mean. They're not so mysterious.

There are times and places for bad words, just like everything else.

I know some people, like my grandmother, can get really hurt by bad words. I don't want to hurt her.

When I get mad, sometimes it helps to say a powerful word.

Mean words are different. It's not OK to call names and use words to hurt people.

Why It Works

Eric was a three-year-old with an extensive vocabulary. One day he got furious at his mother and wanted to call her something awful. He summoned up the biggest word he could find and shouted, "You . . . you . . . you . . . *radiator!*"

Cursing is an exploration into power, say Laura Davis and Janis Keyser, authors of *Becoming the Parent You Want to Be*. Younger children's curses may be "dummy" and "poo-poo head" or even "radiator." Older preschoolers often pick up grown-up curse words. Tim Jay, author of *What to Do When Kids Talk Dirty*, says it's natural that preschool-age children are fascinated by bodies and potty talk, since potty training has played a big part in their young lives.

When children bring home bad words and try them out on you, they are fishing for information. *What's an appropriate response to this word? How does this word affect people?* Young kids understand that curse words are emotionally charged. They try to figure out why the word is so special by trying it out again and again and witnessing the reaction. Sometimes a child uses a dramatic word just to get attention. Davis and Keyser suggest offering information: "If you're trying to get my attention, you could say, 'Mom, I really need you.'"

Stephanie Rottmayer, director at the School for Young Children, says bad words are mostly a big deal for adults, not kids. Young kids lose interest if adults don't reward cursing with a strong reaction. "Sometimes it's just fine for a group of kids to get together and say bad words. They aren't hurting anybody. They are laughing and having fun together," she says. But it's important to give kids information so they understand who feels uncomfortable hearing those words and what times and places are considered socially inappropriate for saying them.

Powerful Language

"Bad words" fall into many categories. There are power words (swear words), body words (potty talk) and family-specific bad words (like "stupid" or "shut up"). These can be dealt with by offering freedom of speech in a limited location. Other bad words are more serious and need additional steps, including mean words (name-calling) and sexually explicit words.

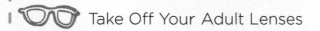 Take Off Your Adult Lenses

We ban bad words because we don't like to hear them. But speech is meant to be controlled, not censored. Lift the ban, but keep your ears happy, too. Teach her what's acceptable by giving her information and a degree of freedom. A child should be free to say anything she wants—in her bedroom or in the bathroom. There's a time and place for everything, even bad words.

Swear Words = Power Words

Think about why adults curse. Why are some words vulgar and "bad" and other words good? Most of us need a few powerful words to call on when times get tough. When we smash our finger in the car door or drop our cell phone in the toilet, even the most mild-mannered mom might yell an expletive. As six-year-old Calvin says in the comic strip *Calvin and Hobbes*, "Life's disappointments are harder to take if you don't know any swear words." Of course, some people love casual cursing, but then the power evaporates. Swear words keep their intensity only when we hold them in reserve for times of extreme stress and anger.

Keeping that reason in mind helps us stay objective when it comes to young kids and swearing. Because, face it, when a three-year-old shouts, "You s***head!" we lose our objectivity. Fast. If your child says something that pushes your buttons, just walk away.

> *If you don't want your child to swear, then don't swear yourself. Model saying "gosh," "dang," "fiddlesticks" and "shoot" or try out something new like "Thundercrackers!"*

Language is generally rated PG at our house. However, my husband loses his cool occasionally, and when he does, three-year-old Zach perks right up. Zach loves the intensity of his papa's voice. He loves its power and the drama of the new words. Then he likes to try it out himself.

One morning at our house we ran out of Rice Krispies.

"Dammit!" shouted Zach. "Oh, goddammit!"

"Where'd he learn that?" my husband asked.

Swear words mean nothing to young kids, but children are attracted to their power. If you don't want your child to swear, then don't swear yourself. This strategy can work temporarily—perhaps until school age, when peers supply new data.

Potty Words

Bodies are fascinating, and many kids delight in bathroom noises and vocabulary. Potty talk is age-appropriate and often hysterically funny to kids. There is nothing wrong in allowing four-year-old friends to giggle together—it can actually be a positive form of social bonding. Most adults don't find it half as entertaining as kids do, so be prepared to shift the conversation's location.

For example, Deb, a teacher at the School for Young Children, set up a "Poop House" in one corner of the classroom when a small gang of kids wanted to do lots of potty talking. She delineated the area with blocks and announced, "Kids can say whatever they want in here. If you want to say poop words, say them in here." The Poop House did its job. It gave a safe, contained area for free speech. Other kids and teachers didn't have to hear it. The children in the Poop House laughed and laughed and had a good time together. Eventually they grew bored with the novelty and moved on to other play. At home, you can do the same: set up a designated area where kids can get their giggles out.

Family-Specific Bad Words

In one house it's "shut up." In another it's "butt." If you have words you don't like to hear, try figuring out what type of word it is. Do you dislike it because it's a mean, name-calling name? Or because it's potty talk? Model language you do want to hear and deal with "bad words" according to their type.

Adult Bombs

An interest in potty talk and common swear words is natural for preschoolers, but be wary if your sweet five-year-old starts dropping truly X-rated adult words. He's being exposed to things he shouldn't. There's no way you can erase an adult word from his vocabulary (let him say it in his bedroom if he has to), but sexually explicit words, along with other warning signs, could indicate sexual abuse. Track down where he heard the word. If the source worries you—say, an older teen or an adult in the neighborhood—investigate your child's safety.

Mean Words

If Suzy calls Sarah a "stupid head," the issue is less about the word, and more about anger and hurt feelings. Don't focus on her word choice ("That's not nice, you shouldn't say 'stupid'"). Focus on the feeling beneath the word. You might say, "You sound mad at Sarah! I wonder what happened?" Use conflict-mediation steps to sort it out.

What about when you're the target? Mean words from your child can really sting. Take a deep breath. Disregard the word and state his feelings: "You're really mad that you can't have another cookie." See more in Rule 6: "I Hate You!" Is Nothing Personal.

Try This—Add to Your Toolbox

Even if you don't swear at home, bad words will someday enter your child's vocabulary. If you don't like hearing it, here's what you can do.

Be Dull

Kids love attention. If your child can get a rise out of you by saying a bad word, what fun! Stop the excitement. Be dull and calm. Talk in your regular voice and give a brief reply. If you can't answer calmly, then just walk away. Deny your child the fun of getting a reaction from you.

Change the Location

When your child swears or talks about poop at the dinner table, give him an option where he can say that word. The bathroom is a great spot. Maybe your child's bedroom with the door closed, or outside. Allow free expression but change the location. This method protects your rights—you don't want to hear it—but avoids falling into the trap of banned words. For example: "If you need to say that word, go into the bathroom. You can say that word as much as you want, but not at the dinner table."

Offer Information

My son came home from school one day when he was five.

"I know a bad word," said Myles. He glanced up at me with a wicked sparkle in his eyes.

"What makes you think it's a bad word?" I asked.

"Katy told me not to say it."

"What is it?" I asked.

"Traction," he said proudly.

Bad words seem especially powerful when kids don't know what they mean. And most kids don't. Words are typically censored, not explained. Little gangs of kids giggle over bad words and spread misinformation. When I was a little girl, I remember experimenting with a swear word in the car one day. My mother was silent for a moment and then told me it meant female dog. I was thoroughly disappointed. Knowing the true meaning robbed it of its zing.

When you first hear your child use a bad word, help her out. Explain what the word means (see Rule 26: Sex Ed Starts in Preschool). Tell her, "You can always ask me what any word means and I will tell you." Discuss where it might be OK to say it and who doesn't like to hear it. Take out the mystery and offer accurate information. Kids are grateful to learn more—no one likes to be embarrassed.

Go Scientific

An interest in bad words may mean your child needs more information about how his body works and what's private and what's not. Get out a book about the human body. Point out parts of the digestive system. Explain which parts of the body are private. Teach your child some new words. Tell them "butt" is short for "buttocks." What about "esophagus"? Kids love big words. Saying a big word like "esophagus" conveys lots of power. Taking the scientific approach often takes the wind out of the little jokesters' sails.

Invent New Power Words

My six-year-old swore at the breakfast table the other day. I smiled. He was trying out the power of his new swear word: "picklerash."

Encourage your child to create his own personal power word. If your child echoes the R-rated words you let slip out, try this: "That's a strong word. That's Mommy's strong word when I get really mad. Do you need a strong word, too?" Help your child pick out a special word that's just her own.

Kids this age get creative, and many delight in having their own personal word. I know a whole family that used to say "Sugarjets." Whenever my husband got mad as a boy he'd yell out "Funnelburgers!" My son Zach chose to shout "Chop! Chop!" Myles favors long words: "Picklerash," "Blumpfenzine" or sometimes "Hippokaloric!" These words tickle kids' funny bones and bestow great power and control. "That's my word," Myles will tell his father. "You can't say it, it's just my word. When I say 'picklerash,' you'll know I'm mad!"

Using a substitute word in another language can work, too. I met a six-year-old who swore in German when he was mad. *"Scheiss!"* he'd call out. This was his code word. Since few people in Maine understood German, he was relatively safe using his powerful swear word. Some kids love this approach because the word is "real."

Investigate Racist and Sexist Slurs

Tread carefully if racist or other offensive slur words show up in your child's vocabulary. They may signal danger. Exactly where did this word come from? Whose company is he keeping? Do you have concern for your child's safety? If a slur is used in name-calling, address the conflict first, then investigate the word's source.

As when children use other bad words, ignorance is often the reason, so offer information and firm social limits. For example, my son Myles likes to name imaginary countries. One time he named one "Nig-ger." I told him his chosen name was already a word and explained its meaning. "That's a very mean word for people with dark-colored skin. It's so mean people don't say it anymore, not even grown-ups. It hurts people very much." Depending on your family's racial background, you might explain it differently.

WORDS TO TRY

If you need to say that word, go into the bathroom.

You can say that word as much as you want, but not at the dinner table.

Do you know what it means? I can tell you.

You can always ask me what any word means and I will tell you.

Let's talk about where it's OK to say that word and where it's not.

Sounds as if you're interested in how bodies work.

That's a word grown-ups say when they're angry.

Do you need a strong word, too? What word could you say when you get really mad?

WORDS TO AVOID

We don't say that word in this house.

That's not a word you can say.

Don't ever let me hear you say that word again!

Don't talk to me like that!

OUT AND ABOUT

Sometimes sending your child to the bathroom to swear isn't an option. You might be nowhere near a private spot like the bathroom. One option is to find one. Move your child outside, sit in the car, find a deserted corner where your child can spout off. Another option is to impose a time delay. "You can say that word as much as you want at home in your bedroom, but not right now in the store." Kids will often comply if they realize they can still do what they want to do—just later. Wherever you are, remember to focus on feelings.

Love Your Kid's Lies

If you're looking for an "honest" answer from your three-year-old, you have about four years to wait. Although kids can lie as young as age two, and many four-year-olds start telling regular fibs, a true understanding of morals, honesty and conscience does not kick in until later.

Don't be a stickler for truth. When "lies" come up, use them to guide your child toward open communication and self-awareness. Young kids lie for many reasons, but mostly they lie to please us—so don't get mad.

Renegade Reason
Young kids lie to express wishes and try to control their world. Your reaction matters more than her lie.

It's a universal shock when your three- or four-year-old tells his first whopper:

"I did. I washed my hands."

"No, you couldn't have, there was no water running. Don't lie to me."

When kids push our lie button, we jump. Lying deeply offends us. Often we lash out when kids lie to "teach" them honesty.

Lying is a natural and normal part of development, and although young kids say things that are not true, these lies are not malicious. If you look at kids' lies, you'll see that often children are working hard to please us. *What could I say that will make Mom happy? She wants me to have washed my hands. I can say, "I did."* Kids tell us what they think we want to hear. They lie to stay out of trouble or get what they want. Children also lie for playfulness. They lie to experiment. Kids try to change the world with their words and make the world match their make-believe.

 Take Off Your Adult Lenses

When a young child "lies," she is doing her best to say the right thing. It's not a morality crisis. She is trying to please you and protect herself. She is not purposefully dodging the truth to anger you and is not being "bad." Punishment doesn't stop lies (kids lie to avoid punishment). Instead, show your child that you like the truth, and she will alter her behavior to please you.

A young child's lie is a wish or an emotion. It's a sophisticated attempt by the child to control her world with language. Recognize her effort to say the right thing, and teach her what to do instead.

Renegade Blessings

Children who experience no shame or punishment when they lie gradually learn these valuable life lessons:

My parents like it when I tell the truth. That's what pleases them.
Wishing about something is fun to do, but it doesn't change reality.

> *If I do something wrong, it doesn't make me a bad person.*
> *It's hard to admit I was wrong or did something wrong, but*
> *I can do it.*
> *It's safe to tell my parents things, even difficult things.*

Why It Works

There's good reason to love your little liars. Ongoing research from psychologist Victoria Talwar and others shows that children lie to make their parents happy. The more we learn about lying, the more we learn it's a complex social skill, often involving a combination of self-protection and increasing another person's happiness. Children alter their stories to please adults.

Children will answer in the best way they see to avoid punishment, please people and get what's best for themselves. T. Berry Brazelton says it's unreasonable to expect children ages three to six to fully understand the benefits of honesty.

Think about why we value honesty. Honest relations help us live in a just and caring community. Lies can hurt people. But, then again, so can blunt honesty, which is why many adults consider white lies to be a form of caring and respect. If you want to teach honesty, model honesty as well as being caring and kind.

Punishment isn't a great way to teach morality. After all, morality is about what's good and right, and how best to live together in a society. One of the main reasons kids (and adults) lie is to protect themselves from punishment. Talwar's research shows punishment doesn't stop lies. Instead, children become more sophisticated at lying. Once children learn that

> *A child's lie is not a crisis in morality. Her conscience will unfold in its own time.*

lies are bad and may get them punished, they don't stop lying, they just try harder not to get caught. They become more ingenious liars.

The ability to lie shows a child is able to think from another person's perspective. *I spilled the paint. But she doesn't know—she didn't see me.* Although this newfound ability to take another's viewpoint may show up as a lie, it's also an important step in developing empathy. Parents can guide this emerging morality, but shouldn't rush it. Complex moral reasoning takes further brain development.

Can Young Kids Lie?

For years psychologists who studied young children thought kids six and under couldn't lie. They just weren't cognitively capable. Today it's believed that kids do lie, but at best it's confused lying. Effective lying frequently starts after age six, when kids have the mental power to spin a consistent story, but even then, moral understanding is not mature.

Robert Coles, a Harvard psychiatrist, has extensively researched morality in children. In his book *The Moral Intelligence of Children*, Coles says that children don't develop full moral reasoning until ages seven to eight. However, just as with emotional intelligence, adults can help guide children as their moral intelligence develops. Australian researcher Kay Bussey confirms that although children may start experimenting with lies at ages two to three, it's not until age eight that children fully comprehend truth and realize that telling the truth can make you feel better.

Young lies, then, fall in their own category. Two- and three-year-olds may confuse reality with fantasy. Kids age four and up may know they are lying, but not fully understand complex concepts like honesty.

Children's "lies" suddenly become less threatening when viewed as what they are: Attempts to please. Experiments with new abilities. The desire not to get hurt. When you look at it this way, the emotional charge drops. You no longer feel so betrayed and maligned. You can stay in the mode of active parenting—trying to understand your child—rather than reacting to the flashpoint of *being lied to*.

Young Lies As Wishful Thinking

If you stop and listen, kids display harmless wishful thinking throughout the day. My son Zach wanted to eat a sticky Popsicle in the house. Since he's usually a mess of drips, Popsicles are outside food for us. Zach wanted to be inside today.

"It's raining," he said.

"No, it's not. It's a nice day."

"It's raining! Wet! Wet! I have to eat inside."

Zach was doing wishful or magical thinking. By stating, "It's raining," he was not lying, but rather expressing a wish and trying to control his world.

Here's a common "lie" uttered by a potty-training child:

"Did you just poop?" asks the father.

"No, I didn't!" says the two-year-old.

"I smell something stinky," says the father. "We have to change your diaper."

The "No, I didn't!" is a wish. Your tot may be thinking, *I wish I hadn't. I don't want to stop playing.*

When this happens, try translating your child's wish. Verbalize the inner wish to bring the real meaning to light. For example: "You don't want to stop playing. You wish you hadn't pooped. But you did. We'll take a quick break and come right back to playing."

Most parents make light of the weather-changing wish or the stinky-diaper denial, but frown on lies that involve breaking rules. To the child's mind, it's all the same. When she breaks a rule or makes up a story to cover a misdeed, the young child is still trying to express wishes and get her needs met.

Avoiding Blame and Lie Traps

"Did you break that lamp?"

"No."

"Don't lie to me. I saw you swinging your Lego plane right into it."

The scenario above is a common lie trap. We already know what the child did, but something drives us to question him and try to extract an "honest" answer. It leads to an unnecessary power struggle about who's right and who's wrong. Don't ask, "Did you do this?" if you already know what happened.

To a young child, *no* is his attempt to protect himself and also please you. Just like the stinky-diaper answer, he wishes he hadn't broken the lamp. He would like someone else to be the one who did it. Maybe he's scared of being punished. Most of all, he doesn't want to lose your affection.

No could mean:

No—I wish I hadn't broken it.

No—I wish someone else had caused the problem.

No—I'm not bad. I'm not the kind of kid who does bad things.

No—I'll say I didn't do it, and then you will still love me.

No—I don't want to be punished.

Nobody likes blame, even if it's rightfully placed. When kids are caught in a fix and don't know how to get out of it, they will often lie to distance themselves from the bad act. Kids respond this way when they feel trapped. "I didn't do it!" or "Brown teddy did it, not me!" Teach them what to do when they feel trapped. Offer statements and questions to guide them to what's right. Here's how it might go:

"I see the lamp is on the floor."

"Yeah, it just fell."

"I know lamps don't fall all by themselves."

"It did! I was just watching and it fell."

"When you break something, you have to tell me about it."

"I didn't do it."

"I bet you wish you hadn't done it."

"I wish I hadn't. I just sort of touched it. I didn't know it would break . . ."

When you show understanding, kids usually share what really took place. When I confront Myles with a transgression, this generally happens right after I say, "I bet you wish you hadn't done it." Like magic, the real story spills out.

Guide, Don't Chide

The other day I caught three-year-old Zach white-handed. His right hand was smeared with something white and glossy, and when he saw me he hastily wiped it on his pants. My husband had just finished a small painting project and had left the brush and paint can out in the barn.

"What's that?" I asked.

"Nothing."

"Looks like you touched Papa's paint," I said.

"No," said Zach.

The white paint streaks stood out boldly on his navy-blue pants.

"Hmm . . ." I said. "Let's go look. Show me where the paint is."

Zach trotted right to the paint can and showed me where he'd dipped his fingers. He helped me wash up the mess.

Keep a lid on your own anger when your child lies. Try to keep your voice neutral even if it irks you. Children often lie because they hope to avoid their parents' anger (even if there is no other punishment). Show him how to make amends, and let him know that telling the truth pleases you.

Don't Suppress Creative Tales

When children come up with obviously outrageous tales, don't worry about true and false. Enjoy the story (My unicorn lives under that tree and every night she . . .) and acknowledge its creativity. "And then what did the unicorn do?" This is the age of freewheeling imagination, and creative kids may concoct elaborate fantasies. No need to point out they're not "real." If she's trying to shift blame for a misdeed to an imaginary friend, then help her deal with mistake-making.

Try This—Add to Your Toolbox

Don't Ignore Lies

Being in a stage of developing morality is not free license to lie. While two-year-olds may not grasp truth or falsehood, older preschoolers ages four to six have a much better idea. Don't ignore young lies when they come up, but rather guide kids in an age-appropriate manner.

Teach your child how to deal with problems, make mistakes, cope with the sting of embarrassment, and get into the practice at a young age of fessing up. She may not have full moral reasoning yet, but she can start to develop good habits. Lies are usually linked to uncomfortable feelings like fear, envy, frustration or shame, so help her grapple with these prickly emotions. Kids crave your understanding. The more practice your child gets in acknowledging missteps in a safe environment, the easier it will be for her to make honest admissions as she grows.

Steps to Unravel a Lie

1. Make observations about what you see. (I see red crayon writing on the wall.)
2. Offer information. (Walls are not for writing. If you want to use crayons, you have to do it on paper.)
3. Acknowledge wishes for what they are. (I bet you wish that's the way it happened.)
4. Empathize. (I don't like making mistakes. Sometimes when I make a mistake, I feel bad and wish somebody else had done it.)
5. Give the child a job, if possible, to fix the situation. (Get a washcloth or broom)
6. Problem solve together. (What can we do to help you remember? Write a reminder sign, "Don't Touch the Fish Tank," move the temptation and so on.)

Guide your child with empathy and then problem solve together. You want your child to understand what went wrong and not repeat it. You also want her to tell you when problems come up, even (or especially) when the situation is hard to talk about. Keep calm and keep communication open: "You can always tell me when something like this happens." All this builds on her emerging moral abilities and sets the stage for her to succeed in the future.

WORDS TO TRY
Responding to young lies
Did you wish . . . ?
I know you wish that's the way it happened.

I bet you wish you hadn't done it.

It's hard not to touch the computer when it's sitting out.

I don't like making mistakes. Sometimes when I make a mistake, I wish somebody else had done it. Do you feel like that, too?

It's hard to be the one who makes a mistake.

Making amends

When you break something, you have to tell me about it.

It's hard, but it's important to tell someone.

You can always tell me. I won't get mad. I really like it when you tell me the truth.

When you make a mistake, you have to help fix it.

There's a mess on the floor. We need a mop.

What can we do to help you remember?

WORDS TO AVOID

Are you lying to me?

Don't lie to me!

You know that's not true. I saw it happen.

OUT AND ABOUT

You'll certainly hear people say, "Don't lie to me!" There's no point in trying to shield your child from hearing adult rage on the topic. What matters most is your personal reaction. Follow up another adult's "Don't lie!" statement with a calm approach to unraveling a lie.

Sensitive Subjects

Courage is what it takes to stand up and speak; courage is also what it takes to sit down and listen.

—Winston Churchill

Sex Ed Starts in Preschool

When I mentioned to a group of parents that I started sex ed with my son when he was only two years old, there was an audible gasp in the room.

"You're kidding," one mother said.

"Oh, my god, I wouldn't say a thing until he was at least thirteen."

"I'm so glad that day is far off. The birds-and-the-bees talk . . . Yikes!"

Of course, with a two-year-old, I wasn't getting too detailed, but we read picture books together and I answered his questions. Besides, how could I dodge it? When Myles was two, I was expecting his brother, Zach.

I looked around the room. Several of the mothers were also pregnant. What on earth were they telling—or *not* telling—their older children?

Renegade Reason
Young kids are curious about birth and bodies. Honest answers help kids develop a healthy body image and begin a lifetime of open parent-child talks.

I was taught young, too. There wasn't a time I can remember when I didn't know how babies were made. Blame it on the 1960s and 1970s, if you like. The sexual revolution had upended old values, books were being published that advocated being open with children about sexuality, and my mother thought it was a sensible idea.

What I remember was a childhood of honest answers. I had reliable, factual information at my disposal and I wasn't embarrassed about it. Plus, when I hit age eight, I was able to cope with the onslaught of misinformation that flourished on the school bus and in the school yard.

Renegade Blessings

When you teach sex ed gradually, it's easier to build on this relationship. You set yourself up to be an "askable" parent from your child's earliest memories. Your son or daughter can learn:

> *I trust my parents. They give me honest answers.*
> *I can always ask my parents anything, even difficult or private things.*
> *Some things we talk about just at home.*
> *Some parts of my body are private.*
> *I know how I was born. I have knowledge.*
> *My body will change as I grow.*
> *Life is fascinating.*

Why It Works

"Sex ed begins at birth," many experts say. This means showing babies right from the start that their bodies are good and that body parts have names. Logan Levkoff, a sexuality educator who often appears on *Good Morning America* and the *Today* show, says adults can convey the message that bodies are good and natural (or dirty and sinful) even when we interact with newborns and very young children. President Obama, Dr.

Levkoff and others support age-appropriate sex education for kids of all ages. What's appropriate for two- to six-year-olds?

Sex ed for the preschool set is mostly focused on babies and body parts. Where do babies come from? What are the differences between male and female bodies? Talk of babies leads to body parts, which leads to males and females, which leads to . . . well, frankly, whatever the child is curious about.

You want your child to:

Be informed and have accurate information.

Have shame-free feelings about his body.

Understand which body parts are private.

Make you the first stop when she has sexual or sensitive questions..

 Take Off Your Adult Lenses

Don't shy away from sex ed. It's not about teaching promiscuity to young kids. Think of it as a biology lesson combined with the gift of open communication. Children learn names for body parts and begin to grasp how babies, puppies and kittens are made. Starting early lets kids know they can always come to you with questions, giving you a chance to continue to share your knowledge and values in the years to come.

Starting Young

When I was five, there was one picture book on our shelf that fascinated me more than all the others. It had a purple cover, and inside was a story so magical, it was hard to believe it was all true (how *could* I have ever been smaller than a pencil dot?). The book was *How Babies Are Made* by Andrew Andry and Steven Schepp. Gently and incrementally, it introduced the concept of fertilization and intercourse, starting with flowers, then moving up to chickens, puppies and people. By the time the story got to people, I knew about eggs and sperm, the holes for them to go in and the hole for the baby to come out. It wasn't surprising or scary. It was comfortable. And marvelous.

Luckily, this 1968 book was reprinted in 1984 and is still available through bookstores online. The cut-paper illustrations make everything clear without being in your face about biological facts. It was written and illustrated by people who understood preschoolers—exactly what kids this age want to know, and no more.

Of course, there are many books to help you offer sex ed to your child, but a lot of them tend to be cartoony, as if sex-related topics are so embarrassing that they can be dealt with only through comic illustrations. Preschool-age kids may find these confusing, rather than helpful. Books with funny cartoons are often better suited for an older child (elementary-school age) who will appreciate the humor. Stick with simplicity, but start soon.

> *If a child is old enough to ask, she's old enough to get an honest answer.*

Early Is Easier

Young kids don't know what the big fuss is. Why would adults be nervous about some parts of their body? Since three-year-olds aren't embarrassed about sex yet themselves, it makes it much easier to talk about. Kids this age are extremely matter-of-fact. Especially if you're nervous about talking about sex with your kids, start young. This way you can practice saying words you might stumble on, like "vagina" or "sperm," and have a mostly forgiving audience.

The first window of opportunity for healthy teaching arrives early. "If your kid can come to you at age six and get an honest answer," says Deb Baillieul, who teaches sex ed to first-graders, "she's going to know she can talk to you as a teenager. If she's not able to talk to you at age six, she's not going to come to you later." Setting up a dialogue about bodies and sexuality early eases the path for everyone. Although the teen years seem far away now, you will be grateful to have laid a healthy foundation for sexuality early on.

When you start early, you also become more in control of the information your child receives. Your child will be encountering both knowledgeable and ignorant peers, ranging from kids who have witnessed the home birth of a younger sibling to kids who are only told "Hush!" but are desperate to gain answers. If you don't teach your children, you can be guaranteed someone else will. Position yourself as a welcoming authority.

Be Askable

When Laura came home from school with a question about sex, her mother exploded.

"That's a word that ignorant people use for what married people do, and don't you ever say it again!"

For many of us, that's the sort of sex education we received. With no model to follow, it's easy to clam up. Take confidence that you will find your path. Crack open a book, practice saying anatomical words aloud if they make you blush, and concentrate above all on being an approachable, welcoming, "askable" parent. It's not a lecture, it's a discussion. Accept their curiosity. A big part of being askable is simply listening to your child.

Try This—Add to Your Toolbox

Keep It at Home

You're at the grocery store, and while the pregnant woman in front of you puts jars of spaghetti sauce on the checkout counter, your child blurts out, "How did the baby get inside her body?"

It's OK to save a big question like that for later. There's no reason to explain about eggs, sperm and intercourse in public. Defer the question, but don't dodge it.

"That's an important question, honey. We'll talk about it on the way home."

Let your child know you heard the question, it's a good question, and you plan to talk to him about it: "That's a big question, and I want us to have plenty of time to talk about it. I'll answer your question about babies when we get home." Even if explaining biology to your preschooler makes you squirm, don't back out on your promise. Once you're safely home from the grocery store, and the milk is in the fridge, answer his question directly.

Of course, if you're comfortable answering a sexual question in public, go ahead. It's always best to answer your child's question as soon as possible, whenever it comes up. This captures the teachable moment most fully and helps create a healthy, askable atmosphere.

Clarify the Question

Find out what your child needs to know and answer just that. Don't overwhelm her. You may think you're in for a huge discussion, but often a child has a simple question. Early questions about sex can often be misleading.

"You were asking about how babies come out. Do you want to know about how babies are made?" Clarify the child's true question and find out what depth of information she is really looking for. She might not care about how the baby gets *in* yet, just where it grows and where it comes out. Give a simple answer to one question. Then stop and see if she asks for more.

When a sexual question comes up, ask, "What do you think?" This buys you more time to clear your head, but it also helps you gauge where her current understanding lies. If she answers, "Babies come from hospitals," then you have a good idea of where to start.

Admit It If You're Nervous

If you're flustered, kids will likely know it. That's not intended to make you even more nervous. Just be prepared to acknowledge it. Tell your child, "We didn't talk about this when I was growing up. I don't know what to say, and it makes me nervous." Most kids will read your body language and tone of voice anyway, so don't try to hide it. Share with them that it's hard for you. Think of this as a benefit if you can. You're modeling an open relationship. Someday your child may share something with you that's hard.

Girls and Boys: Teach Both Sides

"Where's *your* penis, Mommy?"

Many a child learns that boys have penises and girls don't. Remember to mention what girls *do* have. It's important for boys and girls to grow up understanding that both sexes have something unique and special, not focusing on what's lacking. You can say, "Bodies are different. Boys have a penis and girls have a vulva." "Men and women both have nipples, but girls' nipples grow into breasts." "Girls have three holes and boys have two. Everyone has holes for pee and poop, and girls also have another hole for a baby to come out." "Girls have a womb (or uterus) where babies can grow inside of them."

Boys deserve to know about girls' bodies, and girls deserve to know about boys'. It may seem more natural to teach your son about his penis, but not about a vulva or vagina. Tell kids of both sexes facts about the other. For example, many young kids walk in on their mothers in the bathroom and get worried about the sight of menstrual blood. Give both boys and girls a simple explanation, and go on and tell them more if they ask. "Grown-up women have periods. A period is red because it's mostly blood, but it doesn't hurt. That's how women's bodies work."

Reinforce Public and Private

This can be tricky. For the kid who loves to bolt buck-naked across the park, the line between public and private is shaky. My six-year-old dropped his pants on the crowded playground to scratch a mosquito bite. Teaching kids what's public and what's private involves two topics: private places and private body parts.

Private places. Would you take your clothes off in the grocery store? The doctor's office? What about the bathroom or your bedroom? It may be OK to be naked in the living room at your house. Define the places. Ask kids questions to help them figure it out.

Private parts. These are the parts that get covered by your child's bathing suit. Go over who can touch them, including the child himself. This is a good time to delve into good touches and bad touches and what to do if he gets an icky "uh-oh" feeling. Remember kids sometimes play doctor at this age. It's generally innocent and a quest for knowledge, but be aware if there's a power imbalance (a nine-year-old and a five-year-old together).

Adults Only

Emphasize that intercourse and other sexual acts are for grown-up bodies. It's healthy for kids to know about it, but they also need to know that their body won't be ready until many years in the future. "When you're grown up, your body will be ready. Boys and girls don't have sex." This information helps reinforce safety lessons about sexual abuse.

Books Are Allies

Books are a godsend for teaching kids about babies and bodies. Besides offering words and pictures to help the tongue-tied, books can fill in gaps you don't know. It's OK to tell your child, "I don't know," and reach for a book. Just make sure you read the book ahead of time. Several books categorized for preschool kids are actually better for elementary-school-age children. Stick with the basics, and find something that will be both informative and comfortable for your child. Remember, you are not just providing information, you are conveying attitudes. There are plenty of books available to teach sex ed to kids, and you want to choose ones that match your child's needs and your family style.

As a parent, you'll also find in-depth resources to help you navigate common issues surrounding preschool sexuality, including playing doctor, masturbation, media messages and sexual abuse. The free online booklet *Right from the Start: Guidelines for Sexuality Issues, Birth to Five Years*, published by the Sexuality Information and Education Council of the United States, gives good information. See more suggested reading for both adults and children in the appendix.

Over and Over

For families who sit their preteen down for a birds-and-the-bees talk, it's a one-time event. Everyone leaves the room red-faced and relieved it's over. But unanswered questions linger.

When you make sex ed a continuing part of learning about life, questions that are meaningful to your child will naturally come up at many ages. Even if you explain *everything* to your four-year-old, don't expect to be done. Children absorb what is meaningful to them at each age and need to encounter the information again and again. For example, the popular Our Whole Lives sex-ed curriculum works with many age groups and advocates a lifelong approach to sexuality education.

The topics are endless. Whereas a three-year-old might focus on babies, a five-year-old might wonder about adoption or types of families. Media messages become increasingly important as your child uses the Internet and watches movies. This is all part of comprehensive sex ed.

If you can help your child accept and understand her body in preschool, she has a better chance to maintain a healthy body image as she grows. "No child should be ashamed of her body," says Janet Stocker, cofounder of the School for Young Children. "These are beautiful bodies—every single one of them."

Sex Ed for Preschoolers

1. How babies are made

This is the center of sex ed for preschoolers. It's a natural and highly relevant topic.

Young children are often surrounded by babies, their mothers may be pregnant and they see baby pictures of themselves. Tell children how babies form and grow, where they grow and how babies get out. Early talk about eggs and sperm is appropriate, and how it takes one thing from a male and one thing from a female to make a baby.

2. Parts of the body

Kids need accurate vocabulary words for their body parts—bellybutton, nose, vulva and all. They should understand what the parts of their body do (this hole's for pee, that one's for poop, this one is for a baby to come out someday if I want to be a parent) and how to keep them clean. Preschoolers also need to know names for body parts of the opposite sex and how bodies are different. They should know their bodies will change and grow to look like a man's or a woman's.

3. Private parts and safety

Kids may be shaky on what's public and what's private for a while. Model what's private and gently remind them which places are OK to touch and which are not. Tell kids their private parts are the areas covered by their bathing suits. If anyone touches their private parts, they need to tell you right away.

4. Other curious questions

If a child asks, he has a need to know. Be an askable parent. Do your best to explore any topic that interests him. But don't push it—children this age are likely to be more interested in the babies part and think intercourse, kissing or other sexual acts are gross.

WORDS TO TRY

Reacting to the question

I'm glad you asked that.

That's a big question. Let me think a minute.

That's an important question. We'll talk about it in the car.

I want us to have plenty of time to talk about it. I'll answer your question when we get home.

Answering the question

What do *you* think?

You were asking about (fill in the blank). What do you want to know?

Everyone has holes for pee and poop. Girls also have a hole for a baby to come out. It's called the vagina.

I wonder why you asked that.

Did I answer your question?

I see you have more questions. Let's get a book about that.

That's private. It's OK in your room, but not at the playground.

WORDS TO AVOID

The baby grows in her stomach.

Babies are made out of love.

Angels (storks . . .) bring babies.

That's dirty.

A good girl like you shouldn't ask those questions.

It's complicated. You wouldn't understand.

That's none of your business.

(Silence.)

OUT AND ABOUT

Children aren't convenient. So although you may wish your child would bring up personal sexual matters only at home, in your company, with the doors closed, likely she won't. Kids say the darnedest things wherever they may be.

Sometimes you may be on the receiving end of a sexual question with someone else's child. If that happens, make sure you don't overstep your boundaries. It's safest to defer to the other child's parents most of the time. Say, "That's a question for your mommy and daddy."

Other times, a brief answer may be fine. Whatever you do, always tell the other parent. "I want to let you know that Charlie was asking questions about our dog's penis today. This is what I told him. . . ." Tip off the parents as soon as you can that a sexual question has come up, but don't put anyone on the spot. For example, don't announce in front of their child, "Phoebe asked about sex and I told her you'd let her know *everything*!"

When my six-year-old nephew Robin was admiring his new cousin, he told me he loved baby Myles so much he wanted to marry him. Then he paused for a minute and asked, "Can boys marry boys?" Knowing my brother and his wife's values so well, I was able to give Robin a direct and honest answer. Use your judgment.

You might share your views on early sex education, and tell the other parents you're comfortable talking about the subject. Sometimes parents are grateful to have another adult they trust when it comes to navigating delicate waters like sexuality. If your sister admits she's not up to the job, but would be grateful if you described the basics to her daughter, invite the parents to sit in the room while you read a book with your niece. But do this only if you are specifically asked to play this role.

Be Buddies with Dead Birds

Next to the ice cream in my mother's freezer, you might find a hummingbird. Or a cardinal or indigo bunting. If a songbird chances to fly into the house windows and die, my mother lifts the fragile body into a ziplock bag and saves it in the freezer to show her class of three-year-olds. The next day the children examine its still eyes and gently probe its feathers with a Popsicle stick.

"When will it fly away?" they ask.

Renegade Reason:
Beginning to understand the concept of death is a major task of the preschool years.

Often by age three or four, kids ask questions and wonder about life and death. It's common for kids to incorporate talk of death into their imaginary play. For example:

"We are going to die and fall in the deep blue sea and turn into little crumbs of people."

"I have my camel in a cage, but all his legs fell off and he died."

"Sophie's dog died. He ate rat poison. What *is* rat poison? I'm eating rat poison. . . . AHH!"

"Grandpa's in heaven. When's he coming back?"

Exploring ideas of death is a major part of emotional development, and considered to be an important task of early childhood. At this age, kids don't understand the finality of death, and often believe the dead bird will fly again, or Grandpa will come back from his trip to heaven. Questions may begin in preschool but continue on for years as children confront mortality. Accept this striving to understand and do your best to meet questions with calm, age-appropriate answers.

Monica, mother of twin five-year-old boys, spotted a dead raccoon by the side of the road. It lay in plain view for several days, and Monica had to drive right by it every time she took the boys on an outing. She couldn't bear for her kids to see the raccoon's body, so she made sure both boys were thoroughly distracted each time they drove by.

The topic of death brings up conflicting emotions for us as adults. When children ask "Am I going to die?" it forces us to confront our own mortality. We sometimes like to dodge the questions, protect our children, skirt the raccoon on the side of road. But preschool is the time when children first think about death, and it's natural that they want answers. Many children lose a grandparent during these early years. Sometimes they lose a pet. Before kids must grapple with the full intensity of grief, it helps to start with the basics of life cycles and mortality. It helps to start with dead birds.

Renegade Blessings

When you honestly answer your child's questions about death and help her explore dead plants and animals, you help prepare her for changes throughout life.

All living things have a time to live and die. Trees, birds, pets and people.

> *I've seen a dead animal before. I know what death can look like.*
>
> *I can talk to my parents about important topics. They will give me honest answers.*
>
> *Dead things don't have to be scary. They are just part of life.*
>
> *Even if my parents die, there will always be someone to take care of me.*
>
> *I will die someday, too. It happens to everyone.*

Why It Works

"For children, even those quite healthy and never before seriously sick, death has a powerful and continuing meaning," writes Robert Coles, author of *The Spiritual Life of Children*. "Eventually, the questions always come."

The idea of death pops up in multiple ways in a child's life, from books and movies where characters die, to an ant she smushes on the sidewalk. Child development experts like Ellen Galinsky acknowledge that talk of death can be taboo, but say preschoolers naturally have questions and need information.

Some kids voice "dying" thoughts repeatedly during the early years. Some don't take an obvious interest. All kids will be intrigued if you explore a dead bird together. Fascination and mild interest are both healthy and fine.

If your child is fascinated, do the best you can to give matter-of-fact answers to her questions. For a healthy child who frequently plays out death themes, the intense focus on the topic can be unsettling for parents. Just like an intense interest in swinging, painting or superheroes, this is part of your child's development. Remember, religious scholars have grappled with questions about the ultimate for millennia. It's OK for your child to wonder and try to work it out in her own way. Keep in mind your parenting goals. Most likely you want your child to:

Feel comfortable talking to you of death and other difficult topics.

Develop an understanding of life cycles and death.

Experience the full range of human emotion and express her ideas and feelings.

Learn about your family's customs and beliefs related to death.

Over time, develop a healthy attitude toward death.

Don't force it. If your child does not want to talk about death or is worried about going to a funeral, do not insist. There will be plenty of time in the years ahead to explore the subject.

 Take Off Your Adult Lenses

It's not morbid for children to wonder about death. It's healthy and natural. You can help by answering their questions directly and explaining life cycles. Investigating a dead worm or bird together helps introduce kids gently to death before they have to face grief and loss themselves.

Exploring Death and Feeling Safe

The other day at breakfast, my husband was thinking about coffee, and I was thinking about my shower and getting the kids out the door on time. My son Zach, age three, was thinking about death.

"We going to die?" he asked.

"Yes, all people die someday. All living things," I said.

"I going to be dead?" Zach continued.

"Yes, but right now it's your turn to be alive."

"But I going to die?" It was obviously on his mind.

"Yes, Zach."

He paused for a moment and stuck his spoon in his cereal. "You going to die?" he asked.

Echoing words I'd heard all my life, I answered, "Yes, sweetheart, but probably not today. I'm planning to be here for a long time."

Unlike Zach, who likes to pose big questions at breakfast, I asked my mother about death mostly at night when I was little. My questions always came at bedtime, when she was tucking me in and kissing me good night. Being left in a dark room is a bit like a final good-bye to a child. I still remember the inner desolation I felt as my favorite person in the world vanished each night.

"Are you going to die?" I would ask, as she was leaving me. "When are you going to die?"

"I don't know," my mother truthfully answered. "But hopefully not for a long time."

She gave no false guarantees—this is important. But even then I understood her wish was to share life with me for as long as possible. It can be hard to give children an "I don't know" answer. We want to tell them "I will always be here with you." But the truth is, you don't really know. It's more accurate to say, "I will always love you, and I will be with you as long as I possibly can." Or "I will always love you, no matter what happens." The truth is kindest, and children can accept it, even at a very young age.

Someone Will Take Care of You

Even as children ask, "Are you going to die, Mommy?" be prepared to face this fact: It's not all about you. As usual, kids are thinking about themselves. The bottom line for kids is: "Who will take of me?"

When I went out of town on a trip, Zach asked me how he would eat. "Papa will feed you," I said, and also his babysitter, Jenny. "Oh!" said Zach, with obvious relief. "So many feeders!" He felt much better knowing his needs would be cared for.

Reassure children that somebody will always take care of them. "If I'm not here, Mommy will take care of you." Don't be startled by the next question: "But what if Mommy dies, too?" Answer calmly. "We've made a plan to take care of you. If anything happens to both Mommy and me, Aunt Jackie and Uncle Michael will take care of you." It may seem morbid to you, but young children are often comforted by that simple knowledge.

You can take this one step further. For example, Jennifer and Greg's three children, ages five, four and three, wanted to know exactly what to do if both their parents died. They knew Aunt Carrie would take care of them. "But how would we find her and tell her?" they wanted to know. Jennifer showed them her address book and explained they could give it to an adult who could find Aunt Carrie's phone number and call her. Having an actual plan to follow gave the kids comfort.

Grown-Ups Cry, Too

We had a picture book when I was growing up called *Grownups Cry, Too*, by Nancy Hazen. I was fascinated to realize that grown-ups cried for all sorts of reasons—even when they were happy. In real life, I watched, too. My dad cried listening to a piece of music. My mother cried seeing people she loved.

Years later, my friend Dan lost his beloved dog. They buried him in the backyard between the swing set and the garden. Dan was shaken with grief and cried when I hugged him. "I don't know what to tell the kids," he said. "I can't let them see me crying." Dan had two children, ages five and six. "It's OK to cry in front of your kids," I reassured him. "It's good for them to see you sad. Tell them you loved Yukon and you miss him."

He did just that. It was such a relief for Dan to share his feelings and know the kids would be all right. Together, the whole family talked about death and how much they missed their dog.

If you need to cry, don't keep a strong front and hide it from your kids. Part of their emotional understanding comes from watching you. If you're going through a period when you are crying a lot, reassure kids that feelings do change. You won't cry forever, but right now you are feeling very sad.

The Grieving Child

Ideas in this chapter are mainly for kids who are curious about death, but haven't yet experienced a deep personal loss. If your child is coping with the death of a grandparent, parent, sibling or other close family member, her needs will be different. She may be in deep grief or feeling mad, scared or horribly guilty, believing that somehow she caused the death. If a child you know has faced a loss, keep in mind that kids grieve differently from adults. Children may move in and out of intense feelings and intersperse sorrow with periods of happy play. Art therapy helps many grieving children, and there are abundant resources to help families cope with loss.

Try This—Add to Your Toolbox

Accept Death Yourself

If you're like Monica, the mother who shielded her kids from roadkill, you have some work to do on your own beliefs before you broach the topic of death with your child. Children's questions are candid and can be unsettling. Many parents are still uncomfortable with death themselves and avoid the topic. Think about your beliefs and fears. As a parent, you have to come to terms with your own mortality before you can truly help your child.

Consider Life Cycles

Since children understand taking turns, it can help to frame life cycles in this way: "Everyone has a turn to die and a turn to be alive. It's our turn to be alive now."

Looking at old family pictures can help tell the story of life and death in a nonthreatening way. "That's your great-grandmother. She's dead now, but when she was alive, she had a little boy named Henry who grew up to be your grandpa."

The life cycles of trees and other plants offer a safe way to explore death, too. Walk in the woods and find dead trees, logs and stumps. Watch as flowers die in the garden, or dandelions die in a bouquet. Emphasize that all living things have a turn to live and a turn to die.

Start with Worms and Dead Birds

Facing mortality is an enormous issue. Before your child copes with the loss of someone she loves or the beloved family dog, it's good to start with an animal that has no emotional ties to your child's life. A mouse, perhaps. A bird or a worm. Simply having the chance to look at something dead gives kids time to ask questions and digest the very idea of death. Then, when faced with the death of a pet or grandfather, your child can cope better. She's already encountered death and seen it with her own eyes. Her most basic questions have been addressed already, freeing her up to grieve.

Find a dead worm. It's easy to start with a worm, since they frequently wash up on sidewalks after a big rain. A worm won't likely evoke much emotion, but it offers the perfect opportunity for talking about what's alive and what's dead. What makes something alive? How do we know it's dead? Offer plain, concrete physical information. "Dead animals don't eat or move anymore." Or "This worm is dead. It can't get hurt anymore. Look, we can touch it with this stick and it won't get hurt."

Often children will want to fix death and call for a doctor. For example, these preschoolers are trying to help Tessa, the dead classroom rat.

"She needs to go the animal doctor," said Milo, age three.

"She may wake up," said Blake, also three. "I'm just saying maybe."

"She's so sad to be dead," said five-year-old Kent.

"Maybe if I give her some water she'll be alive again," said Hailey, age five.

Be gentle with the dead animal and model respect, but it's OK to investigate. Given all the germs involved, it's best not to use bare hands, but it's just fine to examine the body carefully, turn it over and touch it with a stick. Some people prefer gloves, which let kids feel how cold the body is. If it's a bird, look at its wings, crest and beak. Kids will be fascinated to see it doesn't move on its own anymore.

"It's soft," said three-year-old Madison. "I blew his feathers."

"Its eyes are still open, but it's dead," offered another child.

"We're investigating!"

Roadkill offers another teaching tool. Don't bypass that squirrel you saw squished on the road this morning. Or the baby bird that fell out of its tree. Talk about it. If you're walking by, stop and look at it. How did it die? Will it climb a tree again? Is it like your stuffed squirrel at home? How is a real squirrel different? Kids are often worried about getting hurt, so they may get scared about death because they fear it will hurt. Tell them, "No, it doesn't hurt to be dead. Live things can get hurt, but not dead things."

You may wish to hold a small ceremony for the dead animal or bury it. Rituals like these can make a big impression. Rituals present the emotional side, and model respect for both the living and the dead. In the case of Cattail, a cat who got hit by a train, the lesson continued beyond the burial. Max, Mae and Mateo helped their mom bury Cattail in the backyard, wrapped in a dish towel. A week after their ceremony, the kids began talking about Cattail and wondered where he was. "He went to heaven," said Mateo. "Maybe he's in the hospital," said Mae. "He's in the ground," said Max. They begged their mother to dig him up. "All right, but just once," she agreed. They dug up the spot and saw Cattail's body still lying in the ground.

Focus on Physical Facts

A group of three-year-olds peered at a dead cardinal.

"What does it eat?" one child asked.

"It's not going to eat any more food," said Addie.

"That's right," said the teacher. "It's dead. Dead animals don't need food."

"It's a dead, dead, dead bird," said Scott.

"This bird is not going to eat or poop anymore," said the teacher. "It's not going to fly or sit on a branch or sing again."

Take the time to lay out simple, physical facts about death for children. Knowing that dead animals don't eat or breathe or run—and won't ever do so again—helps kids begin to grasp the finality of death. The full idea may not sink in until elementary school, but children can begin to understand what makes death physically different from life.

The Religion Question

"What happens when you die? Where do people go? Why are we going to die?"

If you have religious beliefs, feel free to share them with your child. But keep it simple and offer practical information about death, too. Kids are literal. The mystery in religion often confuses them. When a young child hears "Grandpa's in heaven," she often thinks he's gone on a trip and is living in another place. Books like *Water Bugs and Dragonflies* may help you explain the idea of spiritual transformation.

If your views are secular, share those. If you fall into the uncertain camp, don't be afraid to say, "No one really knows," or "I don't know, but this is what I think." No matter what your beliefs, let your child know that people have many ideas about what happens after death. She is sure to encounter other families who talk about heaven or explain death in a different way.

Talking to Young Children About Death

Keep it simple. Answer only the question the child is asking at the moment.

Talk about death before your child loses a loved one.

Start with dead worms, birds or other animals. A child can begin to understand the facts and physical side of death before it happens to a pet or person they love.

Give kids concrete explanations about what dead and living things do. Tell them dead animals (and people) can't move, think, breathe, eat or go to the bathroom.

Use the words "dead" and "die." Euphemisms confuse children.

Avoid linking death to sleeping or leaving. Kids can become afraid to go to sleep or let you leave.

Avoid linking death to getting sick. Kids get sick frequently and might mistakenly think they are going to die. If your family knows someone who is dying from a disease, make it clear that a serious illness is different from getting a little bit sick.

Read picture books about death together. Some are secular, some are spiritual. Read the book ahead of time to make sure it's right for your family.

Stay as calm and matter-of-fact as possible.

Reading Resources

Many excellent children's books focus on grief, including the loss of a pet, or sometimes a parent or grandparent. There are also several picture books that present death and life cycles in a gentle, informative way. Some of these books start with the death of plants and animals and move on to the death of people. You might try *The Dead Bird* by Margaret Wise Brown (author of *Goodnight Moon*), *Lifetimes* by Bryan Mellonie or *I Miss You: A First Look at Death* by Pat Thomas.

Reading books like these opens up conversations about death. You can also read a book about a pet dying even if your child has not experienced that loss. During these talks you can explain your personal spiritual or secular views to your child. For older children (ages eight and up), Natalie Babbitt's *Tuck Everlasting* is a gem of a book that has helped generations of children accept change and mortality.

WORDS TO TRY
Talking about animal death
This bird is dead.
The body is cold and stiff. It won't fly or sing or eat or poop anymore.
It got hit by a car and that broke its body.
You can touch the body with this stick. Touch it gently.
We can bury it if you want to.

Talking about human death
She/he died.
All living things die.
Yes, I will die someday. Yes, you will die someday.
Everyone has a turn to die and a turn to be alive.

It's our turn to be alive right now.

I don't know when, but probably not for a long time.

I plan to be with you as long as I can.

I will always love you, no matter what happens.

Someone will always take care of you.

What happens when something dies? I believe . . .

Let's get a book about it.

WORDS TO AVOID

Shh! Don't talk about that, it's not nice.

Don't worry, I'm not going to die.

I'll always be here for you.

Why are you talking about death so much? Think about something more cheerful.

OUT AND ABOUT

Conversations about death are often private, but still culture clash can occur. Some folks don't like death. Some don't think it's appropriate to talk about death with children. Others fear their religious or secular views won't be heard or respected.

If you come across a dead worm or squirrel on the playground and kids from several families crowd around, be careful not to insert your beliefs. Stick to the facts ("It's dead. It won't eat again") and accept whatever beliefs come up. Kids in a group typically banter with the knowledge they've learned at home: "It's in heaven now," one child might say. "No," says another. "It just gets buried in the ground." Or: "Squirrels don't have heaven. Just people." Stay neutral and remind everyone, "Different families have different ways of thinking about these things."

Section VIII

Renegade Rules in the Real World

You have enemies? Good. That means you've stood up for something.

—Winston Churchill

Rule 28

Make Some Enemies at the Playground

"The hardest thing for me," said my friend Rachel, "is when our family interacts with kids who are parented differently from the way I parent."

"I consider myself reasonably independent," another parent told me. "I try not to let others' opinions affect my decisions and actions. On the other hand, I do feel that pressure to conform and to be accepted. There is so much passive judgment by other parents in public settings."

No matter how you parent, you won't please everyone. Part of becoming a parent is navigating a new set of social relationships—whether it's within your family or out in the neighborhood. If you aim to be an effective parent, don't try to be liked at all times. That's true when you set limits on your kids, and it's true for other adults you meet. Do your best, and do what you believe is right.

Renegade Reason

If you're a Renegade, not everyone will like your style.

The first two summers I took my son to the playground, I was intensely aware of other parents' eyes on me. They all seemed so comfortable in their parenting skins, and I was just getting used to the fact that I was a mother.

When I pushed Myles on the swing, I felt enormous pressure to give up his seat when a new family arrived. What would the other parents think? What if they didn't share my ideas about long turns? What about when he went *up* the slide and other parents insisted their kids should only go down? It surprised me how vulnerable I felt parenting in public. Where had all my courage and conviction gone?

It's easy to be overwhelmed. We get embarrassed. We want to look competent. We want to make friends, not cause trouble. It can be incredibly hard to stand alone, whether it's at the park letting your child have a long turn on the swing, or at Grandma's, where no superhero games are welcome. Parenting in public—no matter what methods you use—can be hard.

Renegade Blessings

Your child benefits when she can trust you wherever you are. Parenting is not a popularity contest. Stick to your principles as best you can. Your child will learn:

My parents won't desert me. They'll stand up for my rights in public.

Some places have different rules. That's OK, as long as it's clear.

Not all kids listen when I set limits. I might need a grown-up's help.

Other families do things differently. There are all kinds of people in the world.

Start at Home, Start Small

When you're just beginning to apply Renegade Rules, you may find it easier to parent this way at home. Focus on the new tools and your relationship with your child. Practice in private without judging eyes upon you. As you gain confidence, you'll be ready to take Renegade ideas out in public with you. Not only that, but you'll start to notice every time someone denies a child his rights. As a reminder, a child has:

A right to unstructured free play.

A right to choose her own playmates.

A right to use props and choose his own play themes.

A right to uninterrupted play during playtime.

A right to feel safe.

A right not to have objects taken from her (forced sharing).

A right to move and use his body vigorously.

A right to be outside.

A right to experience and express the full range of her emotions.

A right to ask questions and know things.

A right to stand up for his own rights by setting limits on others' behavior.

A right to be listened to, to be respected, and to have her rights consistently supported by adults.

A right to grow at his own unique pace, following the natural course of child development.

As you start supporting these rights, they will become a way of life. Practice and gather your confidence at home. As you become passionate about what you're doing, you'll find you're reluctant to give it up when you walk out the door.

Becoming a Renegade Parent

Tips to Get Started

1. **Start with sharing**

   Taking turns is an easy concept for all ages to grasp. You can implement this Renegade method at home in just a day or two and get immediate results. Since kids tussle over toys so much, it makes a big difference in daily life. After trying it at home, try it out on a playdate.

2. **Pick one or two Renegade Rules**

   Focus on areas you are struggling with right now. "If something's bothering you," says my mother, "it's time to make a change." Start with those. Don't try to change everything at once. If your child is wild and loud, implement some "Power Actions." If your four-year-old is a potty mouth at dinner, focus on freedom of speech. Letter writing is easy to implement and gets results fast. Become comfortable with those Renegade Rules before moving on to the next.

3. **Focus on the Renegade Golden Rule**

   If you can't remember what to say, think about the Renegade Golden Rule: It's OK If It's Not Hurting People or Property. It truly covers most situations. If you're uncomfortable with your child's play, try changing the timing or location. Remember to set reasonable limits: "All feelings are OK; all behavior isn't."

4. **Share with your spouse or another ally**

   Share your excitement or other reactions to the Renegade Rules. Let people know you're trying new methods; explain some ideas from this book. Not everyone likes to read parenting books, but the more allies you have, the easier it is to adopt

Renegade ideas. Leave the book out where your partner can find it.

5. **Find like-minded support**

It makes a world of difference if you can find one or two other adults who believe in what you're doing. Gather like-minded parents around you. Practice Renegade Rules together at playdates or in the neighborhood. You might find good allies at a progressive preschool. Don't overlook the older generation. Many "renegade" ideas, like unstructured play and allowing rough-and-tumble games, were popular a generation ago.

6. **Stick to your principles**

As a parent, you must be an advocate for your child. This can be a difficult part of raising kids, but it's vitally important. Start now to assert what's important to you. As you move into school years, you'll need to speak up for what's best, whether it's less homework, a new teacher, a special diet or longer recess time. You must be a mother/father lion and staunchly defend what's right for your child. Have courage. Bucking an established system is never easy. Do it respectfully, and you may gain more renegade partners along the way.

7. **Take heart**

Many Renegade ideas can help greatly in the teen years and beyond. Learning new ways can be hard, but it's worth it for the present and the future. If kids like the way they were raised, they will likely repeat it as adults. As you implement changes today, you'll also be helping your future grandkids.

Try This—Add to Your Toolbox

Culture clash will occur no matter how you parent. If you follow Renegade Rules, sharing, social rejection, rough play and weapon play are some of the main ones that may clash with other parents. So will any form of conflict. There's a strong drive to sidestep conflict in our culture, so you'll find parents remove their kids from even small altercations.

In Public

Two-year-old Isabella and her mom were visiting the children's museum. Isabella and another little boy both wanted the same toy, but before Isabella's mother could say anything to help the kids sort out the conflict, the other parents had whisked their son away. "You have to share," they told him sharply. "If you can't share, you're going to have to move." Isabella ended up with the toy she had grabbed.

How do you manage an "it's OK not to share" philosophy in a public place? The other parents move so fast. There's rarely a chance to talk it through with the kids. So many parents insist on sharing on demand that it's hard to voice a different view.

Tips for Renegade Parenting in Public

1. **Act fast**

   Parents do move quickly to avoid conflict and embarrassment. If you plan to say something, it's best to act fast. Get down low at the children's level and engage them both quickly. If you do, parents are less likely to rescue and interrupt.

2. **Speak aloud for all to hear**

   Get in the habit of parenting aloud. Verbalize everything so parents and kids can both hear. This helps reinforce the ideas for you and your child, and also puts the world on notice that you are conscious and comfortable with your parenting. No one has to guess about what you are doing or why, and families listening in can learn from your model.

Your words are not just for your own child. Don't whisper. Your message is for the other child, and especially for his parents. "I see you took that ball out of his hand. He's not done yet. And that's OK. I can't let you take it out of his hand."

If you can, quickly sum up the situation with an observation ("I see you both want this toy"). Then stand up for children's rights ("It's OK to keep playing with it until you're all done"). When you put your views out in the open, the other family knows where you stand. *Oh* (they may think), *that mom is not mad at me. I don't have to force Katie to share right now. I can relax.* Most adults try to minimize conflict immediately. If they know your views and go against them, they are actually creating conflict—something most parents are loath to do.

3. **Explain yourself**

Take a moment to speak politely and directly to the other parents. Explain what you are doing, and appeal to their desire to help. "We're working with Katie to stop grabbing. Thanks for backing me up." Or "We're working on impulse control with Nicky. Do you mind if I help the kids talk to each other?" Once the other parents realize you *want* to take time to sort out small conflicts or that you *want* to stop a behavior in your own child, they are more likely to slow down, watch and give you some latitude. People have a natural desire to help.

4. **Let it go**

You won't be able to apply Renegade Rules every time. That's OK. In some situations, it may not be worth the effort to try, or some days you may not have the energy. Not every parenting moment goes your way.

5. **Set different rules**

You may be most comfortable coming up with "private" and "public" rules for your family. For example, gun play is OK at home but not at the park. We can take a long turn at most places, but not at the children's museum—there are so many kids waiting for turns. Experiment and find what works for you. Set expectations ahead of time with your kids when you can.

6. **Explain to your child**

If things don't work out or you alter your parenting methods in certain situations, make sure you tell your child. Tell them, "Some families have different rules about taking turns." Or "At home we don't do it that way, do we? At home you can have a long turn. Things are different at the playground." There's no need to dwell on it, but your child will appreciate your acknowledgment that things are different.

At Friends' Houses

"What if my child goes to play at another kid's house and the other kid doesn't stop when she says 'Stop'?"

Every child becomes used to the ways her own family does things, and she may indeed be surprised when things are different in another house. This is nothing radical. Kids may notice that you take your shoes off at Ben's house and you get to eat cookies at Katie's house. Kids are also quick to understand that play rules are different in different houses.

If your child is used to setting limits on playmates, she will speak up at a friend's house. "Hey! I said 'Stop,' and you didn't listen. I don't like it when you push me like that." She can ask for adult help if she needs it. The everyday reinforcement you do at home gives kids practice for social situations like this. You can also explain your methods to the other family.

At Home

Views on child raising can be vastly different between parents. Sometimes it's even enough to break up a relationship. However, different parenting styles between parents can work. If you disagree on styles, then agree to support each other. The way he handles bedtime may not be the way you would approach it, but back him up. Try to agree on the big issues and let the little ones go. Differences between fathers and mothers can give kids a broader view of social relationships. It's OK to be somewhat inconsistent between parents—children will recognize the differences.

If one spouse is too busy to read up on child development, don't assume she's not interested. You may be able to share bits and pieces of what you learn—or even better, model the new methods in front of your parenting partner. You might hear her say "Where'd you learn that? That works like a charm." Maybe she'll become a Renegade Parent, too.

At Relatives' Houses

Family can be the hardest. Unlike strangers, you can't leave. Unlike friends, they may not share any of your views. Many parents of young kids feel intense pressure from their in-laws, parents, aunts and uncles. You may not like the way you were raised, or you may not like the way your extended family treats your children. You may feel pressure to have perfectly behaved children—an especially tall order when families get together at exciting holiday times.

Likely your family won't change, so parenting in family groups may be challenging. Here are some ideas to help:

> Support your partner. Pledge to support each other when you are visiting family. Ask your spouse or partner in advance to back you up, and do the same for her.

Set expectations. Tell your kids ahead of time what's expected at Grandma's house. Practice this behavior before you go. Maybe Grandma can't stand loud noise, so practice low voices a few days before your visit.

Be like a duck. Let comments slide off you like water off a duck's back. If you know you don't like your father's views on child rearing, resolve not to let it bother you. Don't get irked.

Keep perspective. Sometimes we get riled up on behalf of our kids. The children will be fine. Unless there's a serious problem (abuse), kids will not be hurt by visits to family. They may not notice the problems you see, and may instead have fond memories of Uncle Jake or Nana. It may be your own baggage that's the problem.

Practice at home. The more comfortable you become with your parenting style, the easier it becomes to parent confidently in front of others. Time and practice make us all better parents.

WORDS TO TRY

At our house, we . . .

It's OK with me if it's OK with you.

It seems as if you're worried when kids do that, but in our family, it's all right with us.

It looks as if you're upset that Jacob is still using the swing.

Jacob, when you're all done, this girl wants a turn.

Sometimes it's hard when kids have to wait. Long turns are OK with me.

We'll be going home in about ten minutes.

I know it's different from how you raised us.

That's something our family does at home.
Every family does things differently.

WORDS TO AVOID
Let me tell you how to handle this.
You need to/Your child needs to . . .

Rule

29 Goof Up

There's no reason to follow this book exactly. I don't. No one can. Parent-child relationships are full of nuances, children are different, and some days we simply have more energy to devote to parenting than others.

When parents at the School for Young Children compare themselves to the teachers, they often despair: "How do you do it? I can never get him to do that. You make it look so easy." Stephanie, the director, reassures them. "We only have your kids for two and a half hours a day," she says. "You have them the rest of the day. You can't be 'on' all the time."

These teachers typically have twenty to thirty years of experience working with the same age group. As a parent, you're brand-new at the job.

Don't berate yourself. Do the best you can, as often as you can.

Renegade Reason
Parenting doesn't follow a rule book—even a Renegade one. There's no one right way to raise a child.

The tools and techniques in this book are based on child development—how your child understands the world and how she grows.

They form the accumulated wisdom of approximately seventy-five early-childhood educators over the course of forty years. If you don't like the way you were raised, try out this new model. The Renegade Rules are designed to make daily parenting easier by giving you new ideas.

It's impossible to say the right thing all the time. Try out new techniques when you have energy. Remember, it gets easier over time. Using these methods, you'll see less yelling, less frustration and more open communication about needs and feelings. As you adopt new ideas, tools and techniques, your family will develop new habits. And you'll be laying patterns for lifelong positive relationships in your family. What works with preschoolers helps with teenagers and beyond. You are creating the framework for your family.

Renegade Guidelines

It's OK if it's not hurting people or property.

Young kids learn best through play.

People are not for hurting—not their bodies and not their feelings.

A child engaged in her own interests is working at her optimal level of learning.

Which really matters more: his action or your reaction?

Trust your child's choices in play.

All feelings are OK; all behavior isn't.

Focus on the feeling underneath the behavior first.

All behavior has meaning. Children are trying to get their needs met.

Don't accelerate the natural pace of child development.

Take off your adult lenses. Adjust your expectations.

A child is ready in her own time.

Renegade Blessings

These blessings are for you, the mother, father, teacher, grandparent or caregiver. This Renegade Rule book can bestow multiple lessons on your life:

I don't always have time or energy to parent the way I want. That's OK—nobody does.

When something's bothering me, I can make a change. I have tools to draw on.

My child's needs are not my entire world. I have needs and rights, too.

I can try out ideas gradually. New habits take time, but someday they may be second nature.

I don't have to reinvent the wheel. I can parent with confidence by drawing on collective wisdom.

The hard work I do now will pay off. Patterns of conflict mediation, open communication and trust will help in the teen years. My children are likely to use these methods when they become parents.

May you hit your parenting stride with confidence.

Appendix

Recommended Books for Adults

PLAY
Bos, Bev, and Jenny Chapman. *Tumbling over the Edge: A Rant for Children's Play*. Roseville, CA: Turn the Page Press, 2005.

Cohen, Lawrence J. *Playful Parenting*. New York: Ballantine Books, 2001.

Elkind, David. *Miseducation: Preschoolers at Risk*. New York: Knopf, 1987.

————. *The Power of Play: How Spontaneous, Imaginative Activities Lead to Happier, Healthier Children*. Cambridge, MA: Da Capo Press, 2007.

Hirsh-Pasek, Kathy, and Roberta Michnick Golinkoff. *Einstein Never Used Flash Cards: How Our Children Really Learn—and Why They Need to Play More and Memorize Less*. Emmaus, PA: Rodale Press, 2003.

Jones, Elizabeth, and Gretchen Reynolds. *The Play's the Thing: Teachers' Roles in Children's Play*. Rev. ed. New York: Teachers College Press, 2011.

Paley, Vivian Gussin. *A Child's Work: The Importance of Fantasy Play*. Chicago: University of Chicago Press, 2005.

CONFLICT MEDIATION
Excellent resources for learning more conflict management skills with children:

Bailey, Becky. *There's Gotta Be a Better Way: Discipline That Works!* Oviedo, FL: Loving Guidance, 1997.

Faber, Adele, and Elaine Mazlish. *How to Talk So Kids Will Listen and Listen So Kids Will Talk*. Rev. ed. New York: HarperCollins, 1999.

EMOTIONS AND CHILD DEVELOPMENT
Dreikurs, Rudolf. *Children: The Challenge*. Rev. ed. New York: Plume, 1990.

Faber, Adele, and Elaine Mazlish. *Liberated Parents, Liberated Children: Your Guide to a Happier Family*. New York: William Morrow, 1990.

Galinsky, Ellen. *Mind in the Making: The Seven Essential Life Skills Every Child Needs*. New York: William Morrow Paperbacks, 2010.

Ginott, Haim, Alice Ginott, and H. Wallace Goddard. *Between Parent and Child: The Bestselling Classic That Revolutionized Parent-Child Communication.* Rev. ed. New York: Three Rivers Press, 2003.

Goleman, Daniel. *Emotional Intelligence: Why It Can Matter More Than IQ.* Rev. ed. New York: Bantam, 2010.

———. *Social Intelligence: The New Science of Human Relationships.* New York: Bantam, 2007.

Greenspan, Stanley. *Building Healthy Minds: The Six Experiences That Create Intelligence and Emotional Growth in Babies and Young Children.* Cambridge, MA: Da Capo Press, 2000.

Kurcinka, Mary Sheedy. *Kids, Parents and Power Struggles.* New York: William Morrow Paperbacks, 2000.

Turecki, Stanley, with Sarah Wernick. *Emotional Problems of Normal Children: How Parents Can Understand and Help.* New York: Bantam, 1994.

ACTIVE PLAY, ROUGH-AND-TUMBLE PLAY AND BOYS

Carlson, Frances. *Big Body Play: Why Boisterous, Vigorous and Very Physical Play Is Essential to Children's Development and Learning.* Washington, DC: National Association for the Education of Young Children, 2011.

DeBenedet, Anthony T., and Lawrence J. Cohen. *The Art of Roughhousing: Good, Old-Fashioned Horseplay and Why Every Kid Needs It.* Philadelphia: Quirk Books, 2011.

Gurian, Michael. *The Wonder of Boys: What Parents, Mentors, and Educators Can Do to Shape Boys into Exceptional Men.* New York: Tarcher, 1996.

Hodgins, Daniel. *Boys: Changing the Classroom, Not the Child.* Flushing, MI: Self-published, 2009.

Pollack, William. *Real Boys: Rescuing Our Sons from the Myths of Boyhood.* New York: Random House, 1998.

Thompson, Michael, and Teresa H. Barker. *It's a Boy! Your Son's Development from Birth to Age 18.* New York: Ballantine Books, 2009.

Tyre, Peg. *The Trouble with Boys: A Surprising Report Card on Our Sons, Their Problems at School, and What Parents and Educators Must Do.* New York: Three Rivers Press, 2008.

POWERFUL PLAY AND WEAPON PLAY

Explore more about the benefits and purpose of children's powerful play, including weapon play:

Edmiston, Brian. *Forming Ethical Identities in Early Childhood Play.* New York: Routledge, 2008.

Jones, Gerard. *Killing Monsters: Why Children Need Fantasy, Super Heroes and Make-Believe Violence.* New York: Basic Books, 2002.

Katch, Jane. *Under Deadman's Skin: Discovering the Meaning of Children's Violent Play.* Boston: Beacon Press, 2002.

Kindlon, Dan, and Michael Thompson. *Raising Cain: Protecting the Emotional Life of Boys.* New York: Ballantine Books, 2000.

Kirsh, Steven. *Children, Adolescents and Media Violence: A Critical Look at the Research.* 2nd ed. Thousand Oaks, CA: Sage Publications, 2011.

Levin, Diane E., and Nancy Carlsson-Paige. *The War Play Dilemma: What Every Parent and Teacher Needs to Know.* 2nd ed. New York: Teachers College Press, 2005.

PRAISE AND MORAL DEVELOPMENT

Bronson, Po, and Ashley Merryman. *NurtureShock: New Thinking About Children.* New York: Twelve, 2009.

Coles, Robert. *The Moral Life of Children.* New York: Atlantic Monthly Press, 1986.

Damon, William. *The Moral Child: Nurturing Children's Natural Moral Growth.* New York: Free Press, 1988.

Kohn, Alfie. *Punished by Rewards: The Trouble with Gold Stars, Incentive Plans, A's, Praise, and Other Bribes.* New York: Houghton Mifflin, 1999.

———. *Unconditional Parenting: Moving from Rewards and Punishments to Love and Reason.* New York: Atria Books, 2005.

Riley, Sue Spayth. *How to Generate Values in Young Children.* Raleigh, NC: Boson Books, 2005.

SEX EDUCATION

Davis, Laura, and Janis Keyser. "Learning about Bodies." Chap. 17 in *Becoming the Parent You Want to Be: A Sourcebook of Strategies for the First Five Years.* New York: Three Rivers Press, 1997.

Rothbart, Betty et al. *Right from the Start: Guidelines for Sexuality Issues, Birth to Five Years.* New York: Sexuality Information and Education Council of the United States (SIECUS), 1998 (free booklet online http://www.siecus.org/_data/global/images/RightFromTheStart.pdf).

PARENTING

All-around good resource books on most topics:

Davis, Laura, and Janis Keyser. *Becoming the Parent You Want to Be: A Sourcebook of Strategies for the First Five Years.* New York: Three Rivers Press, 1997.

Rogers, Fred. *You Are Special: Words of Wisdom for All Ages from a Beloved Neighbor.* New York: Penguin, 1995.

Recommended Books for Children

ANGER

Riana Duncan, *When Emily Woke Up Angry*

Edna Mitchell Preston, *The Temper Tantrum Book*

Thierry Robberecht, *Angry Dragon*

Maurice Sendak, *Where the Wild Things Are*

Norma Simon, *I Was So Mad*

Linda Urban, *Mouse Was Mad*

Rachel Vail, *Sometimes I'm Bombaloo*

FEAR

Dr. Seuss, *What Was I Scared Of?* (sold alone or in *The Sneetches*)

Ed Emberley, *Go Away, Big Green Monster!*

Mercer Mayer, *There's a Nightmare in My Closet*

Martin Waddell, *Owl Babies*

GENERAL FEELINGS

Eric Carle, *The Grouchy Ladybug*

Dr. Seuss, *My Many Colored Days*

Ed Emberley and Anne Miranda, *Glad Monster, Sad Monster*

Mem Fox, *Tough Boris*

Cherryl Kachenmeister, *On Monday When It Rained*

Ezra Jack Keats, *Peter's Chair*

Robert Kraus, *Leo the Late Bloomer*

Jeanne Modesitt, *Sometimes I Feel Like a Mouse*

Fred Rogers, *Making Friends*; *The New Baby*

Ann Herbert Scott, *Sam*

Judith Viorst, *Alexander and the Terrible, Horrible, No Good, Very Bad Day*

SEPARATION

Audrey Penn, *The Kissing Hand*

Judith Viorst, *The Good-bye Book*

Karma Wilson, *Mama Always Comes Home*

Jane Breskin Zalbin, *Don't Go!*

EARLY SEX EDUCATION

Andrew C. Andry and Steven Schepp, *How Babies Are Made*

Joanna Cole, *How You Were Born*

Lennart Nilsson, *Life* or *A Child Is Born* (Kids are fascinated by the stunning photos.)

Mark Schoen, *Bellybuttons Are Navels*

BETTER FOR OLDER KIDS (AGES 5–8+)
Laura Krasny Brown and Marc Brown, *What's the Big Secret?*
Robie H. Harris, *It's Not the Stork!*

EARLY DEATH EDUCATION
Margaret Wise Brown (author of *Goodnight Moon*), *The Dead Bird*
Robie H. Harris, *Goodbye Mousie*
Bryan Mellonie, *Lifetimes: The Beautiful Way to Explain Death to Children* (secular)
Fred Rogers, *When a Pet Dies*
Doris Stickney, *Water Bugs and Dragonflies* (spiritual)
Pat Thomas, *I Miss You: A First Look at Death*
Judith Viorst, *The Tenth Good Thing About Barney*
Barbara Walsh, *Sammy in the Sky*

FOR OLDER KIDS (AGES 8+)
Natalie Babbitt, *Tuck Everlasting*
Leo Buscaglia, *The Fall of Freddie the Leaf*

Acknowledgments

Thank you to my agent, Joëlle Delbourgo, who was confident from day one and believed the world was ready for this book. Thanks go to the entire team at Tarcher/Penguin, especially Molly Brouillette and my editor, Sara Carder. Deep gratitude to Sara: Her vision truly shaped this book and turned it into a renegade.

Grateful thanks to my team of test readers, who took time from their busy lives as parents and grandparents of young children to read early chapters: Elizabeth Dell, Anne Donn, Kathy Fey, Brad Gerlach, Clare Hurtgen Kwan, Lucky McKeen, Sarah Payette, Tanya Schlam, Ty Schmidt and Zane Kathryne Schwaiger. Thanks go to my writing group, the Powerfingers: Mardi Link, Cari Noga, Anne-Marie Oomen and Teresa Scollon. You are my renegade blessings.

Hugs and special thanks to the School for Young Children (SYC) family who inspired, advised and welcomed me into their classrooms. Big thanks to the team of SYC review readers: Deb Baillieul, Joanne Frantz, Angela LaMonte, Ann Rigney, Susan Roscigno, Stephanie Rottmayer, Janet Stocker and Jan Waters. An extra hug to Stephanie for her boundless enthusiasm and commitment to this book and for always being there when I needed her. Thanks to the First Unitarian Universalist Church of Columbus, which has hosted the SYC program for forty-two years and counting. And, of course, this book would not exist without the visionaries who founded SYC years ago: my eternal thanks and respect to Lee Row and Janet Stocker.

Deep appreciation goes to Alison Burns, Jeannette Wildman Downes, Margaret Hoagg, Ariel Love and Cruz Paniagua. Without your care watching my children while I was at my writing desk, this book truly could never have been written. And finally, to my children and my husband, Rick. You are my inspiration.

If you enjoyed this book, visit

www.tarcherbooks.com

and sign up for Tarcher's e-newsletter to receive
special offers, giveaway promotions, and
information on hot upcoming releases.

TARCHER
PENGUIN

Great Lives Begin with Great Ideas

New at **www.tarcherbooks.com**
and **www.penguin.com/tarchertalks**:

Tarcher Talks, an online video series featuring
interviews with bestselling authors on everything from creativity and prosperity to 2012
and Freemasonry.

If you would like to place a bulk order
of this book, call 1-800-847-5515.

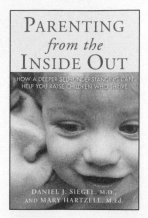

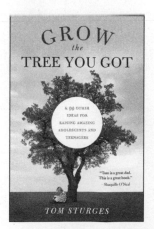